The Movement:
British Poets of the 1950s

Twayne's English Authors Series

Kinley Roby, Editor
Northeastern University

TEAS 502

The Movement: British Poets of the 1950s

Jerry Bradley

Indiana University Southeast

Twayne Publishers ■ New York

Maxwell Macmillan Canada ■ Toronto

Maxwell Macmillan International ■ New York Oxford Singapore Sydney

The Movement: British Poets of the 1950s
Jerry Bradley

Copyright 1993 by Twayne Publishers

Twayne Publishers   Maxwell Macmillan Canada, Inc.
Macmillan Publishing Company 1200 Eglinton Avenue East
866 Third Avenue   Suite 200
New York, New York 10022   Don Mills, Ontario M3C 3N1

Library of Congress Cataloging-in-Publication Data

Bradley, Jerry, 1948-
    The movement: British poets of the 1950s / Jerry Bradley.
    p. cm. – (Twayne's English authors series; TEAS 502)
    Includes bibliographical references and index.
    ISBN 0-8057-7040-2
    1. English poetry – 20th century – History and criticism. 2.
Movement, The (English poetry) I. Title. II. Series.
PR605.M68B73. 1993
821'.91409 – dc20   93-7653
                                                CIP

The paper used in this publication meets the minimum
requirements of American National Standard for Information
Sciences – Permanence of Paper for Printed Library Materials,
ANSI Z39.48-1984.

10 9 8 7 6 5 4 3 2 1

Printed in the United States of America.

To Lou Thompson

whose inspiration and support have proved

invaluable to my work and life

Contents

Preface

The Movement comprises a curious episode in British literary history. A group of nine writers (Kingsley Amis, Robert Conquest, Donald Davie, D. J. Enright, Thom Gunn, John Holloway, Elizabeth Jennings, Philip Larkin, and John Wain), the Movement formed in the 1950s as a repudiation of the previous decade's verse, but ironically enough had its origins in the 1940s. While some of its members have disputed the group's existence, the effects of the Movement have nonetheless extended well beyond the 1950s.

Organized or not, the Movement poets found a practical use for poetry. Owing no obeisance to the Muses, the gods of poetic inspiration, they crafted a skeptical postwar poetic in which comedy and melancholy became the prime means of self-discovery. They brought everyday life back to poetry, and their no-nonsense stance, often modestly informal and conversational, sought to rehabilitate the corrupted public taste of the 1940s by employing a spoken diction that rendered authentically and in an offhand fashion observations about midcentury life. Their emphasis on clarity and democratic values proved a courageous endeavor, for it demanded rigorous self-examination; they were forced to explore openly their own capacity for self-deception and foolishness. The results of that venture are still being debated, but it is generally conceded that the Movement produced a host of brilliant if ambivalent works and at least one truly extraordinary poet, Philip Larkin.

While the majority of these nine writers have published a substantial body of literature other than poetry and while the characteristics of Movement verse are discernible in their fiction and criticism, their poetry remains their most important contribution. They have persevered for more than three decades at the forefront of British letters (all but Larkin are still alive), but the majority have not been studied in much critical depth. Larkin has, at last, rightfully begun to be acknowledged as England's finest postwar poet, and readers can be grateful for the commentary that his work has prompted, but over the decades the work of Jennings, Conquest, Holloway, and Enright in particular have been far too ignored. This study hopes to bring new attention to the contribution of all the Movement's members.

Acknowledgments

I would like to acknowledge the following for the use of quotations from copyrighted works:

Ballantine: *A World of Difference* by Robert Conquest, 1964.

Barnes and Noble: *Twentieth-Century English Poetry: An Introduction* by Anthony Thwaite, 1978.

Bernard Bergonzi: "Pound and Davie" by Bernard Bergonzi, in *Donald Davie and the Responsibilities of Literature*, 1983.

Alan Bold: *Thom Gunn and Ted Hughes* by Alan Bold, 1976. By permission of Alan Bold.

The British Council: *The Poet Speaks* edited by Peter Orr, 1966.

Anthony Burgess: *The Novel Now: A Guide to Contemporary Fiction* by Anthony Burgess, 1967.

Cambridge University Press: *These the Companions* by Donald Davie, 1982; *The Slumber of Apollo: Reflections on Recent Art, Literature, Language, and the Individual Consciousness* by John Holloway, 1983; *A History of Modern Poetry: Modernism and After* by David Perkins, 1987; *D. J. Enright: Poet of Humanism* by William Walsh, 1974.

Canto, Inc.: For portions of *Trying to Explain* by Donald Davie, 1979, originally published in *Canto* 2, no. 1 (Spring 1978).

Jonathan Cape: *What Became of Jane Austen? And Other Questions* by Kingsley Amis, 1976.

Carcanet Press Ltd.: *Collected Poems 1950-1970* by Donald Davie, 1972; *Collected Poems 1970-1983* by Donald Davie, 1983; *The Poet in the Imaginary Museum* by Donald Davie, 1977; *Purity of Diction in English Verse* by Donald Davie, 1967; *Under Briggflatts: A History of Poetry in Great Britain 1960-1988* by Donald Davie, 1989; *Consequently I Rejoice* by Elizabeth Jennings, 1987.

Chatto & Windus Ltd.: *Conspirators and Poets* by D. J. Enright, 1966; *Memoirs of a Mendicant Professor* by D. J. Enright; *Shakespeare and the Students* by D. J. Enright, 1970; *The Terrible Shears: Scenes from a Twenties Childhood* by D. J. Enright, 1973. Reprinted by permission of Watson, Little Limited.

Robert Conquest: *The Abomination of Moab* by Robert Conquest, 1979.

George Dekker: *Donald Davie and the Responsibilities of Literature* edited by George Dekker, 1983.

Howard Erskine-Hill: "Two Hundred Years Since: Davie, the Eighteenth Century, and the Image of England" by Howard Erskine-Hill, in *Donald Davie and the Responsibilities of Literature*, 1983.

Essays in Criticism: "Auden's (and Empson's) Heirs" by F. W. Bateson, 1957; "New Critics and New Lines" by Robert Conquest, 1958; "New Lines and Mr Tomlinson" by D. J. Enright, 1957; "The Middlebrow Muse" by Charles Tomlinson, 1957.

Faber and Faber Ltd.: *Fighting Terms* by Thom Gunn, 1962; *The Occasions of Poetry: Essays in Criticism and Autobiography* by Thom Gunn, 1982; *The Sense of Movement* by Thom Gunn, 1967; *Collected Poems* by Philip Larkin, 1989; *Required Writing: Miscellaneous Pieces 1955-1982* by Philip Larkin, 1983; *Larkin at Sixty* edited by Anthony Thwaite, 1982.

Fantasy: *Poems* by John Holloway, 1954.

Gale: *Contemporary Authors Autobiography Series*, 1987; *Contemporary Authors*, New Revision Series, Volume 28, 1990; *Dictionary of Literary Biography*, Volume 27, 1978.

Victor Gollancz Ltd.: *My Enemy's Enemy* by Kingsley Amis, 1962.

Harvard University Press. *A History of Modern Poetry* by David Perkins, 1987.

John Holloway: *New Poems* by John Holloway, 1970; *Language and Intelligence* by John Holloway, 1951.

Hutchinson: *Memoirs* by Kingsley Amis, 1991.

Kenkyusha: *Poets of the 1950s* edited by D. J. Enright, 1955.

Listener: "Marble Fun" by Alisdair Maclean, 1973.

London: "The Two Languages" by John Holloway, 1959.

London Magazine: "Context" by Robert Conquest, Elizabeth Jennings, and Thom Gunn, 1962; "Ten Comments on a Questionnaire" by Robert Conquest and Elizabeth Jennings, 1964; "The Climate of Pain in Recent Poetry" by Martin Dodsworth, 1964; "Ted Hughes and *Crow*" by Egbert Fass, 1971; "The Difficult Balance" by Elizabeth Jennings, 1959; "Four Conversations" by Philip Larkin and Thom Gunn, 1964.

London Sunday Times: "Books of the Year" by Somerset Maugham, 1955.

Longman Group U.K.: *Poetry To-Day, 1957-60* by Elizabeth Jennings, 1961.

Macmillan: *Language and Intelligence* by John Holloway, 1951; *Collected Poems* by Elizabeth Jennings, 1967; *Relationships* by Elizabeth Jennings, 1972; *Contemporary Poets* edited by James Vinson, 1980.

Marvell Press: *The Minute and Longer Poems* by John Holloway, 1956.

Methuen: *An Anthology of Modern Verse 1940-60* edited by Elizabeth Jennings, 1961.

New Statesman: "Amis Goes Pop" by Alan Brien, 1967; "Underwriter" by Douglas Dunn, 1974; "The Examined Life" by Clive James, 1979; "Lucky Jim's Political Testament" by Paul Johnson, 1957; "New Minted" by Frank Kermode, 1961; "Clean and Clear" by Julian Symons, 1967.

New York Times Book Review: "Images and Reality" by William Meredith, 1959; for portions of *Trying to Explain* by Donald Davie, 1979, originally published in the *New York Times Book Review,* 9 November 1975.

Overlook Press: *Jill* by Philip Larkin, 1984.

Oxford University Press: *Collected Poems* by D. J. Enright, 1981; *Fields of Vision: Essays on Literature, Language, and Television* by D. J. Enright, 1988; *Oxford Book of Contemporary Verse* edited by D. J. Enright, 1980. Reprinted by permission of Watson, Little Limited. *Thomas Hardy and British Poetry* by Donald Davie, 1972.

Poetry: "Pointless and Poignant" by John Matthias, 1977; "A Poetry Chronicle" by John Thompson, 1959.

Routledge Books: *Articulate Energy: An Enquiry into the Syntax of English Poetry* by Donald Davie, 1955; *The Charted Mirror: Literary and Critical Essays* by John Holloway, 1960; *The Colours of Clarity: Essays on Contemporary Literature and Education* by John Holloway, 1964; *The Fugue and Shorter Pieces* by John Holloway, 1960; *The Landfallers* by John Holloway, 1962; *The Lion Hunt: A Pursuit of Poetry and Reality* by John Holloway, 1964; *Planet of Winds* by John Holloway, 1977; *The Poet Speaks* edited by Peter Orr, 1966; *The Proud Knowledge: Poetry, Insight, and the Self 1620-1920* by John Holloway, 1977; *Wood and Windfall* by John Holloway, 1965; *The Movement: English Poetry and Fiction of the 1950s* by Blake Morrison, 1986.

Rutgers University Press: *Poetry and Fiction* by Howard Nemerov, 1963.

St. James: *Contemporary Poets*, 1970.

St. Martin's: *Between Mars and Venus* by Robert Conquest, 1962.

Secker & Warburg Ltd.: *The Apothecary's Shop: Essays on Literature* by D. J. Enright, 1957; *Heaven Knows Where* by D. J. Enright, 1957; *The World of Dew: Aspects of Living Japan* by D. J. Enright, 1955. Reprinted by permission of Watson, Little Limited.

Simon & Schuster: *Coasting* by Jonathan Raban, 1987, courtesy of Gillon Aitken.

Southern Illinois University Press: *The New University Wits and the End of Modernism* by William Van O'Connor, 1963.

Spectator: "Editor's Notes" by Kingsley Amis, 1955; "Hock and Soda-Water" by Kingsley Amis, 1954; "A Sense of Movements" by Thom Gunn, 1958.

Stein and Day: *No! In Thunder* by Leslie Fiedler, 1972.

Times Literary Supplement: "Too Good for This World" by John Bayley, 1974; "The Dual Role of Critic and Poet" by John Holloway, 1960; "Poetic Personality," 1955.

Twayne: *Kingsley Amis* by Philip Gardner, 1981; *Philip Larkin* by Bruce K. Martin, 1978.

University of Chicago Press: *Under Briggflatts: A History of Poetry in Great Britain 1960-1988* by Donald Davie, 1989.

Viking: *Collected Poems 1944-1979* by Kingsley Amis, 1979.

H. W. Wilson: *World Authors 1950-1970* edited by John Wakeman, 1975.

Yale Review: "Things, Voices, Minds" by *Thom Gunn*, 1962.

Acknowledgment is also due to the following:

My Enemy's Enemy. Copyright 1962 Kingsley Amis. Reprinted by permission of Jonathan Clowes Ltd., London, on behalf of Kingsley Amis.

Collected Poems 1944-1979. Copyright 1979 by Kingsley Amis. Reprinted by permission of Jonathan Clowes Ltd., London, on behalf of Kingsley Amis.

Reprinted by permission of Farrar, Straus & Giroux, Inc. Excerpts from *Moly and My Sad Captains* by Thom Gunn. Copyright 1973 by Thom Gunn. Excerpts from *Selected Poems 1950-1975* by

Chronology

1917   Birth of Robert Conquest.

1920   Birth of D. J. Enright and John Holloway.

1922   Birth of Philip Larkin, Kingsley Amis, and Donald Davie.

1925   Birth of John Wain.

1926   Birth of Elizabeth Jennings.

1929   Birth of Thom Gunn.

1951   F. W. Bateson founds the periodical *Essays in Criticism*, a platform for the Movement.

1952   Davie's *Purity of Diction of English Verse.* John Lehmann begins his *New Surroundings* broadcasts.

1953   Enright's *The Laughing Hyena* and Wain's *Hurry On Down.*

1954   *Spectator* article officially names the Movement. Amis's *Lucky Jim* and Gunn's *Fighting Terms.*

1955   The Movement comes of age with the publication of major volumes of poetry: Enright's *Poets of the 1950s*, Larkin's *The Less Deceived*, Conquest's *Poems*, and Davie's *Brides of Reason.*

1956   Conquest's *New Lines* and Holloway's *The Minute and Longer Poems.*

1962   Wain's reminiscence *Sprightly Running.*

1963   Conquest's *New Lines II.*

1964   Larkin's *The Whitsun Weddings.*

1966   Holloway's *A London Childhood.*

1967   Jennings's *Collected Poems* and Amis's *A Look round the Estate: Poems 1957-1967.*

1972   Davie's *Collected Poems 1950-1970.*

1973	Enright's *The Terrible Shears*.
1974	Larkin's *High Windows*.
1980	Wain's *Poems 1949-1979*.
1981	Enright's *Collected Poems*.
1983	Larkin's *Required Writing: Miscellaneous Pieces 1955-1982*.
1985	Death of Larkin.
1986	Jennings's *Collected Poems 1953-1985* and Blake Morrison's critical history *The Movement*.
1988	Larkin's *Collected Poems*.
1991	Amis's *Memoirs*.

Chapter One

The Movement:
Origins and Influences

In the 1950s there was no one British poet who embodied the spirit of the age as T. S. Eliot and W. B. Yeats had for previous generations. *Poetry To-Day, 1957-60*, Elizabeth Jennings's update of Geoffrey Moore's British Council booklet, announced that in place of a singular voice British poetry was being influenced by a group "vaguely called The Movement," writers who had been "hustled into a group often very much against the will of the poets themselves."[1] Robert Conquest's *New Lines* anthology (1956) was largely responsible for this perception, for its grouping of nine poets publicly defined the Movement's membership and consolidated it around a new poetic emphasizing clarity, intellectual detachment, and formal perfection. It was a poetic built upon the old but was decidedly new. "In one sense, indeed, the standpoint is not new," Conquest writes in the book's introduction, "but merely the restoration of a sound and fruitful attitude to poetry, of the principle that poetry is written by and for the whole man, intellect, emotions, senses and all. But restorations are not repetitions. The atmosphere, the attack, of these poets is as concentratedly contemporary as could be imagined. To be of one's own time is not an important virtue, but it is a necessary one."[2]

For Donald Davie a poetry of the time meant one imbued with Augustan restraint. His *Purity of Diction in English Verse* (1952) came closest to being a manifesto around which Movement poets could rally. It called for a retrenchment from experimentation and from those verses employing grand themes by stressing instead the dignity of ordinary things through a revitalized if predictable imagery. That same year John Lehmann's BBC radio series *New Soundings* began broadcasting the work of five new poets, Davie among them, to a wider public. Proposing to define this fresh direction in poetry,

1

Lehmann intended to counter prevailing tastes by offering anti-romantic poetry conveyed in a conversational tone. Though Philip Larkin was not among them, like Lehmann he felt that as far as poetic technique was concerned, "no device is important in itself. Writing poetry is playing off the natural rhythms and word-order of speech against the artificialities of rhyme and metre."[3]

John Wain's six *First Reading* programs followed Lehmann's in 1953 and continued to publicize this new generation of writers. So by the time that J. D. Scott actually gave name to the Movement by capitalizing it in his 1954 *Spectator* article, "In the Movement," many observers of the literary scene were already aware that the literary tastes of modern Britain were changing. Dylan Thomas and the pre-war old guard whose work frequented the pages of *Poetry London* in the 1940s were being supplanted by a group of poets who took a more modest, less elitist approach to verse.

Although Scott's anonymous article named three novelists (Wain, Kingsley Amis, and Iris Murdoch) and two poets (Davie and Thom Gunn) as composing the Movement, two representative anthologies soon expanded the membership of the group. D. J. Enright included the names of Conquest, Jennings, Larkin, John Holloway, and himself (while retaining Amis, Davie, and Wain) in his *Poets of the 1950s* (1955), and Conquest's *New Lines* added Gunn to Enright's list of eight. Discussion of the Movement has generally been limited ever since to the work of these nine writers.

The Movement platform, set forth as it was in Conquest's introduction to *New Lines*, met with some uneasiness in the group. Amis wanted it tougher, Larkin more genial. Conquest himself had attacked the Movement by name in his original draft, but that attack was deleted from the published manuscript. "I can't remember why this sentence was dropped. . . . I wish, all the same, that I'd kept it in: it could, or might, have spared us all the brouhaha about *New Lines* and the Movement which still goes on. To be fair to myself, I did say in that introduction that all we had in common was no more than a wish to avoid certain bad principles. As Thom Gunn put it later, all we shared was what had been the practice of all English poets from Chaucer to Hardy."[4] Conquest admitted that his *New Lines* introduction "was not a balanced or judicious piece. Nor was it intended to be – it was a provocative showing of the flag, or trailing of the coat. In this it succeeded: at any rate the collection attracted a remarkable volume of abuse and some equally noisy championship" (*Sixty*, 33).

While a study of their early poetry confirms how little some of these poets actually had in common at the time Conquest assembled them to his seminal anthology, his collection nonetheless emphasizes the characteristics by which these poets would be read for some time: a wry honesty and a technical coolness that made them wary of the seriousness of poetry itself. These qualities are most evident in the works of Larkin, Enright, and Amis, but Conquest discovered them in the works of other contemporaries who were striving to write an unemotional sort of poetry, one that eschewed symbolism, abstractions, and allegory. What was noticeably lacking in all this unsentimental verse, however, was the passion of a personal philosophy, a characteristic Anthony Hartley praised in his *Spectator* review of *New Lines*, boasting that the Movement was producing a disciplined verse void of emotional mushiness.

Despite its federation in various anthologies, the Movement was not assembled around acknowledged shared beliefs, intriguing technical experimentation, or the powerful personality of a great poet. To the contrary, what the group shared was more a lack of belief and a refusal to engage in silly verbal gymnastics. Furthermore, the Movement's most important poet, Philip Larkin, was dreadfully reclusive and consequently reluctant to become spokesman for any group; moreover, he had not even been mentioned in Scott's *Spectator* article. The Movement was democratically constituted; its members were friends and cronies, or eventually became so, and as professional equals delighted in one another's work and companionship and championed one another's talents. For the most part they emerged from similar backgrounds, born in the 1920s to working-class families (Conquest himself a notable exception on both counts), and they were sent off to Oxford and Cambridge in the 1940s to complete their studies. University trained – six at Oxford, three at Cambridge – they developed as writers, reviewers, and readers of poetry and banded together as middlebrow critics whose awareness of literary tradition and the practicalities of analytical criticism led them to wrest poetry from control of the institutions with which they were affiliated. It was an ambivalence both fitting and confounding to their purpose.

> On the one hand, the Movement enjoys and exploits the sense of belonging
> to an academic élite; on the other hand, it disapproves of writing aimed at
> such an élite. On the one hand, it asserts the importance of university teach-
> ers and critics; on the other, it questions and satirizes their function. On the
> one hand, it declares that to write for a large audience is damaging; on the
> other, it declares that it is valuable and necessary. On the one hand, its work
> is dense, allusive, intimate with fellow intellectuals; on the other, its work is
> simple, "accessible," intimate with an imagined Common Reader.[5]

As university poets, they bit both hands by retaining a class consciousness governed by modesty and informality; they were academics who distrusted the academy. Larkin demurred, "I can't
understand these chaps who go round . . . universities explaining
how they write poems: it's like going round explaining how you
sleep with your wife" (*Required*, 71).

They also distrusted critics who fashioned their careers at the
expense of writers. The first important critical piece by a Movement
author may have been John Wain's article in *Penguin New Writing*
(1949) praising, for the most part, the poetry of William Empson.
Empson's verses were most appealing, Wain maintains, when clearly
rejecting the experimental excesses of 1940s romanticism; intellectual objectivity should be, according to Wain, the first requirement of
the critic. Critical theory should not supplant a consideration of the
text, for, whatever literature is, it is generally more interesting than
the criticism about it. Enright's "The Rise of Criticocracy" similarly
targets critics who saw themselves as being larger than the works
they criticized.

Enright was one of three with ties to Cambridge (Davie and
Gunn being the others). Although they attended at different times
and did not know one another there, all studied with F. R. Leavis.
Leavis, a demanding critic, inculcated in his students a regard for
artistic discipline and a skepticism for effete, precious, neoromantic
poetry, attributes shared by the Oxford six. (Oddly enough the Cambridge three became acquainted with the Oxford group before
meeting one another. Gunn, for example, so admired the poetry of
Elizabeth Jennings that he went to Oxford to meet her in 1953, and
while there he also met Wain.) Yet all nine Movement poets seemed
to concur with Davie's assessment in *The Poet in the Imaginary Museum* (1977) that a poem needn't suffer from the lively rationality of
the poet. The demands of textual analysis had made them under-

standably self-conscious, and there was no common message in their poetry, but they were united by their lack of common belief, their refusal to be taken in.

The group eventually dispersed about provincial Britain – only Conquest remained based in London – though they did not hold jobs as professional poets. Seven of the Movement authors were published together in *Essays in Criticism*, founded in 1951 by F. W. Bateson, a periodical that served as their platform for several years. Their poetry may have lacked a distinct program, but it was welcomed by Bateson and other editors as an antidote to the poetry of the 1940s, particularly that of Dylan Thomas, which struck them as "thoroughly despicable."[6] Thomas had been virtually canonized on the strength of his fervent romanticism, but pretentious imitators had embraced that romanticism and recast it in their own faddish and emotionally bloated measures. To Movement poets Thomas's mysticism was as unappealing as the soft Marxist literature of the 1930s, and it was considerably more obscure. "To many of the new young, Thomas has come to seem the apotheosis of the False Poet: operatic, sodden, all shapeless dithyrambics and professional Welshness" (Fiedler, 200).

David Perkins alleges that "Dylan Thomas was too relentlessly melodious and rhetorical, making the fifties poets all the more conscious of the morality of plainness. Moreover, they could not recognize their world in the sentimental clichés of Thomas' "Fern Hill" or *Under Milk Wood*, and thus they were motivated all the more toward an honest realism. That Thomas' archetypal symbols seemed vague and obscure to the point of self-indulgence impelled them with stronger conviction toward lucid, rational discourse."[7] Those traits (and Thomas's drunkenness) were satirized in two powerful pieces of Movement fiction, John Wain's *Living in the Present* (1955) and Kingsley Amis's *That Uncertain Feeling* (1955), novels of the sort detested by Somerset Maugham and other members of the literary establishment because they were funny at the expense of ensconced literary and social institutions. Such works – including Wain's *Hurry On Down* (1953), Murdoch's *Under the Net* (1954), an unfinished novel by Larkin, and, of course, Amis's *Lucky Jim* (1954) – deploy educated underachievers, even dropouts, as their protagonists. These idealistic philistines, nurtured on popular culture, serve as spokesmen for their creators whose political and artistic conservatism are testament to their lost innocence. Amis and Wain were soon linked with the Angry Young Man phenomenon which shared the Movement's distrust of pretension.

Though their work was full of political implications, Movement authors tended to express their ideas without fervor. In some this conservatism hardened as their careers became more established. While they had written little about World War II (Wain's "A Song about Major Eatherly" being an important exception), Larkin displays a reluctance toward change and an inherent suspicion of the naïve liberalism of the 1950s in "Homage to a Government" and "MCMXIV," and Amis and Conquest became staunch supporters of the Vietnam War. Leslie Fiedler contends that this "militant middle-browism . . . [was] a useful weapon in the fight against a quiet, upper-class reign of terror based on a frozen high style and a rigidified good taste" (Fiedler, 200-1). Ted Hughes similarly reports:

> One of the things those poets had in common I think was the post-war mood of having had enough . . . enough rhetoric, enough overweening push of any kind, enough of the dark gods, enough of the id, enough of the Angelic powers and the heroic efforts to make new worlds. They'd seen it all turn into death-camps and atomic bombs. All they wanted was to get back in civvies and get home to the wife and kids and for the rest of their lives not a thing was going to interfere with a nice cigarette and a nice view of the park.[8]

But a number of the Movement's personnel – particularly Larkin and Gunn – had disavowed the existence of any organized group. The very notion of committing to any idea, especially a literary movement, seemed ridiculous to them, so they discredited association with the group. Larkin believed that the poets had been lumped together for critical convenience as a result of the furor created by Wain's radio broadcasts. Gunn claimed that the nine writers never publicly agreed on any poetic program, but Davie suggested that their defensiveness, their craven denial of participation in a movement, was but one aspect of their group sensibility.

Davie emphasized that the group worried about not appearing to act in concert. Conquest himself had denied intending to start any alliance with his *New Lines* anthology, but G. S. Fraser grouped six Movement poets together as Empsonians and Academics in his anthology *Springtime* (1953), and Conquest's 1953 P.E.N. anthology placed four of them together. Over a three-year period (1953-56) over 240 poems by eight Movement poets were published in the *Spectator* – only Enright was not a regular contributor – where Wain and Amis had been hired to write book reviews.

Clearly, in advance of Scott's essay and despite protestations to the contrary, friendships and professional relationships had already been formed that contributed to a group aesthetic, and that aesthetic had been broadcast and publicly criticized over a period of years. So when Scott's essay on the idea of a movement was printed as part of a circulation-building scheme, it achieved almost immediate currency. Less than four months later the *Times Literary Supplement* announced that the characteristic poetry of the midcentury had been established.

In assessing the Movement's accomplishments in *The Poet in the Imaginary Museum* Davie remarked that his Movement colleagues were putting the house of English poetry in order by getting rid of its pretentiousness and cultural arrogance. But in 1957 Wain declared that the revolt was over, its work done. A. Alvarez issued a similar judgment in 1958. And in July 1959, Davie penned "Remembering the Movement," all but announcing the death of a movement that most of its members claimed never existed and calling for abandonment of poetry as private and public therapy. According to Blake Morrison, Davie's essay established "a connection between the Movement's poetic manner and the refusal of its members to acknowledge the existence of a group endeavour" (Morrison, 99). They tried to pretend that the Movement had been an invention of journalists, that it had never existed because its members never agreed that they had anything in common. But despite having renounced the hold of the Movement, Davie still acknowledged it four years afterward in his *Thomas Hardy and British Poetry* (1973), claiming that the Movement had been in keeping with the strong tradition of English verse exemplified by Hardy. He had taken a similar position in 1956 in the Movement's heyday, when in *Delta*, a Cambridge literary magazine, he defended its traditional origins. Larkin's edition of *The Oxford Book of Twentieth Century English Verse* (1973) likewise reiterated the Movement's importance in an uninterrupted tradition of British poetry, a tradition emanating from the nineteenth century but interrupted by World War I, which claimed the lives of its promising talents. But Davie attacked Larkin's anthology for including too many minor but traditional poets as a way to avoid including more experimental poets.

The Movement became in time the establishment it had once rebelled against. It succeeded, as Hartley notes in his *Spectator* article "Poets of the Fifties," in bringing discipline, empiricism, and a skeptical distrust of intense feelings to verse. By recognizing the "new tradition" of Movement verse, organized or not, editors presumed its existence. Soon other movements sprang up against them, most notably the *Mavericks* anthology (1957) spawned by Dannie Abse and Howard Sergeant, who thought the Movement more a publicity campaign than a poetic revolution; Malcolm Bradbury's *Eating People Is Wrong* (1959) similarly wonders whether the Movement had been entirely made up by Hartley and Scott, the literary editors of the *Spectator*. Elizabeth Jennings herself called it a journalistic creation of the 1950s, but she has not been wholly consistent in her views about the Movement. She confessed in a 1966 interview with John Press, later recorded in *The Poet Speaks*, that she thought at the time that it was unhelpful to have been identified with the Movement "because I tended to be grouped and criticized rather than be grouped and praised. I think now that the Movement has really broken up, and each of the members of this movement, such as Davie, Gunn, Amis and Larkin, have found their own styles and are really so different you could scarcely call them a movement any longer."[9] She thought the Movement had indeed been a genuine one and was not contrived, that its members had an affinity for one another at the time, but being the Movement's only woman and only Catholic she wanted to write about those subjects which the others did not find quite so engaging. She felt that her poetry had been too rigid and formal, although she wrote swiftly and revised little, and she wanted "to loosen up" her verse" (*Speaks*, 92) by experimenting with prose poems and a libretto for an opera.

It is unsurprising, then, that the Movement poets began to turn away from a group identity. The characteristics of their verse were hardly unusual, and their group identity had been so strong to begin with. Clarity was important to them. Lacking spontaneity, they began to try writing poetry that was different from the *New Lines* format. Since they were distrustful of other literary movements, the Movement poets rightly became distrustful of their own. Having achieved a group identity, members of the Movement began to throw off their label in order to assert their individual identities, which at times led them away from a concerted program of verse. Friendships that once formed the core of the Movement began to strain. Philip Larkin sniped: "Isn't England a marvellous free, open country? Take a fellow like old John Wain, now. No advantages of birth or position or wealth or energy or charm or looks or talent – nothing, and look where he is now. Where else but in England could a thing like that happen? You know, a few years ago I think he got to be Professor of Poetry at Oxford. Just imagine."[10] Wain became miffed on another occasion when Magnus Magnusson introduced him as "the poor man's Kingsley Amis" (*Memoirs*, 44). And Amis, who taught with Davie at Cambridge, recalls, "All I can clearly remember of Donald Davie of Caius is his accusing me, accurately enough, of thinking him square" (*Memoirs*, 221).

Like Jennings, Amis has displayed characteristic ambivalence when speaking about the Movement. He has called it a "phantom"[11] but has also admitted that he had something in common with the other poets lumped into it. Gunn claimed, "I found I was in it before I knew it existed,"[12] and he suspected that it may indeed have never existed. Conquest himself, whose first *New Lines* anthology was the high-water mark of the Movement, added 16 supplementary poets in *New Lines II* (1963), including writers such as Ted Hughes and Thomas Blackburn, whose style was clearly antipathetic to the Movement sensibility. Enright claimed that even as a member he knew nothing about the Movement, an assertion Douglas Dunn partially supports:

> Reading [Enright's] poems, I find myself thinking he was a non-member, a subversive associate from the very beginning. And bother his inclusion in *New Lines*. On the other hand, in a few poems he writes as if he had been the only poet to take what The Movement allegedly stood for with any seriousness. . . . But Enright's poetic antagonisms do appear to have arisen more from urgent social necessity than concern for the health or otherwise of poetry-writing. Lucidity is humane, obscurantist symbol-making and verbosity little more than dandified avoidance of important realities. While Enright believed something on these lines, The Movement as a whole approved of "purity of diction," an altogether more literary concern, urgent enough in their eyes, but an animating impulse which, if not drastically opposed to Enright's more thematic concerns, was at least strikingly different.[13]

If the Movement never existed, then it could never have disbanded. Consequently though the history of the Movement per se may be limited to the 1950s, its antiromantic sensibilities and the careers of its members have extended long beyond the period. Their unemotional calm and their predilection to oppose deceit, set forth as early as 1946 in an editorial in the Oxford-based little magazine *Mandrake*, remain an important part of their work. And given their longevity – all but Larkin are still alive and publishing – the moderation and skeptical rationalism that were hallmarks of their verse more than three decades ago continue to influence British verse today. And the friendships endure. Donald Davie, who preferred a neutral tone with all its formal elegance in the 1950s for his *Brides of Reason*, decades later, even though he has publicly broken ranks with the Movement and come to acknowledge some virtues of romanticism, still writes rational, controlled verse and remembers his colleagues fondly. The Movement was, in the estimation of Blake Morrison, "a literary group of considerable importance – probably the most influential in England since the Imagists" (6).

Chapter Two

Philip Larkin

While the Movement may have been somewhat undecided about its membership and program, it was uniform in its admiration of Philip Larkin as its poetic exemplar. Larkin never claimed membership in any literary school, but his work exhibits the blend of technical formalism and conversational diction characteristic of the Movement. He was practical and tough-minded and avoided lofty rhetoric, preferring instead a lyrical simplicity that postwar readers found attractive. According to Kingsley Amis, Larkin "always knew where he stood, never fooled himself or said anything he did not mean; when he told you he felt something, you could be quite sure he did feel it – a priceless asset to a poet, and a poet of feeling and mood at that. The same quality ensured that when he had nothing to say he said nothing, a turn of mind that helped him not to write any bad poems" (*Memoirs*, 58).

Larkin was born on 9 August 1922. His parents, Eva Emily Day and Sydney Larkin, were timid and reserved, and Larkin himself developed a severe stammer. His father was city treasurer of Coventry, but Larkin's childhood there was hardly cosmopolitan. It was largely uneventful, and his recollection of it, particularly in "I Remember, I Remember," lacks all sentimentality. The poem shows little attachment to the past. Rather, in it Larkin demystifies his upbringing and concludes that "Nothing, like something, happens anywhere."[1]

Larkin was a mediocre student. Though plagued by nearsightedness, he spent much of his time reading, often at the rate of a book a day, and looking for cigarette cards in the Coventry gutters, a habit to which he comically attributed his slouched posture as an adult. He traveled little. His father took him to Germany once, a trip that spawned in him a hatred of all foreign travel, "not being able to talk to anyone, or read anything. . . . I wouldn't mind seeing China," he wrote, "if I could come back the same day. . . . I think travelling is very much a novelist's thing. . . . The poet is really engaged in recreating the familiar" (*Required*, 47, 55). As Larkin matured, his view remained substantially unchanged; he saw little benefit in studying cultures other than his own. "I don't see how one can ever know a foreign language well enough to make reading poems in it worthwhile," he griped. "A writer can have only one language, if language is going to mean anything to him. . . . In fact poets write for people with the same background and experiences as themselves, which might be taken as a compelling argument in support of provincialism" (*Required*, 69). Larkin's conservative views may have been more than provincial; they may in fact have been xenophobic. Anthony Thwaite and Andrew Motion, Larkin's literary executors, have respectively in their *Selected Letters of Philip Larkin, 1940 to 1985* (1993) and *Philip Larkin: A Writer's Life* (1993) offered evidence of Larkin's prejudices.

Larkin attended King Henry VIII School and wrote humorous pieces for the *Coventrian*, the school magazine. In 1940, because of the war, his father thought Philip should go to Oxford a year early at his expense rather than spend an extra year in school and sit for scholarships. He enrolled in St. John Baptist College there, reading the Honours School of English Language and Literature, and for the first time was exposed to a circle of friends who shared his interests. But the reclusive Larkin was initially terrified by Oxford, and his anxiety exacerbated his already pronounced stammer.

Larkin expected to have only three or four terms at Oxford before being called into national service, but he was deemed unqualified to serve because of his poor eyesight. He stayed on, taking his B.A. in 1943. Upon leaving Oxford, he was twice rejected for civil service positions before being appointed to a library post in Shropshire that enabled him to continue his graduate studies at Oxford. Shropshire was but the first in a series of sublibrarian appointments for Larkin; he also worked at the University College of Leicester and the Queen's University of Belfast before becoming head librarian at University of Hull in 1955, where he remained until his death in 1985. Librarianship suited Larkin, for he could not imagine himself a "professional" poet working in a university; "it would embarrass me very much. I don't want to go around pretending to be me" (*Required*, 51). Like Donald Davie and John Wain, he objected to the "cunning merger between poet, literary critic and academic critic (three classes now notoriously indistinguishable): it is hardly an exaggeration to say that the poet has gained the happy position wherein he can praise his own poetry in the press and explain it in the class-room" (*Required*, 81). The arrangement was offensive, putting the poet in "the unprecedented position of peddling both his work and the standard by which it is judged" (*Required*, 82).

Larkin began writing poems as a teenager, selling his first one at 19 to the *Listener*. He continued his writing at Oxford, publishing some work in the *Cherwell*, the undergraduate magazine, and in William Bell's *Poetry from Oxford in Wartime* (1944). On the basis of those poems Fortune Press, which had issued Bell's anthology, invited Larkin to submit a collection of his poetry. The result was *The North Ship* (1945). "I spent the next three years [1943-45] trying to write like Yeats, not because I liked his personality or understood his ideas but out of infatuation with his music" (*Required*, 29). Yet Larkin's prosody in *The North Ship* is generally unmusical, monotonous, and full of romantic symbolism. Excessive and unfocused, his syntax is too complex and his rhymes far too predictable. Moreover, little of his personality is exhibited in the poems. Though there is little of the formal stuffiness one might expect from an Oxford poet, Larkin's posturing in *The North Ship* gives little evidence of his becoming England's most important postwar poet. His themes of lost love remain unrealized, vague, and bleak, and there is none of the wry humor that characterizes his mature work. He was so disappointed in the poems that he was reluctant to allow the volume to be reprinted in 1966. "They are such complete rubbish, for the most part, that I am just twice as unwilling to have two editions in print as I am to have one" (*Sixty*, 43).

Larkin turned to fiction and soon issued two novels, *Jill* (1946) and *A Girl in Winter* (1947). *Jill*, dedicated to his friend Amis, took about a year to write and uses their days at Oxford as a primary source. Larkin's protagonist is a shy scholarship boy named John Kemp, an inexperienced youth from a northern industrial district. In his *Postwar British Fiction*, James Gindin calls Kemp the first example of the displaced working-class hero common to British fiction in general and to Movement novels in particular. Alienated and lonely, Kemp equivocates between two worlds. Kemp's personal disaffection is characterized by his closest companions at Oxford: his roommate Christopher Warner, an unlikable womanizer and a rugby-player, and an ill-mannered, sulky young scholar named Whitbread, who shares

Kemp's proletarian background. Kemp's isolation is further heightened when his hometown, Huddlesford, is bombed. Though his parents' house survives intact, he feels distanced from his past and the society that has nurtured him, so he invents for himself an imaginary girlfriend named Jill. He writes letters to her and fabricates a diary and short story in her name, but, when he meets a young girl in a book shop, he attempts to make real his fantasy. Even her name – Gillian – approximates that of his fantasy girl, but Gillian refuses to be called Jill. Moreover, she is Warner's girlfriend's cousin and is only 15 years old.

Obsessed by his fantasy and the girl who might fulfill it, Kemp pursues Gillian. Hoping to impress her, he invites her to a lavish tea. With wartime rationing in effect, Kemp is nonetheless able to assemble a seductive feast of cakes and tarts and jellies. But when her cousin prevents Gillian from taking tea with Kemp, he gets drunk. Emboldened by alcohol, he finds her party and forces a kiss. Warner knocks him down and with the help of others throws him in the school fountain. As a result of his dousing, Kemp contracts pneumonia and is unable to finish the semester. He returns home to Huddlesford with his parents. Dismayed and disillusioned, Kemp learns the first lesson of adulthood, that one has little control over life, even one's own.

A Girl in Winter, less comic than *Jill*, conveys similar sentiments. Larkin thought of the work, originally called *The Kingdom of Winter*, as a kind of prose poem. So did John Bayley, who called the book "one of the finest and best sustained prose poems in the language."[2] It deals with one day in the life of Katherine Lind, a 22-year-old refugee from an unspecified European country. Katherine is a librarian without status, and because of her nationality she is given only odd jobs. Much of the novel is taken up by her adolescent reverie of a visit with Robin Fennel, a classmate, and his family. As a teenager Katherine was enamored of Robin, a feeling he didn't return. Some years later as a soldier, however, he slips away from his base intending to sleep with Katherine. Intoxicated, he coarsely presses her sexually. Though she does not refuse him, she is not deceived by any illusions of love for him and comes to feel that life no longer holds for her any promise of romantic fulfillment. "There's a limit to what you can get from other people and there's a limit to what your own personality is in itself. That's really the story of *A Girl in Winter*" (*Required*, 56).

Jill gained considerable local success at Oxford, and *A Girl in Winter* attained even wider acceptance. Larkin tried for the next five years to write a third novel, but he couldn't finish it. According to Kingsley Amis, whom Larkin consulted in some detail about the work, it was "a serio-comic account of the gradual involvement of a rising young executive in the motor industry, Sam Wagstaff, with a working-class girl he knocks down in his car coming home from the factory" (*Sixty*, 28). An avid reader of fiction, Larkin later confessed to Jonathan Raban: "I *love* novels. I've started novels. Five of them, I think. Five lost novels. No, it's not the writing that's so difficult with novels, it's the plots. Keeping them up. I don't know. Kingsley always seems to manage to find stories in his life; I'm afraid that mine's not the sort that easily lends itself to stories."[3] Though Larkin's novels never proved as popular as his poetry, his interest in fiction surely prepared him in some measure for the specificity of detail and clarity demanded of Movement verse. Ever the reductionist though, Larkin succinctly distinguished between the two genres: "A very crude difference between novels and poetry is that novels are about other people and poetry is about yourself."[4]

In January 1948, Larkin turned again to poetry and submitted to Faber a collection called *In the Grip of Light*. It is uncertain whether T. S. Eliot, then an editor at Faber, ever saw the manuscript, but it was rejected within a month. Larkin moved to Belfast in 1950 and began to hone his craft. In addition to working at the Queen's University, each day he would write for two hours, then drink and play cards. His style matured. "I felt for the first time I was speaking for myself" (*Required*, 68).

In 1951 Larkin published his next collection, *XX Poems*, at his own expense. He printed only 100 copies, and the book received little notice. He sent review copies to selected writers and critics, but he did so at a time when postal rates had just been increased. He affixed insufficient postage to the books, and many never reached their intended readers. Copies did, however, find their way to D. J. Enright and G. S. Fraser; both men praised Larkin's work, and Fraser included Larkin in his *Springtime* anthology (1953). Despite being otherwise ignored, 13 of the 20 poems did become the basis for *The*

Less Deceived (1955), which brought Larkin his first significant critical attention.

Written between the immature *The North Ship* and the accom-
plished *The Less Deceived*, *XX Poems* is clearly a transitional work.
In it Larkin began to abandon the musicality of Yeats and to turn toward a more personal verse, embracing Hardy as his spiritual influence. From Hardy he learned to celebrate the commonplace and to
focus on moral issues. He began to write more from personal experience and in his own vernacular, qualities that were to enrich Larkin's
greatest poems. Discovering his own voice in *XX Poems*, Larkin uses
the first-person "I" as the basis for his poems. In "IX: Waiting for
breakfast, while she brushed her hair," for example, the reflective
narrator and the emphasis on observable details – an empty hotel
yard, wet cobblestones, a misty sky – disclose Larkin's movement
away from the vague symbolism of earlier poems and toward a more
conversational poetic. It begins:

> Waiting for breakfast, while she brushed her hair,
> I looked down at the empty hotel yard
> Once meant for coaches. Cobblestones were wet,
> But sent no light back to the loaded sky,
> Sunk as it was with mist down to the roofs.
> Drainpipes and fire-escape climbed up
> Past rooms still burning their electric light:
> I thought: Featureless morning, featureless night. (Larkin *CP*, 20)

George Hartley, editor of Marvell Press, wanted the poem added to
the second edition of *The Less Deceived*, but Larkin declined. He
added it instead to the reprinted edition of *The North Ship*; "though
not noticeably better than the rest," he writes, "it shows the Celtic
fever abated and the patient sleeping soundly" (*Required*, 30).

Larkin's friends began to publish in the *Spectator* and other periodicals and in Oscar Mellor's Fantasy Press pamphlets; Larkin's
collection of five poems (1954) was number 21 in the series. But
when the *Spectator* printed its "In the Movement" essay, it did not
mention Larkin. Critical notice did come the following year, however, when Marvell Press issued *The Less Deceived*. Larkin submitted
the typescript under the title *Various Poems*, but Hartley was convinced by Larkin to base it on a phrase from one of the volume's
poems, "Deceptions." *The Less Deceived* is a fitting title, for the

complications of self-deception form the book's major theme and had been at the core of *Jill* and *A Girl in Winter*.

"Deceptions" is based on an account in Matthew Mayhew's *London Labour and the London Poor*, in which a Victorian girl is drugged, raped, and forced into prostitution. Ironically, the girl – while clearly the victim in the most obvious sense – is less a victim of self-deception than the perpetrator of the rape, who brings to the act expectations that are not fulfilled. Addressing the girl, Larkin concludes:

> For you would hardly care
> That you were less deceived, out on that bed,
> Than he was, stumbling up the breathless stair
> To burst into fulfilment's desolate attic. (Larkin *CP*, 32)

Larkin heightens the poem's drama by exploring in a casual tone the gulf between expectation and achievement. By understating the horror of what has transpired, his conversational technique has the effect of underscoring it. The casual familiarity of the language renders the rape commonplace, and so all the more disturbing.

The difficulties of romance represent another important theme in *The Less Deceived* and in Larkin's two later collections. In one poem, "Maiden Name," a woman's maiden name is seen as an artifact of her failure to find love. And in another, "Places, Loved Ones," Larkin explores the problem in awaiting that special person whose love might make life redemptive and purposeful. To find her would absolve the poem's narrator of responsibility for his amatory failures ("So that it's not your fault / Should the town turn dreary, / The girl a dolt" [Larkin *CP*, 99]), but not to love necessitates a recognition of personal culpability. Are romantic fantasies responsible for disappointment, or are they the impetus to throw off from time to time the shackles of self-limitation?

Larkin never married, and his poetry expresses considerable bewilderment about the prospects of sexual happiness and wedded bliss. "I don't want to sound falsely naïve, but I often wonder why people get married. I think perhaps they dislike being alone more than I do. . . . I think living with someone and being in love is a very difficult business anyway because almost by definition it means putting yourself at the disposal of someone else, ranking them higher than yourself" (*Required*, 54). Kingsley Amis recalls that as Larkin

aged he developed a crasser, more disenchanted view of the possibilities of love: "you promise to give someone half your money for
the rest of your life and not to fuck anyone else" (*Memoirs*, 61). In
the poem "Reasons for Attendance" he suggests that in a humanist
society art may be a higher calling than sexual happiness, but he
leaves open the possibility of error ("If no one has misjudged himself. Or lied" [Larkin *CP*, 80]). Still, he equates losing touch with
sexual happiness "to losing one's faith in a religious age" (*Required*,
292).

Such self-debate is at the heart of Larkin's best poems, poems in
which the speaker's pragmatism challenges his impulsive, idealistic
side. According to Bruce K. Martin, "because Larkin carefully depicts
his speakers . . . as witty, we can enjoy their expressions of dissatisfaction, but . . . he [also] exposes them as rationalizers. . . . Each
finds himself trying to justify a situation ultimately unjustifiable."[5] By
having his speakers question their own credibility, Larkin appears
reasonable and temperate himself. The speaker's dissatisfaction with
himself becomes acceptable, as in "Poetry of Departures," only because the alternatives to the drab routine of his life are
"artificial / Such a deliberate step backwards" (Larkin *CP*, 85).
Further, in "Toads" he confronts his own dislike for work but
ultimately concedes he is too cowardly to cry out "Stuff your
pension!" (Larkin *CP*, 89). Larkin writes as if there were a happy
median of existence to which one might adhere and thereby appear
neither too stuffy nor too foolish. Indeed, averageness is his peculiar
birthday blessing for Sally Amis in "Born Yesterday." He would wish
her beauty and happiness, but they are unlikely accruals, and,
unwilling to appear fatuous or absurd, he wishes for her instead

> An average of talents:
> Not ugly, not good-looking,
> Nothing uncustomary
> To pull you off your balance,
> That, unworkable itself,
> Stops all the rest from working. (Larkin *CP*, 84)

The emotions here are typically subdued. Larkin was aware that
such poetry was different from the radical urgency of the apocalyptic
poets of the 1940s who immersed themselves in grand gesture.
Larkin sought to write a quieter verse rooted in the real world, and

he explained his objective as follows: "I tend to lead the reader in by the hand very gently, saying this is the initial experience or object, and now you see that it makes me think of this, that and the other, and work up to a big finish – I mean, that's the sort of pattern. Other people, I suppose, will just take a flying start several yards off the ground, and hope the reader will ultimately catch up with them" (Morrison, 125).

Larkin's use of the self-critical persona reached its apex in "Church Going," perhaps the paradigmatic Movement poem. It was one of Larkin's contributions to *New Lines*, and it is the most powerful poem in the collection. The dispute in "Church Going" is not whether to believe in God; rather it is what shall replace God in the modern consciousness. Larkin tacitly accepts society's post-Christian condition, but shows no pessimism at the notion of God's absence. "The days when one could claim to be the priest of a mystery are gone: today mystery means either ignorance or hokum" (*Required*, 83-84).

Larkin insists the poem "isn't religious at all. Religion surely means that the affairs of this world are under divine surveillance, and so on, and I go to some pains to point out that I don't bother about that kind of thing, that I'm deliberately ignorant of it . . . the poem is about going to church, not religion" ("Conversations," 73).

Larkin's persona in "Church Going" adopts his common mask of skepticism and wryness ("bored, uninformed"), an agnostic cyclist who has stopped to inspect a deserted country church. The poem implies that even God is not there, for once inside the church the narrator becomes flippant; he drops an Irish sixpence in the collection box and, mounting the lectern, delivers a mock sermon. But he becomes increasingly deferential as the poem proceeds. Even Larkin's diction is elevated, reverential. The narrator's church going does not connect him with God, but it does link him with humankind. He turns isolating cynicism aside by recognizing a positive and communal "hunger in himself to be more serious" (Larkin *CP*, 98). That this movement, this shift in thinking, has happened to a free thinker makes its message more striking and palatable. The irony is unmistakably Larkinian: the church merits importance because it sanctifies humanity, and the speaker's sarcastic method enables him to render the world intelligible. He moves from solitariness to solidarity as the first-person singular pronoun gives way to the plural form in the final stanza.

In 1964 Larkin issued his most compelling volume, *The Whitsun Weddings*, for which he was awarded the Queen's Gold Medal for Poetry and the Arts Council Triennial Award. It built upon the reputation of *The Less Deceived*, and the first printing of 4,000 copies was soon exhausted as the British public discovered a poet who was not only sensible but imminently readable. The poetry is straightforward and easy to interpret, and it speaks to a mass culture identified in billboards, religious faith healings, graffiti, and department stores. Asked to comment on the poems, Larkin teasingly allowed, "the poems were written in or near Hull, Yorkshire, with a succession of Royal Sovereign 2B pencils during the years 1955 to 1963, there seems little to add. I think in every instance the effect I was trying to get is clear enough. If sometimes I have failed, no marginal annotation will help now" (*Required*, 83).

Truly little context is required for a successful reading of the poems; there is nothing much referential about them at all. They are the culmination of the guiding principle Larkin set forth in Enright's *Poets of the 1950s*, "that every poem must be its own sole freshly created universe, and therefore have no belief in 'tradition' or a common myth-kitty or casual allusions in poems to other poems or poets" (*Required*, 79). Larkin stringently avoids classical and historical allusions. In fact, World War I (in "MCMXIV") seems at the dim edge of memory, existing in an age of innocence from which modern culture retreats more and more every day. The poems are distinctly modern, yet not "avant-garde." Unlike the three P's (Ezra Pound, Charlie Parker, and Pablo Picasso) who "seemed crazy when they were new and seem crazy now" (*Required*, 72), Larkin strives to be understood.

Because Larkin's cultural references are so recognizable, he is able to achieve a kind of personal detachment. In "Wild Oats," for example, he tallies the statistics of a failed romance: over 400 letters in seven years, one 10-guinea ring, five rehearsals in parting, two wallet snapshots of a "bosomy English rose" (Larkin *CP*, 143). But this reckoning is but a mask to avoid painful introspection. After 20 years the narrator still bears regret over the episode, but the numbers provide an impersonal way to speak of failed expectations and personal inadequacy.

Larkin's narrators never seem to sow their wild oats before oblivion overtakes them, and *The Whitsun Weddings* is an inventory of such failure and despair: Mr. Bleaney, whose fusty room becomes a grave for his narrow dreams ("Mr Bleaney"); Larkin's schoolmate Dockery, who thought fatherhood would save him from extinction ("Dockery and Son"); the bewailing, suffering women of "Faith Healing"; "the boy puking his heart out in the Gents" in "Essential Beauty" (Larkin *CP*, 144); Arnold, who "married a woman to stop her getting away / Now she's there all day" ("Self's the Man" [Larkin *CP*, 117]). Larkin once admitted, "Deprivation is for me what daffodils were for Wordsworth" (*Required*, 47), and poem after poem, like "Dockery and Son," reminds with trenchant dread that

> Life is first boredom, then fear.
> Whether or not we use it, it goes,
> And leaves what something hidden from us chose,
> And age, and then the only end of age. (Larkin *CP*, 153)

Jonathan Raban called them "lines that you can frighten yourself with in the dark" (266). Larkin was certainly not humorless, but for him sad thoughts were more appropriate for poetry. "I suppose there must be some people who think life is first fun, then contentment. Wouldn't wash in a poem, though, would it? 'Life is first fun, then contentment.' Doesn't sound at all right to me" (Raban, 266). Larkin liked to think of himself as being funny, and humor is definitely present in many of his poems, but he knew that unhappiness propels a poem in a more fundamental way than does happiness. "I think it is very much easier to imagine happiness than to experience it" (*Required*, 55), but the trouble with using humor is that "it makes them think you aren't being serious" (*Required*, 73). Despite his humor, Larkin never considered himself a satirist; a satirist thinks he knows "better than everyone else" (*Required*, 73).

In a series of poems – "Essential Beauty," "The Large Cool Store," and "Sunny Prestatyn" are the best examples – Larkin employs humor to mark the gulf between the lure of advertising and the keenness of romance's failure. In them reality is glamorized into a perversion of the platonic ideal. In "Mr Bleaney" Larkin feared that how a man lived was a measure of his worth; in "Essential Beauty" that dread is transcended by advertisers whose distortions

> cover slums with praise
> Of motor-oil and cuts of salmon, shine
> Perpetually these sharply-pictured groves
> Of how life should be. (Larkin *CP*, 144)

Imperfect life cannot match its unearthly and natureless dreams, and Larkin's panorama of ecstasy, of "unfenced existence" (Larkin *CP*, 137), serves to clarify his loneliness. In "Here," the opening poem of *The Whitsun Weddings*, the ideal remains out of reach, but in the title poem seems attainable, a force "ready to be loosed with all the power / That being changed can give" (Larkin *CP*, 116). Larkin must not have come to that optimism easily; never prolific, he composed that poem over a three-year period, and its optimism is visible in only one other poem in the collection, "An Arundel Tomb," which closes the volume with the observation that "What will survive of us is love" (Larkin *CP*, 111).

One of Larkin's great loves was jazz. As a boy he wanted to be a jazz drummer, and he confessed it would be easier for him to live without poetry than jazz. He introduced Amis to it in Oxford and became jazz feature writer for the *Daily Telegraph* in 1961. Those jazz reviews were assembled into *All What Jazz* (1970), a collection that displays the no-nonsense attitude of the Movement. "There could hardly have been a conciser summary of what I don't believe about art" (*Required*, 293). Larkin resented the move from traditional to improvisational jazz, equating it with a move away from realism and toward modernism in art. In his reviews he attacks the confusion and pretentious elitism of modern art; "they are irresponsible exploitations of technique in contradiction of human life as we know it" (*Required*, 297).

Larkin also edited *The Oxford Book of Twentieth Century English Verse* (1973), which includes six of his own poems. "I spent five years reading everyone's complete works, ending with six months in the basement of the Bodleian Library handling all the twentieth-century poetry they had received. It was great fun. I don't say I made any major discoveries, but I hope I managed to suggest that there are good poems around that no one knows about. At any rate, I made a readable book. I made twentieth-century poetry sound nice. That's quite an achievement in itself' (*Required*, 73).

And in 1974, a decade after the publication of *The Whitsun Weddings*, Larkin issued *High Windows*. It sold 6,000 copies in three weeks, a record for his publisher. He considers the familiar themes of love and death in *High Windows*, but he does so from the stoical perspective of advancing age. His fundamental are not so much re-peated as reconfirmed, though the comedy is more open. Change is accepted sardonically, Larkin recognizing that the passage of time brings only death and oblivion. But what other choice is there? To protest time will not stop it, so Larkin's humor is a form of self-de-fense that enables him to endure. In *High Windows*, though, he is more a parodist than in earlier works, rendering serious subjects comically and trivial ones with touching pathos.

"Annus Mirabilis" and "This Be the Verse" begin comically enough, and both derive their humor from the advanced age of their personas. In the former Larkin gives a brief appraisal of the sexual revolution:

> Sexual intercourse began
> In nineteen sixty-three
> (Which was rather late for me) –
> Between the end of the Chatterley ban
> And the Beatles' first LP. (Larkin *CP*, 167)

The latter tersely explores the lineage of misery:

> They fuck you up, your mum and dad.
> They may not mean to, but they do.
> They fill you with the faults they had
> And add some extra, just for you.
>
> But they were fucked up in their turn
> By fools in old-style hats and coats,
> Who half the time were soppy-stern
> And half at one another's throats.
>
> Man hands on misery to man.
> It deepens like a coastal shelf.
> Get out as early as you can,
> And don't have any kids yourself. (Larkin *CP*, 180)

One of the most touching poems in the collection is "Vers de Société," in which, by responding to a social invitation the narrator is forced to confront his aloneness. "All solitude is selfish" (Larkin *CP*, 181), the narrator ultimately decides, accepting the invitation; there is time enough to be alone.

According to Clive James, "Larkin's poetry draws a bitterly sad picture of modern life but it is full of saving grace" (*Sixty*, 107). Andrew Motion similarly praises Larkin's ability to "assert the value and resilience of human charity" (*Sixty*, 67). His resilience and charity are tested in two "institutional" poems, "The Building" and "The Old Fools." His subjects are those confined to hospitals and nursing homes wherein they "struggle to transcend / The thought of dying" (Larkin *CP*, 192-93). They don't know what's happening to them, but Larkin does, and he views those places as modern cathedrals in that they concern themselves with the final disposition of life. As priest-substitute Larkin mediates the distance between himself and "the old fools" both thematically and grammatically. In moving from the third-person subject of the first stanza to the first-person conclusion of the last, he writes in second person in the second stanza: "At death, you break up: the bits that were you / Start speeding away from each other for ever / With no one to see" (Larkin *CP*, 196). The procedure is inverse to the three stages he described as typical to his poetic method: "the first is when a man becomes obsessed with an emotional concept to such a degree that he is compelled to do something about it. What he does is the second stage, namely, construct a verbal device that will reproduce this emotional concept in anyone who cares to read it, anywhere, any time. The third stage is the recurrent situation of people in different times and places setting off the device and re-creating in themselves what the poet felt when he wrote it" (*Required*, 80).

There is little disapproval from Larkin for how things are, merely understanding. His is the view from above, the solitude of the high-windowed perspective. The protests he does issue are fairly muted and mundane. He does complain mildly now and again about money ("Homage to a Government" and "Money") and the dreariness of work, but these complaints spring, according to Kingsley Amis, from "a general reluctance to let go of anything he felt belonged to him or was part of him" (*Memoirs*, 61). Like Conquest and Wain, Larkin worried about the public role of poetry and opposed its being subsidized as a form of public entertainment, but he was reluctant to use poetry as a platform for bardic pronouncements, endorsing instead poetry to "be read silently from the printed page" (*Required*, 87).

In the decade following *High Windows* Larkin wrote few poems. "Aubade," his last great one, was published as a little pamphlet in

1977. It conveys familiar sentiments about death, "the anaesthetic from which none come round" (Larkin *CP*, 208), and expresses Larkin's hardening impassivity toward it: "Being brave / Lets no one off the grave. / Death is no different whined at than withstood" (Larkin *CP*, 209). He seemed to be preparing himself for the end. He once claimed he did not give up on poetry so much as it gave up on him, and the same might be said of life. Larkin's critics have confused his phlegmatic persona with a refusal to take poetic risks. They have found him unnecessarily ordinary, narrow, and provincial. But these are precisely the Movement virtues Larkin wished to attain. He wanted his poems to be compressed and communicative. According to Donald Mitchell, the strengths of Larkin's verse are "its precision, clarity, formal mastery and above all its marvellous rhythmic organization" (*Sixty*, 78). Alan Bennett observes, "One of the good things about Larkin is that he still has you firmly by the hand as you cross the finishing line" (*Sixty*, 73).

Larkin believed that reading poems should be a pleasure, and, though fear of death was his favorite theme, the reading public found his verses pleasurable enough. So did other poets. Upon the death of poet laureate John Betjeman in 1984, a survey of prominent poets favored Larkin to succeed to the position. It was an honor he did not want and managed to avoid. He died of throat cancer in 1985, leaving a legacy of unforgettable verses, his substantial reputation based on fewer than 200 mature poems. Jonathan Raban eloquently commemorated his passing:

> Until his death, I hadn't grasped how much he was loved in England. People minded about his dying, and mourned him, in a way that seemed strange for a poet, however admired his work. He had kept himself profoundly to himself. His word-perfect, world-imperfect, poems were as rare to show as famous comets. He wrote of being alone, of private dereliction, of living without love – inconsolable poems, teased and haunted by the beauty, only just out of reach, beyond the window of the railway carriage or the solitary room. The separating glass of windows figures again and again in his work. Yet he showed how such a life (a life from which most people would shrink in panic) could be managed with, if not quite gaiety, at least great dignity and grace. His poems are heartbreakingly exact. If poems can teach anything, Larkin's teach that there is no desolation so bleak that it cannot be made habitable by style. If we live inside a bad joke, it is up to us to learn, at best and worst, to tell it well. (269-70)

Chapter Three

Kingsley Amis

Although his most famous work was issued in the mid-1950s, Kingsley Amis has remained a popular and endearing writer. Born Kingsley William Amis on 16 April 1922 near Clapham Common, he was reared in Norbury, 10 miles south of London. His low-church, lower-middle-class childhood, much like that of Philip Larkin, was unremarkable; Amis claims he was often bored and "very lonely. . . . I never had fun."[1] Kingsley was the only child of Rosa Annie and William Robert Amis, a senior export clerk for Colman's Mustard. His parents had no particular interest in the arts, but they were concerned that he receive a good education. Although his father approved of Kingsley's writing, he also feared that his son would never be able to earn a living by it. He cautioned him to prepare for a business career, perhaps even one at the mustard factory. Ironically enough in 1963, the year his father died, Kingsley Amis began to support himself full-time as a writer.

Amis wrote his first story, "The Sacred Rhino of Uganda," at 11, and it appeared in the Norbury school magazine. The following year he won a scholarship to the City of London School, which he attended from 1935 to 1939, commuting to the city, like his father. The daily commute ended with the outbreak of World War II, when the school was evacuated for two years to Marlborough College, Wiltshire. Amis greatly enjoyed the City of London School, and he wrote poetry there, publishing "Prelude" in the 1938 school magazine. The poem, modeled on Eliot's *The Waste Land*, shows Amis's talent for imitation and mimicry, which he amiably employed in his fiction and in *The Evans Country* (1962) poems.

In 1941 Amis won a scholarship to St. John's College, Oxford. Larkin was already enrolled when he arrived, and their friendship began when they encountered each other on a flight of stairs at Oxford in the first week. Larkin warmly recalls that friendship in his introduction to *Jill*, a friendship instrumental to the formation of the

Movement. From the beginning the two were enthusiasts of each other's work, though Larkin thought Amis the greater talent. He praised Amis for "a style that will exasperate only those who cannot see when a poem is being funny and serious simultaneously."[2]

Besides literature Amis and Larkin shared an interest in beer and jazz, and both eventually became regular reviewers of jazz records. Amis wrote a monthly column for the *Observer* in the 1950s and later penned two book-length treatises on drinking, *On Drink* (1972) and *How's Your Glass?* (1984). Larkin and Amis found each another immensely entertaining, and they swapped jokes – Amis's apings could render Larkin "incapable with laughter."[3] Larkin later admitted that one of the shaping visions for *The Less Deceived* had been the simple desire to make Amis laugh. "Born Yesterday" is affectionately dedicated to Amis's daughter Sally. Amis repaid the compliment by dedicating *Lucky Jim* to Larkin, who also proved a close and helpful reader of the manuscript in its early stages, and the name of Amis's protagonist (Jim Dixon) was derived from Larkin's home address on Dixon Drive.

As a young man Amis did have a serious side, but Larkin recalls "to some extent he suffered the familiar humorist's fate of being unable to get anyone to take him seriously at all. Kingsley's 'serious side' was political. . . . He became editor of the University Labour Club Bulletin and in this capacity printed one of my poems" (*Jill*, 14). Their comradeship was interrupted, however, when Amis entered the British Royal Signal Corps, where he served from 1942 to 1945, although they continued to visit in Oxford during the time that Amis was stationed nearby. Amis saw duty in Normandy shortly after D day and in Belgium and West Germany, but he faced no combat. He was a lieutenant when he left the military, while Larkin had been deemed unfit for service and had graduated from Oxford during Amis's tour of duty.

Amis's first book was *Bright November* (1947). It was issued by Fortune Press, whose proprietor, R. A. Caton, had recently published *Jill* and *The North Ship* by Larkin and earlier Dylan Thomas's *Eighteen Poems* (1934). Caton was also the model for L. S. Caton, a character who appears in several of Amis's early novels. The poems in *Bright November* are fairly traditional in structure and show the strong influence of Auden, but years later Amis expressed his displeasure with this early posturing, glad that the book's limited publication and the intervening years had kept it from a wider public. Amis's lack of appreciation for *Bright November* is evident; he omits it from his *Who's Who* entry, and he included only six poems from it in his *Collected Poems, 1944-1979*.

Most of *Bright November*'s 31 poems were written while Amis was in the service, the earliest dating from 1943. "Radar" praises his countrymen Kolster and Dunmore, the inventors of radar, but the poem concludes ironically with a consideration of the suffering of the enemy. Other military poems include "Belgian Winter," "Aviator's Hymn" (which shows the influence of Dylan Thomas), and "O Captain, My Captain!" whose title, though borrowed from Walt Whitman, seems patterned after Henry Reed's "Lessons of the War," wherein an experienced military officer speaks to a young recruit. Demobilization inspired "Release," the longest poem and the one from which a phrase was lifted for the volume's title. "Release" is the book's one poem that best exhibits the plainness and honesty characteristic of much Movement verse. "The colloquial touch, the casual self-deprecation, and the subterranean moral concerns all indicate that Amis was beginning to emerge from the shells of other poets."[4]

Amis also used his military experiences as the bases of three stories in *My Enemy's Enemy* (1962). In the somewhat autobiographical "I Spy Strangers," Lt. Archer, a Labour party supporter, writes letters to an Oxford friend who is unfit for service, expressing his desire for a postwar England replete with "girls and drinks and jazz and books and decent houses and decent jobs and being your own boss."[5]

Amis returned to Oxford after the war, taking his M.A. with first-class honors in 1947. Upon his return he met John Wain, and both were soon "united in homage to Larkin."[6] The three supported one another's literary efforts. Wain and Amis shared Larkin's humorous disdain for pretension, and both read *Jill* soon after it appeared; the book inspired each to write his own novel. While Amis's offering, *The Legacy*, was never published, it too encouraged Wain.

> When I first knew him, at Oxford, he was writing a novel: of course every second or third undergraduate one met was "writing a novel," but Amis spoke of his with such enjoyment, and seemed to be having so much fun writing it, that I caught the virus. . . . He had made it seem, as none of the others did, simple and natural to be trying to shape one's day-to-day reaction to life into fiction. I'm quite certain I would never have written *Hurry On Down* without the example of that first, undergraduate novel of Amis's – which, as I recall, was

never published. And if I had not written *Hurry On Down*, I might never have turned professional at all. (*Sprightly*, 204)

Amis also befriended Elizabeth Jennings at Oxford and for a time became her literary mentor, though she was hardly an ironist in the vein of Amis, Wain, and Larkin. They were all composing poems at the time, and Amis published two along with a review of Larkin's *A Girl in Winter* in a 1947 issue of *Mandrake*, an Oxford-based literary magazine coedited by Wain. One of the poems, "Retrospect," seems to have influenced Jennings's poem "Delay," for their endings are strikingly similar. Amis's conclusion, "And love is always moving somewhere else,"[7] resonates in Jennings's words, "And love arrived may find us somewhere else."[8] Their poetry appeared together in *Oxford Poetry* (1948), and, when Amis and James Michie edited *Oxford Poetry* the following year, they included six poems by Jennings, more than from any other contributor.

While at Oxford Amis was commissioned by an Argentine university to write a book on Graham Greene. Amis finished the work, but it was never published, and he failed to win a research degree with his thesis "English Poetry, 1850-1900, and the Victorian Reading Public." Despite the academic setback, his affinity for the Victorians has remained strong. He confesses:

I think of myself like a sort of mid- or late-Victorian person, not in outlook but in the position of writing a bit of poetry (we forget that George Eliot also wrote verse), writing novels, being interested in questions of the day and occasionally writing about them, and being interested in the work of other writers and occasionally writing about that. I'm not exactly an entertainer pure and simple, not exactly an artist pure and simple, certainly not an incisive critic of society, and certainly not a political figure though I'm interested in politics. I think I'm just a combination of some of those things.[9]

Amis married in 1948 and left Oxford the following year, but he kept in contact with his thesis supervisor, F. W. Bateson, who in 1951 established *Essays in Criticism*, which was to become a powerful platform for the Movement. Amis and most of his Movement colleagues contributed frequently to the magazine in its early years.

In 1949 Amis began his teaching career at the University College of Swansea, Wales, where he taught until 1961. In the spring of 1951 he met Dylan Thomas, who lectured at the college. Though suspicious of romanticism's excesses, Amis was sympathetic toward Thomas at the time. Amis's experiences in Wales influenced much of his work, and it is the setting for two of his novels – *That Uncertain Feeling* (1955) and *The Old Devils* (1986) (both contain biting parodies of Thomas) – and for one book of verse, *The Evans Country*.

At Swansea Amis came upon a copy of Davie's *Purity of Diction in English Verse* in the public library. He reviewed the book favorably, as did Wain and Enright, and met Davie shortly afterward at a teachers' conference. Davie remembers the episode: "One of my pleasant memories is of Kingsley Amis, when we met for the first time. . . . What pleased me was that Amis had liked the book, not in his capacity of university teacher (as he then was), but from the point of view of himself as poet. . . . All this was at a time when Amis and I and one or two others discovered that we had been moving, each by his own route, upon a common point of view as regards the writing of poems. That point of intersection, or an area of agreement around it, came to be called the Movement."[10]

Amis's Oxford companions were beginning to attract literary notice, and Amis frequently left Swansea to join them in London. As membership in the Movement began to become fixed, the group found itself purporting an unadorned style, one in which toughness and plainspokenness were brought to bear. Amis's own creative activities gained attention as well. John Wain was at the time conducting a BBC broadcast called *First Reading*, and in 1953 Amis read on the program from *Lucky Jim*, which was then in progress. His poetry was also included in Conquest's *New Lines* and Enright's *Poetry of the 1950s* anthologies.

Amis met Robert Conquest at a P.E.N. party to launch the first of its yearly anthologies, *New Poems, 1952*. Both writers had been included in the collection and soon discovered they were affable allies. Amis claims that Conquest told him 50 bawdy limericks at the party. The friendship grew, and that November Amis defended Conquest against an attack in the *Listener*. Over the years the two collaborated on a number of projects, most notably one novel, *The Egyptologists* (1965), and a science fiction series.

The influence of the Movement "friends" on the face of modern letters became increasingly evident. Delivering a statement of purpose on behalf of his fellow contributors to *Poets of the 1950s*, Amis determined that "No one wants any more poems on the grander

themes for a few years, but at the same time nobody wants any more
poems about philosophers or paintings or novelists or art galleries or
mythology or foreign cities or other poems."[11] Amis was not always
true to his word, however, for his poems "Beowulf," "The English
Novel, 1740-1820," "A Dream of Fair Women," "A Note on Wyatt,"
and "The Triumph of Life" depend, although somewhat derisively
so, on the themes of a grand literary tradition; he uses these themes
as well as easy targets in *Lucky Jim*. If the tradition could not be ignored, it could at least be condemned. And when he went to Princeton in 1958 as a visiting professor, Amis shunned traditional literary
matters almost altogether in favor of science fiction. These Princeton
lectures formed the basis of *New Maps of Hell* (1960), one of the first
detailed overviews of the genre.

Amis noted two things Movement poets held in common: "a desire to be lucid if nothing else, and a liking for strict and fairly simple
verse forms" (Brennan, 19). Amis's first published work from Wales,
A Frame of Mind (1953), certainly displays those characteristics. The
collection was issued in a limited edition by the University of Reading
School of Art, where Wain was on staff as a lecturer. Wain's *Mixed
Feelings* had been issued under the same imprint, inaugurating the
series in 1951, and *A Frame of Mind* is dedicated to Wain.

Amis was understandably more satisfied with *A Frame of Mind*
than with *Bright November*; the work includes some of his best
verse, and 15 of the 18 poems are reprinted in his *Collected Poems*.
"Against Romanticism" presents Amis's disavowal of romanticism
and, one of the Movement's most enduring poems, fixes its credo in
both positive and negative terms. He explains the growth of romanticism, but he makes no choice between its forceful principles and the
dilemma it poses for adherents unable to harness its force. He contrasts those misled by prophecies and visions with the pragmatic,
those governed by rule and reason. Amis further mocks romantic
pantheistic doctrine in "Ode to the East-North-East-by-East Wind."
Amis's wind – "a cheery chap I can't avoid," a "sweating, empty-
handed labourer," a "mailless courier" (Amis *CP*, 54) – seems more
real than Shelley's, and he addresses it, not as a supplicant but with
reproof. "The virtue . . . of the anti-romantic view of life" is that "it
expresses itself in ways which appeal to humour as well as reason."[12]

"Something Nasty in the Bookshop" (later retitled "A Bookshop
Idyll") is another poem that helped establish Amis as one of the

Movement's chief critics of romanticism. In it the speaker explores a thin anthology of modern poetry and discovers a moral of sorts in its table of contents. Making a division by gender, he facetiously contrasts the titles of poems by male and female poets. The women seem open-hearted, personal, and honest, but the poetry by men seems hypocritically smug and self-satisfied, their strong egos creating distances that impede gentle honesty. The tone turns serious, and the speaker decides "Women are really much nicer than men: / No wonder we like them" (Amis *CP*, 57). But his "A Dream of Fair Women," a sexual fantasy about "a squadron of draped nudes" (Amis *CP*, 31), satirically warns of the "boredom on the way" (Amis *CP*, 32) to love's unreal embraces. The humor heightens his argument that man's romantic daydreams are not sustained by life's realities.

In 1954 Amis authored the one book against which all his others have been compared: *Lucky Jim*. The work seems to have been engendered by a visit to Larkin, who was then working as an assistant librarian at the University College of Leicester. Amis became bored by the stuffy, colorless people he met in the common room there, and *Lucky Jim* is his attempt to puncture all academic snobbery and pretense. Appealing to both literary critics and the reading public, the book was a great success, going through 10 printings in 1954 and 10 more in the next three years. It has since been translated into 20 languages and been made into a successful motion picture and a British television series.

Lucky Jim contains many of the qualities of Movement verse and was quickly grouped by critics alongside the works of Britain's rebellious young writers – John Braine's *Room at the Top*, John Wain's *Hurry on Down*, Iris Murdoch's *Under the Net*, and John Osborne's *Look Back in Anger*. While the works do share certain similarities in that they are contemporaneous, populist, somewhat antiintellectual interpretations of the postwar welfare state written in colloquial English, Amis's book – like Wain's, for that matter – displays little anger. But it did identify a new type of hero, "the working- or lower-middle-class university graduate who has been educated out of his own class but who has no ambition to become a 'gentleman'; who has been taught to relish the perquisites of power but who regards the power game, as it is played in Britain, as ridiculous and immoral" (*World*, 45-46). Anthony Burgess called its protagonist "the most popular anti-hero of our time."[13]

Lucky Jim Dixon is the product of a grammar school from the industrial north, the Royal Air Force, and (Larkin's influence again) Leicester University. A junior lecturer in medieval history, he is not only ill-qualified for his job, but he hates medieval history and the provincial university that employs him. He reviles all affectation, all phonies, but he has not been trained for any other kind of work. While he has the lower-middle-class drive to improve himself socially, he is essentially a self-indulgent and inept boor. His probationary period nearly over and wanting to avoid dismissal, Jim is driven to retain a job he vehemently despises.

So Jim is forced to ingratiate himself with the pretentious fool who heads the department, Professor Welch. He spends arty weekends listening to madrigal singing and recorder blowing to impress his chairman, then tries through beer to assuage his self-loathing for having done so. Additionally, his amatory relationship with Margaret Peel, a cliché-ridden and neurotic colleague, also proves embarrassing. He pities her, but he fears her influence. Hating sham, he is nonetheless forced to repress his qualms about his position. He enacts small revenges instead, including making faces at his detractors (his Edith Sitwell face, his lemon-sucking face, his Eskimo face, his Martian face, and so on). When at last he delivers his lecture on Merrie England, it is a drunken disaster. Yet with his academic career ruined, he manages to land both a well-paying job and the girl to whom he is attracted.

The novel was not universally praised. Although it won the Somerset Maugham Award, Maugham himself attacked Dixon and the generation of youth represented in the book.

> They do not go to university to acquire culture, but to get a job, and when they have got one, scamp it. They have no manners, and are woefully unable to deal with any social predicament. Their idea of a celebration is to go to a public house and drink six beers. They are mean, malicious, and envious. They will write anonymous letters to harass a fellow undergraduate and listen in to a telephone conversation that is no business of theirs. Charity, kindliness, generosity are qualities which they hold in contempt. They are scum. They will in due course leave the university. Some will doubtless sink back, perhaps with relief, into the modest class from which they emerged; some will take to drink, some to crime, and go to prison. Others will become schoolmasters and form the young, or journalists and mould public opinion. A few will go into Parliament, become Cabinet Ministers and rule the country. I look upon myself as fortunate that I shall not live to see it.[14]

Amis defended the position of the mid-1950s intellectual who preferred beer to brandy: "To the charge of holding defiant dour scholarship-boy views on culture, he may retort, rather uneasily perhaps, that anyway he is thereby rescued from the 'real' Philistinism of the dilettante. And it might be seriously argued that, for the practitioner if for nobody else, culture made in one's own private still is more potent than that which comes to table in a decanter."[15]

If Jim Dixon is fundamentally a philistine in the eyes of certain critics, Amis sees his philistinism more as a sign of intellectual health than moral corruption. It is true that Dixon hates the madrigal-singing, recorder-blowing weekends, and he confesses that he cannot sing or act. He can barely read English, much less music. Yet he is nonetheless inventive in a vulgar sort of way. He can sing and does so leaving a pub; he can act, for he is a great mimicker and maker of droll faces; and he does write fiction, signing one of his letters Joe Higgins. But his "artistic" interests are personal and therefore less imitative. Amis's defense of philistinism is similar to that set forth by Conquest in *The Abomination of Moab* (1979), and he asserts:

> Jim and I have taken a lot of bad mouthing for being philistine, aggressively philistine, and saying, "Well, as long as I've got me blonde and me pint of beer and me packet of fags and me seat at the cinema, I'm all right." I don't think either of us would say that. It's nice to have a pretty girl with large breasts rather than some fearful woman who's going to talk to you about Ezra Pound and hasn't got large breasts and probably doesn't wash much. And better to have a pint of beer than to have to talk to your host about the burgundy you're drinking. And better to go to see nonsensical art exhibitions that nobody's really going to enjoy. So it's appealing to common sense if you like, and it's a way of trying to denounce affectation.[16]

This attack on affectation is evident in Amis's subsequent novels. In *That Uncertain Feeling* (1955) his protagonist, John Lewis, is an impoverished assistant librarian in the small Welsh town of Aberdarcy. He considers trying to improve his social position by having an affair with Elizabeth Gruffydd-Williams, a married socialite who attended school with Lewis's wife. Lewis is uncertain about committing adultery, and he is equally uncertain about the ramifications of rising to a "higher" social class, represented in some ways by the character Gareth Probert, who has written a dreadfully sentimental play called *The Martyr*. Probert, a thinly veiled parody of Dylan Thomas, is "the apotheosis of the False Poet: operatic, sodden, all shapeless dithyrambics and professional Welshness" (Fiedler, 200). Like Lucky Jim, Lewis seeks money and women, but he rejects the false values they can represent. He doesn't want to betray himself for Elizabeth and the promotion she has arranged through her husband, Vernon. His ambivalence is typical of that in Movement literature, and Lewis eventually resolves it by going back, like Larkin's Kemp, to his origins. His redemption lies in the coal mines, not the library, and in returning to his not-so-glamorous wife.

In *I Like It Here* (1958) Amis's protagonist, Garnet Bowen, a failed playwright, is forced to go abroad to prove the authenticity of a manuscript by an author who may no longer be living. He too is suspicious of European high culture, believing it offers little more than churches, museums, bullfighting, and galleries. Amis himself, as winner of the Maugham award, was required to travel abroad against his wishes, but his attack in *I Like It Here* is not against art; it is against people's pretensions to art. Though Bowen's job is scholastic by nature, his aspirations are more monetary than artistic. The book abounds with literary references – more than 50 authors are mentioned in its pages – allowing Amis to have his satirical say in a survey of English literature from the Anglo-Saxon period to Graham Greene.

If these early novels form a philistine conspiracy, it is, as Blake Morrison observes, one conducted by an intellectual (Morrison, 132). Amis considers the issue of philistinism at some length in his poetry too. In "After Goliath," for example, he questions whether philistines are the real enemies or "the shrill hangers-on of culture" (Perkins, 439). The poem is written from David's pragmatic point of view, and its headnote is a quotation from the first book of *Samuel*: "What shall be done to the man that killeth this Philistine?" (Amis *CP*, 77). The answer is that he shall be applauded by social charlatans:

> Academics, actors who lecture,
> Apostles of architecture,
> Ancient-gods-of-the-abdomen men,
> Angst-pushers, adherents of Zen,
> Alastors, Austenites, A-test
> Abolishers . . . (Amis *CP*, 77)

Amis adds in afterthought, and perhaps with some self-directed scorn, "even the straightest / Of issues looks pretty oblique / When a movement turns into a clique" (Amis *CP*, 77). What giants may be slain by a movement that loses its momentum? If David is the Movement, ready to challenge the established literary order, who is its Goliath? Is his sword a trophy "or means of attack / On the rapturous crowds at his back" (Amis *CP*, 77)? Whatever the answer, Amis avers that such battles must be "fought in the mind" (Amis *CP*, 77).

Although most Movement poets were politically liberal, Amis's philistinism coincides with his disenchantment with communism, intensified by the hardline response to the Hungarian uprising in 1956. He turned aside his liberalism and moved toward the political right, a switch that he traces in some detail in *Socialism and the Intellectuals* (1957), a Fabian pamphlet in which he defines romanticism as "an irrational capacity to become inflamed by interests and causes that are not one's own" (Brennan, 19). Paul Johnson called the treatise "Jim's last will and testament."[17] Amis further explores this conservatism, which led him and Conquest to support the war in Vietnam, in *Lucky Jim's Politics* (1968).

A Case of Samples (1956) also shows Amis's levelheadedness in poetry, his willingness to see verse more as product than prophecy. The book is largely made up of poems from *A Frame of Mind* and Amis's Fantasy Press pamphlet (1954), although it includes two poems from *Bright November* ("Beowulf" and "Bed and Breakfast"), which were substantially rewritten. The title comes from "A Song of Experience," a poem about a traveling salesman's sexual conquests: "What Blake presaged, what Lawrence took a stand on, / What Yeats locked up in fable, he performed" (Amis *CP*, 69).

Howard Nemerov praised the volume: "Kingsley Amis writes a clever, neat sort of verse whose major visible ambition, not to be taken in, is well expressed by the cheerful vulgarity of that title, *A Case of Samples*. . . . It is as though he had decided that the world exists only as literature, that he and his readers are too wise to be fooled any longer by so much literature, and that, in consequence, the remaining job for poetry (aside from cleaning up after the grand Ball of History) is to be more or less benevolently amused at itself and its former pretensions."[18]

Before Amis left Swansea in 1961 to become director of studies in English at Peterhouse, Cambridge University, he completed one other novel, *Take a Girl Like You* (1960), the first of a string of satires about philanderers. At Cambridge Amis found the demands of teaching were taking more and more time away from his writing, and he disliked Cambridge's tutorial system, its declining academic standards, and its prim social life. In 1963 he resigned his position there to devote himself full-time to writing, a departure he discussed in *Encounter* the following February. When he took a temporary position at Vanderbilt in 1967, it marked his last employment in academia.

While at Cambridge Amis published *The Evans Country* poems, whose main character, Dai Evans, is a lecherous traveling salesman. Evans is a working-class optimist and opportunist whose territory is South Wales. The poems' titles are all names of Welsh towns. Though some are imaginary, every one holds promise of another pleasure. For Evans carnal desire deflects mortality for a time, and his scheming nature is best revealed in "Fforestfawr," where after his father's funeral he invites a woman to meet him at a pub, and in "Maunders," where Evans is asked to help judge a local beauty contest. Though drawn to Miss Clydach he sees in her pulchritude

> Two threats: his own destruction
> By passion's fell embrace,
> Or else (a bit more likely)
> Not getting to first base. (Amis *CP*, 111)

Since it is likely that the contestant will neither sleep with him nor overwhelm him with passion, Evans turns his amorous flirtations to Mrs. Pugh, the town clerk and a fellow judge.

Though Evans's morality is questionable, he is sympathetic in that he is a working stiff bound to a timetable that ensures there's "much in life he's never going to know" (Amis *CP*, 116). In the volume's finale, "Aberdarcy: the Chaucer Road," Amis indulgently asks, "Who's doing better, then? What about you?" (Amis *CP*, 116). The query is well put. While Evans may evade questioning his own moral decadence, the reader is not allowed the same ethical self-deception. Donald Davie for one, however, resented being forced to identify with a protagonist whose prime concern is his next sexual conquest, and in his essay "Lucky Jim and the Hobbits" he indicts the poems' lack of political significance. But any sentiment – either for or against Evans – is a distraction from the issue of poetic, rather than moral or political, honesty. And, as Alan Brien notes, Amis "has always been an expert at showing us how we deceive ourselves in the very act of congratulating ourselves on not being deceived."[19]

This discrepancy between appearance and reality, the core of his dark comedy, operates in virtually all of Amis's books. In *One Fat Englishman* (1963) Roger Micheldene, an unscrupulous publisher who has distinguished himself in a number of the deadly sins, journeys to Budweiser College in Pennsylvania, presumably to locate manuscripts worthy of publication. In actuality he is trying to restore his relationship with his exmistress, Helene, who is married to a visiting lecturer there. Micheldene is a snob, but he can't stand the snobbish bore who claims him aboard ship on his passage home. Though he finally discovers that he really loves Helene, like Dai Evans he does not allow sentiment to prove an obstacle to future sexual conquests. Romance must ultimately be tempered by logic; it's better to be a bastard, he reasons, than a bloody fool.

In *The Anti-Death League* (1966), Amis's favorite book, young British weapons developer James Churchill becomes convinced that there is a secret, malignant force far more predictive than the secret military program (Operation Apollo) on which he works. Although this project, a plague to be used against the Chinese Communists, may kill millions, it is still a lesser evil than the wickedness of God, who threatens the woman he loves with breast cancer. The Human Beings Anonymous who compose the Anti-Death League rally together to oppose God's evils, but the novel's final scene, that of a chaplain's dog dying beneath the wheels of a truck, suggests that in matters of religion there are also possibilities of deception. The book's conclusion shows humankind's inability to steer itself consciously away from death, and it compresses the novel's ambivalence into a single image reminiscent of Norman Mailer's *Why Are We in Vietnam?* in which a polar bear is fired upon from a helicopter. And although *The Anti-Death League* is less humorous than most of Amis's other novels, Churchill's inability to distinguish easily between what is admirable and what is despicable gives the book no small amount of comic irony.

The Anti-Death League is part science-fiction, part espionage novel and prepared Amis to undertake *Colonel Sun* (1968), the first post-Ian Fleming James Bond novel. The book, written under the pseudonym of Robert Markham, had been preceded by *The James*

Bond Dossier (1965), an analysis by Amis of Fleming's hero, and by *The Book of Bond, or Every Man His Own 007* (1965), which he wrote under the name of William Tanner. Amis's treatment of Bond met with mixed response. The most frequent complaint was that he humanized Bond too much. By making him more believable Amis consequently made Bond less interesting to many readers who expected Bond to stand above them. In his appendix to *Colonel Sun*, Amis defends his form of escapism, in which the reader is required both to identify with and distance him- or herself from the hero, asserting that there is no more escapist notion than thinking life organized and purposeful.

A quick glance at *A Look round the Estate* (1967), a gathering of poems written between 1957 and 1967, demonstrates this same balancing technique at work. "Coming of Age" is in fact about a "spiritual secret agent" (Amis *CP*, 96) who, having spied on a town for 20 years, becomes one of its most typical citizens.

> At the first christening played his part so well
> That he started living it from then on,
> His trick of camouflage no longer a trick.
> Isn't it the spy's rarest triumph to grow
> Indistinguishable from the spied upon,
> The stick insect's to become a stick? (Amis *CP*, 96)

Ian Hamilton's review in the *Observer* also noted Amis's method, that "when he starts off with a straight face, we know he is just limbering-up for a deflating climax; and when his first lines are all smiles and pubby bonhomie, we tense ourselves for that soggy final couplet in which the hairy philanderer will find a presence at his back 'as cold as ice.' "[20] A seriousness lurks beneath every joke.

Redemption by love is the most prevalent theme in the eight satiric novels Amis has written since 1968. In *I Want It Now*, Ronnie Appleyard, a manipulative London television personality, seduces an heiress at the very time she loses her inheritance. In *The Green Man* (1969), the owner of an ancient country pub near Cambridge is haunted by the ghost of a seventeenth-century homicidal parson named Dr. Underhill. Maurice Allington, the owner of the pub, is typical of Amis's protagonists: middle-aged, selfish, alcoholic, and lustful, characteristics the ghost misinterprets as marks of satanism. But Allington is no ally of evil. He has his virtues, and, when he sets up a sexual threesome of his wife (Joyce), his mistress (Diana), and himself, he does not even participate in the orgy. Joyce and Diana run off with each other, but Allington, who has never understood the needs of women, is somewhat redeemed when he arrives at some understanding of his daughter, Amy.

Every sexual joke cuts two ways for Amis, and he was Movement colleague Donald Davie's favorite novelist primarily because of his ability to render sex comically, "producing though it does both woes and exaltations; . . . he acknowledges and values the tenderness that ennobles decent sexual relations even at their most farcical."[21] Several novels bear out this observation. In *Girl, 20* (1971) classical musician and conductor Sir Roy Vandervane, 53 years old, turns his back on his art and his wife, Kitty, when he becomes intrigued by Sylvia Meera, the title character. Sylvia's youth seems to be her only appealing attribute, and Vandervane attempts to join her culture by growing long hair and dressing in faddish clothes. He looks ridiculous trying to look "cool." *Ending Up* (1974) moves in the other direction, as it concerns Tuppenny-hapenny Cottage, a commune for old folks, and shows that Amis can be just as unsympathetic to the elderly. Though nearing death – Bernard Bastable, for one, has only three months left to live – the lives of these characters are nonetheless no more futile than anyone else's. All five residents of the cottage die, but so will we all eventually, though who among us is ready to confront his or her own death philosophically? Since life is finite, it may matter little whether one commits good or evil. Yet simultaneously, since life is finite, moral values, temporal as they may be, may also be the only ones that matter.

The Alteration (1976) poses similar conundrums. The book, which won the John W. Campbell Memorial Award, is set in a counterfeit world, one denied the historical effects of the Reformation. Amis's hero is a young boy, Hubert Anvil, whose father, Tobias, consents to his castration to preserve his ethereal voice. To preserve one of God's gifts he is willing to relinquish another. John McDermott comments:

> The opposite of such emasculation is fulfilment, whether sexually or artistically, and both spheres are involved in Hubert's case, though other characters experience them singly. There is no fulfilment without experience, and experience is less valuable if it is enforced and not the product of free choice. Hu-

bert's situation forces him to consider manhood while knowing he will not fully achieve it, to try to understand a sexuality that will be irreversibly denied him. In keeping with a pattern familiar to victims of tyrannies, he is being denied experience before he can discover what it is. (McDermott, 140)

By contrast, Jake Richardson in *Jake's Thing* (1978) doesn't suffer from lack of sexual experience; loss of libido is his problem. Although he has bedded more than 100 women, now an aging Oxford lecturer in early Mediterranean history, Jake lacks the vitality to continue his lechery. Apparently no physical malady attends him; he merely lacks sufficient sexual desire. His dilemma presents the essential problem of the Movement perspective, how to unite heart and head. He yearns for a single experience to arouse him both physically and emotionally, but in Amis's fiction sex is the one area in which the two seem least likely to unite. Jake is dissatisfied with his third wife, who is young but overweight. He turns to a psychiatrist, Dr. Proinsias Rosenberg, who connects him to a machine (the nocturnal mensurator) to monitor his erections, and he enrolls in a variety of sexual workshops. Jack lacks sexual appetite, and his wife runs away with her best friend's husband, Jake is left behind with another man's unwanted wife, whom he finds not worth the bother. Jake can raise his testosterone level, but he can't raise his hopes. His virility means nothing if it must be spent on the unwanted sexual partners available to him. Jake is disappointed with his choices, but like Larkin's poetic persona, he ultimately opts for undeceiving intellect over bamboozling romance.

Amis had difficulty finding a U.S. publisher for *Stanley and the Women* (1984) because of what was misinterpreted as his misogynistic viewpoint. The book's villains are all women – Stanley's exwife, Stanley's current wife, Stanley's son's wrongheaded psychiatrist – but they provide as many complications for one another as they do Stanley, although it is Stanley's schizophrenic son, Steve, who seems most victimized. But the men are also soundly ridiculed in the book; the destroyed men are no more admirable than the destructive women. Stanley himself is shallow and hypocritical, but he has also been wrongly blamed by a psychiatrist for his son's instability. Amis has defended the novel against the charges of misogyny on the grounds that humor always seems unfair to whom it focuses on, yet even in *Stanley and the Women* his humor seems derived from the dilemma of the Movement perspective, yearning for romantic fulfillment but unable to escape the bluntness of the truth.

In a sense proving his even-handedness, in 1986 Amis issued *The Old Devils*, in which his women characters get the best of their rotten husbands, who start their daily drinking binges immediately following breakfast. The film version of *The Green Man* contains a brief but self-parodying reference to the book when a copy appears opened by the toilet while an inebriated Allington, played by Albert Finney, bathes in anticipation of a sexual rendezvous. Though the screenplay was written by Malcolm Bradbury, not Amis, it displays the same lack of seriousness with which Amis and other Movement writers typically viewed their own work. Yet the novel is more than "bathroom reading"; it received the most esteemed book award in England, the Booker-McConnell Prize, for which Movement sympathizer and Larkin editor Anthony Thwaite was chairman of judges.

The versatility of Amis, also visible in his detective novel *The Riverside Villas Murder* (1973) and in *Russian Hide-and-Seek* (1980), a futuristic tale about non-Marxist Soviets ruling England, has proven one of his great strengths. The difficulty with which Amis defies categorization was unmistakable as early as 1968 in a fictitious obituary that appeared in *Punch*:

> We record with deep regret the death of Baron Amis in the microfilm library in his home in Nassau. . . . Born in 1922, Amis rose to immediate success with his brilliant first novel, *Lucky Jim*, the film rights which soon freed him from the heavy responsibility of struggling for further literary recognition, as his subsequent books testified. During the 1960s, Amis grew less and less *terrible* as he grew more *enfant*, finally becoming, at the same moment, both a Conservative and Robert Markham, the pseudonym under which he began producing a lucrative range of new James Bond thrillers. . . . He became, in quick succession, Harold Robbins, Barbara Cartland, Godfrey Winn, [and] Mao Tse-Tung.[22]

Although Amis has achieved his greatest recognition and popularity as a novelist, he believes poetry a greater art. "I would have been a poet entirely if I had had my way," he admitted to interviewer Jean W. Ross (*CA*, 11). And with the publication of his *Collected Poems, 1944-1979* came fresh reminders of his importance as a poet. The work is a testimony to a lifetime of refusing to be taken in and may be read as a corrective to the lure of romantic ideology and faddish poetic rhetoric. His verse, generally more sober than his fiction, is seldom confessional and lacks extremes in both content and technique. It seems governed by a practical sensibility that allows the down-to-earth reader to meet him- or herself continually in the poems. Amis explained his general technique for beginning a poem as follows: "I ask myself: Is this idea likely to interest anyone besides myself? and try to forget about it if the answer seems to be No; and – if I do go ahead with the poem – I try to work it into a verse form I haven't used before, or at any rate not recently" (Brennan, 20).

Amis's wit is renowned. A *Times Literary Supplement* reviewer concedes: "Indeed, one's only reproach is that he seems to be in danger of taking too seriously his refusal to take certain things seriously: to refuse to be gulled by certain postures can itself become a posture" (Brennan, 20). While Amis does not take criticism gracefully, like most Movement poets he is frequently self-deprecatory. When the *New Statesman* sponsored a contest for the best addition to his *Collected Poems* and asked Amis to judge it, his own entry, "After Ralph Hodgson," submitted under the Markham pseudonym, came in only second. Such slights not withstanding, William Van O'Connor has praised Amis, despite his small body of poems, as possibly the best poet of the Movement poets, and Clive James has observed that "Only the fact that he is so marvellously readable can now stop Kingsley Amis from being placed in the front rank of contemporary poets."[23]

Chapter Four

D. J. Enright

Perhaps the most liberally compassionate of the Movement wits, Dennis Joseph Enright was born in Leamington, Warwickshire, on 11 March 1920. His father, George, an Irishman, enlisted in the British Army at a young age after his own father died prematurely. Demobilized in England after World War I, Enright's father, a Catholic, married Grace Cleaver, an Anglo-Welsh Wesleyan Methodist. Enright dryly observed that this lower-middle-class union predisposed him toward certain themes: "These circumstances deprived me pre-natally of the ability to comprehend religious or political ideologies, race, nationality and nationalism – phenomena which one needs to have a firm grasp of if one is to lead a stable and balanced life" (*World*, 448).

In school Enright was adept at passing examinations, and, though poor, earned a series of scholarships to support his education at Leamington College, then Downing College, Cambridge, where, as was the case with Donald Davie and Thom Gunn, F. R. Leavis oversaw his studies. These scholarships were resented by some, Enright recalls in "Class," who did not want to see the elevation of the working class:

> I can't help it, I still get mad
> When people say that "class" doesn't mean
> A thing, and to mention one's working-class
> Origins is "inverted snobbery."
>
> The wife of a teacher at school (she was
> Mother of one of my classmates) was
> Genuinely enraged when I won a scholarship.
> She stopped me in the street, to tell me
> (With a loudness I supposed was upper-class)
> That Cambridge was not for the likes of me, nor was
> Long hair, nor the verse I wrote for the school mag.

> Her sentiments were precisely those of the
> Working class. Unanimity on basic questions
> Accounts for why we never had the revolution.[1]

Enright took his B.A. with honors at Cambridge in 1944 and an M.A. there in 1946. Under Leavis's direction he contributed articles, mainly on German literature, to *Scrutiny*, and he began to publish tart book reviews critical of contemporary poetry, once protesting that there ought to be a society for the prevention of cruelty to metaphors. In attacking the dead conventions of traditional verse, these first reviews by Enright present some of the earliest writings to disclose what would come to be known as Movement poetics. He attacks the bombast of latter-day romantics, their lack of clarity, and their general disregard of the reader. In a review of Henry Treece's poetry, Enright crabbed about the specific failure of neoapocalyptic verse: "It strikes me that the semi-surrealist poet occupies a highly privileged position on Parnassus: when he can't go on meaning any longer he can always slip into a stanza or two of non-meaning (which relieves him of the strain genuine poets must occasionally suffer under)" (Morrison, 33). Though Enright was at an early age an insightful critic who aptly perceived the direction the next decade's poetry would take, he considered teaching English literature his profession, and he went abroad to begin that career.

Enright's first post was at the University of Alexandria, known then as Farouk I University (1947-50), where he took his D. Litt. in 1949. Enright's first novel, *Academic Year* (1955), was based on his experiences there. A savagely sardonic work involving English lecturers in Egypt, *Academic Year* concerns the last years of Farouk's rule, during which secret police closely monitored the activities of all foreigners. It records the difficulties of a trio of expatriate English teachers in adjusting to what appears to them as Egyptian corruption. Packet, the youngest and born like Enright to a working-class background from which his scholarships have freed him, is in his first lectureship. He loses the last remnants of his youthful idealism, however, when he has a disenchanting affair with a westernized Syrian named Sylvie. Brett, the cultural officer, is both embarrassed by and apologetic for the poverty he witnesses in Egypt on a daily

basis. And Bacon, the senior lecturer and a failed scholar, is murdered by the supposed relatives of a Muslim girl he has befriended.

Enright had witnessed similar cruelty himself in Egypt. Once on
his way to have tea with another professor, he and an Irish colleague
were accused of being Jewish spies by a small group of Egyptians.
Taken into custody by the police, the pair were rudely interrogated
at length. At last a clerk at the university vouched for them, and they
were released, though considerably late for their engagement. Apparently, Enright had come under police suspicion because he had
proclaimed himself a Wesleyan Methodist on his entry papers; university administrators later explained that the police had misinterpreted his entry as having something to do with Judaism.

Published shortly after Amis's *Lucky Jim* and Wain's *Hurry On
Down*, *Academic Year* was praised as a witty comedy in the manner
of his Movement colleagues. The novel also contains one of Enright's
earliest published poems ("Children, Beggars and Schoolteachers"),
which the inebriated Bacon offers as a substitute for his formal lecture on education. Although he had a strong interest in poetry, Enright in fact had written his novel out of gratitude to his publisher for
issuing *Season Ticket* (1948), a small illustrated pamphlet and Enright's first collection of verse. The publisher showed no interest in
Academic Year, however, although Secker and Warburg did issue the
book seven years afterward.

A number of the poems in *Season Ticket* were also included in
The Laughing Hyena (1953), Enright's second collection, which con-
tinued to show his distrust of 1940s romanticism. Despite the Egyp-
tian topics of many of the poems in *The Laughing Hyena*
("University Examinations in Egypt," "The Egyptian Cat," "Deir El
Bahari: Temple of Hatshepsut," "The Voice," and "An Egyptian in
Birmingham"), Enright did not publish it until he had returned to
England, where he served as extramural lecturer at Birmingham University from 1950 to 1953. One of the poems, "On the Death of a
Child," reinterprets Dylan Thomas's well-known "A Refusal To
Mourn, the Death by Fire, of a Child in London" in a manner less as-
suring of a universal life force but distinctly more conversational
than the original elegy. Although Enright thought Thomas a second-
rank poet, he readily acknowledged Thomas's ability to pen "a large
number of brilliant lines."[2] While his poem expresses a sentiment resembling Thomas's, Enright refrains from excessive metaphors and

religious symbols – "How odd that in this age of precision instruments in literary criticism it is still supposed that to call something a symbol is to make a meaningful statement" (*Conspirators*, 43-44) – preferring economical, simple sentences instead to bear the weight of the poet's grief. "The big words fail to fit. Like giant boxes / Round small bodies. Taking up improper room, / Where so much withering is and so much bloom" (Enright *CP 87*, 10).

"The Laughing Hyena, after Hokusai," the title poem, also concerns a dead child, one whose severed head rests in the hands of an evil demon. Enright uses the Noh figure as an unconventional means to examine the universality of death in all its cruelty and irrational brutality. On first reading the subject seems at odds with his technique, for Enright employs lilting long lines and mellifluous descriptions to overcome the dread. Donald Davie found the long lines particularly apt, for they generate "looping and leaping rhythms . . . language [which] leaps and falls and undulates in sympathy with an energy that is, like Hokusai's 'volcanic.' "[3] Though his topic in "The Laughing Hyena" is more unfamiliar and exotic than those found in poems by his Movement colleagues, Enright's purpose is not dissimilar, for he detects intelligible humanity at the wild Hyena's core. "It, at least, / Knows exactly why it laughs" (Enright *CP 87*, 13).

"The Laughing Hyena" disproves Eliot's dictum that poetry should be an escape from personality rather than an expression of it, and in it Enright displays characteristic Movement skepticism about the academy, believing poetry should achieve "a degree of order . . . out of the surrounding anarchy; to secure a modicum of temporary mercy from the midst of cruelty, to tame one small beast in a jungle of wild beastliness. . . . Poetry is written on a battlefield, not in a library, not in the imaginary museum crammed with all the cultural objects of the past which you must have fingered carefully one by one, the theory has it, if you wish to be more than minor and provincial these days" (*Conspirators*, 59).

For Enright culture (and therefore poetry) was better represented by distant Asian locales than by the artifacts of Davie's "imaginary museum," and his satiric "University Examinations in English" shows how an intermingling of cultures brings hilarious results: " 'Falstaff indulged in drinking and sexcess,' and then, / 'Doolittle was a dusty man' and 'Dr. Jonson edited the Yellow Book' " (Enright *CP 87*, 9). In "The Mosaics at Daphni" the fiery mo-

48 THE MOVEMENT

saic artworks are incongruously located next to an insane asylum.
These poems seem to take a disparaging tone toward aesthetics, but
Enright's indignation is but another form of self-mockery, for, he
questions, how can art ennoble in the midst of cruelty, disease, and
starvation? Although his foreign travels were the basis of his poetry,
his observational techniques remained humanely attuned to the universality of human suffering.

When *The Laughing Hyena* was coolly reviewed by G. S. Fraser,
Robert Conquest wrote a letter to the *New Statesman* vigorously defending Enright. Conquest may have been returning the kindness Enright had shown him the previous year when he had praised Conquest's "Reflections on Landscapes" in a critique of the Festival of
Britain poetry contest. But Conquest was not the only Movement
poet Enright had befriended. Enright (as mentioned in chapter 2 of
this volume) was among the few critics to receive a review copy of
Larkin's 1951 *XX Poems*, Larkin having failed to affix sufficient
postage to the copies he sent out. Enright's favorable review of the
collection in the *Month*, a Catholic periodical, was thus singularly
important to Larkin. Enright praised Larkin's old-fashioned respect
for language and encouraged publishers to take notice of his work; it
would be four more years before Marvell Press would heed his
advice and issue *The Less Deceived*. In the interim a correspondence
ensued between the two, Enright buoying Larkin's spirits at a time
when the shy librarian was having little success as a poet.

Enright's admiration of Larkin was long-standing. When *The
Whitsun Weddings* appeared, Enright praised it lavishly, comparing
it favorably with the poems of Edward Thomas, Emily Dickinson, and
Stevie Smith (the only poet to whom Enright confessed to having
written a fan letter). Larkin's growth as a poet was most evident to
Enright, and he rightfully acknowledged Larkin as the best poet of
his generation:

> For not only does Mr Larkin write like an angel, as many a poor devil does
> once in a long while, he *always* writes like an angel. . . . Practically nothing
> here disappoints, and practically everything here reminds us how distinct Mr
> Larkin's poetry is . . . from all the verse which might be thought to be like it.
> How distinct and superior. . . . [*The Whitsun Weddings*] not only deserves to
> be greatly successful, it will be – and, it seems likely, successful beyond and
> above and below the small dutiful mob who have already made Mr Larkin their
> poetry choice. (*Conspirators*, 141, 146)

In 1953 Enright again left England to accept a series of teaching appointments overseas. In 1955, from the far remove of Konan University in Kobe, Japan, where he taught until 1956, Enright issued *Poets of the 1950s*, which was to prove one of the most important volumes in the history of the Movement. Prior to the book's publication, Movement poets had supported one another's work individually and written complimentary reviews, but the poets had not been collected together in a single anthology. While Enright's itinerancy may have appeared at odds with the Movement's conservative precepts – Larkin, for example, believed that poets should remain at home and re-create the familiar – had Enright not traveled to Japan, he would most likely have never issued this crucial anthology. Enright compiled *Poets of the 1950s* for his Japanese students to acquaint them with the new commonsense poetry that was being written in postwar England, "the poetry of civility, passion, and order."[4] The anthology was intended to navigate his readers "between the rock of Wastelanditis and the whirlpool of Dylanitis" (*World*, 448).

Enright's friendship with Conquest was instrumental in shaping the volume. He and his wife had stayed overnight at Conquest's house in Hampstead, and Enright dedicated his poem "Frankenstein" to him. In return Conquest, as one of the coeditors of the 1953 P.E.N. anthology, included Enright's work alongside his own and that of Kingsley Amis and Elizabeth Jennings. When Enright asked Conquest for advice on what writers *Poets of the 1950s* should contain, Conquest recommended the nine Movement poets. Enright had prepared a roster himself, and his preferences were identical to Conquest's except for Thom Gunn, whose work he had not read. Although Enright and Conquest were in almost total agreement, Enright stuck with his original selections, and, despite Gunn's absence and the limited audience for which the book was intended, *Poets of the 1950s* became the first "unofficial" Movement anthology.

That Enright designed the work more as a text or reader than as tangible evidence of some poetic revolution reveals the tenuous nature of the Movement's origins. Although they possessed no plan to organize along the lines of a common agenda, the eight poets clearly preferred measured wit and cynicism to the extravagances of the neoapocalyptic poets, "the self-shriekers, the wombers and tombers: what we expect from them, and what we get, is dull nonsense whipped up into fancy nonsense. . . . No comparable artificiality can be found in the so-called 'Movement' poets, except at their very worst. They have minds, and they use them."[5] Enright intended no specific program and had no conception of a poetic "movement" in mind, but with the issuance of *Poets of the 1950s* the Movement arrived nonetheless.

It is odd that such a significant work was never published in England, although Conquest had encouraged Enright to release the book there. But Enright was wary of poetic popularity; he had achieved little himself and he warned in the volume's introduction that a poet should worry when his sales approximate half those of the typical nondescript novel. So when Macmillan commissioned Conquest to do a similar anthology shortly afterward, the impetus to see *Poets of the 1950s* printed for English readers declined. Conquest's *New Lines* appeared in 1956, firmly fixing in place the full slate of nine Movement poets.

Upon Enright's return to British Council teaching, his life seemed to parallel that of Packet, his protagonist in *Academic Year* and *Heaven Knows Where* (1957), Enright's second novel. The narrative in the latter book begins with Packet, having completed his Egyptian novel, returning home to England, jobless, availing himself of free dentistry. But he quickly comes to mistrust the luxurious living of his homeland – the cinemas and dance halls – and he feels less safe in England than in Egypt. Although his friends have encouraged him to wait for some professor to die so that he might fill the vacant position, Packet applies to the Institute of Humane Studies on Velo, a mythical Far Eastern island. He discovers upon his arrival in Velo that H. M. King, with whom Packet had been corresponding as director of the institution, is in reality the monarch of the island, His Majesty the King. The king is no despot; rather he governs with liberal doses of Burton's *Anatomy of Melancholy*. And though a monarchy, Velo displays less class consciousness than Packet finds at home in England. According to the king, the real moral power in society is the teacher whose talent to instruct children to behave decently and to blow their noses is more meaningful than that of any politician or king. The Velonians themselves are quite apolitical; "Velo is neither tribe nor society – it's merely persons and things!"[6] Therefore the Institute's main purpose is to further fundamental human concerns, such as erecting earthquake-proof toilets.

In contrast, the neighboring island of Dertha does not welcome foreign intellectuals, and it has even constructed a host of mad sculptures as proof of their hostility. "Dertha was a Principled State, one of its principles being that other states should not be left to go unprincipled," and in time the Derthans invade the docile Velonians. But the Velonians concoct a clever ruse to scare off the Derthans. The Velonians are allowed to celebrate the Night of Wrath, but their celebration is predicated upon Derthan misunderstanding of folk customs on Velo. The Velonians expel the Derthans by means of fireworks, amplified recordings of frogs in mating season, painted phosphorescent monkeys, and a Japanese film projected on the hazy Velonian sky. Afterward Packet meets a farmer's daughter at an island wedding, and a good but primitive life seems all but assured; man, woman, daughter, rice, cottage, and cow seem the clear keys to serenity. When Packet leaves the island, however, the king tells him that what the world does may be offensive and distressing, but he should be immersed in it nonetheless, even if only to dissent.

That gentle dissent extends into Enright's Japanese experiences. Although he intended to be, as he said, one of the few foreigners to live in Japan without writing a book about it, Enright relented. Having witnessed the exploitation of millions of Japanese in their postwar slums, Enright was unable to ignore the power of his experiences there. Ever the sympathetic observer of humankind, he noted startling differences between his Egyptian and Japanese students. "The Egyptians are predominantly comic in spirit – slovenly, a bit brutish, cavalier, unpredictable but yielding to elucidation, orotund and occasionally superb. Those of the Japanese, on the other hand, are predominantly tragic – contorted, agonized, tight-lipped, sometimes baffling, consistent and insistent, and occasionally poetic in a gently sad sort of way."[7] He recorded his observations in four books: *The World of Dew: Aspects of Living Japan* (1955), a collection of essays; in two volumes of poems, *Bread Rather than Blossoms* (1956) and *Some Men Are Brothers* (1960); and fictionally in *Figures of Speech* (1965), a novel in which George Lester, a teacher of English literature in Bangkok, serves as Enright's vehicle to satirize cultural and academic targets, both foreign and domestic.

In *Figures of Speech* Enright intentionally blurs the line between sorrow and humor. In a hilarious reversal of the famous drunken lecture episode in Amis's *Lucky Jim*, a sober George Lester delivers his

British Council address to an inebriated audience. Still he is sent home as an academic failure, though he returns in a more prosperous occupation with new clothes and a large expense account. His young Confucian student Chung Lu experiences similar upheaval. He strives to be a scholarly correct student, but Chung Lu has been addled by his love for Mattie, an attractive and rational girl on vacation from Singapore. Their principles are noble but impede their progress as lovers.

What Enright perceived as the tragic natures of the Japanese also made them appear considerably comic to him. In "The Noodle-Vendor's Flute," for instance, he playfully describes the crude instrument, "Merely a rubber bulb and metal horn" (Enright *CP 87*, 32), by which the vendor advertises his wares as he pedals about town. The song is commonplace, universal, and in it stupidity and sadness coalesce into a celebration of survival. It is precisely this comic view of life, even when "squeezed from a bogus flute" (Enright *CP 87*, 33), that enables the vendor, and by implication the reader, to endure. Enright may seem impertinent in such poems, but his flippancy, much like that in Larkin's verse, keeps the most dire circumstances from appearing hopeless. Inner and outer experience interpenetrate in Enright's work. The poem's detachment is closely akin to that found in Yeats's "Lapis Lazuli," wherein humankind's clownish suffering finds greater expression in the symbolic gaiety of carved Chinese figures.

"The Noodle-Vendor's Flute" is prototypical of Enright's verse in that it focuses without undue pity on a humble character. Moreover he further declares in "How right they were, the Chinese poets" that there is "only one subject to write about: pity, / Self-pity: the only subject to avoid" (Enright *CP 87*, 22). In "The Short Life of Kazuo Yamamoto" he considers a 13-year-old boy with no personal belongings other than a headache who, discovering no hope in the noble ideals of his political leaders, finds rat poison cheaper than aspirin. Paradoxically, the greater Enright's detachment, the greater sympathy his poem invokes, as in "A Polished Performance," where a girl develops dropsy from a short lifetime of eating polished rice. These ironic but humane sketches of Asia's beggars and paupers, its misfits, outcasts, and prostitutes, so powerfully depicted in "The Poor Wake Up Quickly," "The Rag-Picker's Feast," and "Akiko San," underscore the universality of pain. Life is sorrowful wherever it takes place, and Enright makes clear in "The Interpreters (or, How to Bury Yourself in a Book)" that art can offer no lasting relief for its sadness.

All human beings are kin, Enright reminds, although they may not like to acknowledge all their relatives. Margaret Willy writes, "The shock of large-scale misery and squalor to a caring Western sensibility is frequently registered through the accent of deliberate, almost casual understatement which allows the recorded fact to speak for itself; and this powerful restraint serves to intensify by contrast the impassioned force of the writer's pity and indignation. In common with his fellows of the 'Movement,' Enright has resolutely refused to sentimentalize the apparently picturesque."[8]

Enright's humanity was further tested when he went to the Free University, Berlin, in 1956; he found the postwar Germans efficient and polite but antagonizingly uncouth. And there were constant reminders of Stalinism and Nazism. Although he was no admirer of the German people, he had long admired their literature. His commentary on Goethe, written originally for *Scrutiny* in 1945, had been reprinted by New Directions in 1949 as *A Commentary on Goethe's "Faust,"* and he had elsewhere published essays on Thomas Mann, Heinrich Heine, Günter Grass, Heinrich Boll, and other German authors. "Unlike much of our most brilliant modern writing, they send us back into life, not terrified into despair or dullness or quiescence by the sight of others' follies, but cheerfully prepared to commit our own" (*Apothecary's*, 120).

Yet the work of these Germans found little favor with most readers, and Enright hypothesized about the unpopularity of German literature. He believed that in some cases the failure to appreciate German literature rested in non-Germans' inability to like Germans themselves, but Enright's own admiration for German authors was intrepid. The distrust of foreigners, so evident in the work of Larkin and other Movement writers, is distinctly absent from Enright's. His high regard for the exhaustive vision of Goethe, in particular, led Enright to take a most dramatic chance in *A Faust Book* (1979).

A Faust Book is more than a poetic exercise; it is a lyric cycle with occasional prose interludes based on the German Faust story. The lyrics are not based solely on Goethe's rendering of the legend, for Enright's unheroic mockery blends Goethe's account with those of Marlowe, Mann, and others to create a separate version decidedly and humorously his own. He picks and chooses as he pleases, including certain elements from one source but ignoring others. He heightens the drama of the poem by reducing the terms of the satanic contract by half to 12 years. There is no Helen of Troy, as in Marlowe, and no Walpurgisnacht, as in Goethe, but Enright does introduce new characters to the legend. One meets Faust's parents and Meretrix, a lusty go-go dancer. Even Hamlet appears as one of Faust's young pupils.[9]

The lyrics themselves are in differing styles. The line lengths vary; some rhyme while others do not. The book displays Enright's most effective use of poetic personas, a tack he had experimented with to some extent in his *Paradise Illustrated* sequences (1978). The theatrical qualities of *A Faust Book* were such that it was performed by the National Poetry Centre in London in 1983.

Although in Enright's version Faust does not forfeit his soul to Hell, it is largely through a matter of luck. As he explains in "Lucifer advises Mephistopheles of the device known as sprats and mackerels," Lucifer will allow Faust to escape damnation as an encouragement to other sinners. Faust, theologically insignificant himself, is to be used, ironically, as bait to tempt other souls. Apparently Enright, a lapsed Catholic, could find little in his faith to encourage and sustain, as did Elizabeth Jennings.

Though a great admirer of German literature, Enright didn't stay long in Germany, taking a position at Chulalongkorn University in Bangkok in 1957. He used Bangkok as the setting for his third novel, *Insufficient Poppy* (1960), a bleak work in which his protagonist, another teacher of English of working-class origins, is shot trying to wrest a pistol away from an obsessed friend, the Colorado Kid.

Enright experienced violence in Bangkok, and after an altercation with the police his stay was cut short. Returning from a birthday party, Enright and his wife were beaten by 15 drunken Thai policemen in front of a brothel across the street from their house, an account he includes in *Figures of Speech*. Although he was released from incarceration later that night when his identity as a university professor was confirmed, Enright opined, "Writers, above all, ought to know that where they are concerned there is no such thing as diplomatic privilege."[10] The incident was an embarrassing one all around. "In addition it seemed that some carelessly worded poem of mine had wounded the feelings of Marshal Sarit (Prime Minister and a well-known anti-Communist of the day). With tempered regret on both sides, the British Council and I decided to part company" (*World*, 447).

Enright still had one year remaining on his British Council contract, so he was allowed to return to London to serve his final year as a bureaucrat in the program. He then took a position as Johore Professor of English at the University of Malaya (University of Singapore since 1961), where he faced additional adversity. His inaugural lecture there in 1960 created quite a disturbance. The lecture, "Robert Graves and the Decline of Modernism,"[11] was excerpted in the Singapore press along with some of Enright's remarks about the newly constituted host government. Enright's address argued for cultural openness, which Malayan authorities mistakenly interpreted as reproachful criticism. "I had spoken of 'culture' in the sense of the production of works of art, whereas to the Singapore government it signified the reduction of race riots. Students demonstrated in favour of academic freedom, and the fuss died down as it became plain that the professor was neither a colonialist nor a Communist but merely rather simple" (*World*, 447).

The Acting Minister for Law and Labour threatened to revoke Enright's work permit, and the Minister of Culture wrote an open letter denouncing Enright's remarks, calling him a "mendicant professor," an epithet Enright wittily adopted in the title of his autobiography, *Memoirs of a Mendicant Professor* (1969). Enright had unwillingly become a symbol of academic freedom, and the controversy was even debated in the London *Times*, but what came to be called the "Enright Affair" ended quietly when conciliatory letters from both sides were printed in the *Straits Times* and the students' union was mollified. Novelist Paul Theroux, who taught with Enright in Singapore, contends that "his idea of fun is being in hot water. He is anything but a prig, but I think he regards hot water as the natural habitat of a moral person" (*Life*, 29).

Enright continued to teach in Singapore until 1970, although not without continued notoriety. In 1966, speaking at an international conference, he complained about the difficulties in teaching English abroad, claiming that there was a dire division between teachers of literature on one hand and teachers of linguistics on the other. Enright lamented that his noble calling had fallen so obviously out of step with governmental authority and with the proscriptions of language teaching. "The literature teacher actually wants his pupils to be changed by literature; the language teacher merely wants them to be made more efficient members of a given society, to fit in more neatly, to be more efficient citizens" (*Life*, 24).

Enright taught in Singapore for 10 years, issuing two books of poems, *Addictions* (1962) and *The Old Adam* (1965), although he wrote no novel about his experiences there as he had done with Alexandria in *Academic Year* and with Bangkok in *Insufficient Poppy*. (His second novel, *Heaven Knows Where*, set in the imaginary Pacific island of Velo, was also largely autobiographical despite its mythical setting.) Enright's alienation in Singapore, perhaps brought on by years of teaching humane letters to a heedless audience, began to reveal itself as self-deprecation in his verse, the old Adam giving way to an altered, more embittered view of humankind. That humanism has much to recommend it is no excuse, however, for its appearance in a poem, he says resolutely in "Works Order," and in his Singapore poems Enright alternates between declarations of troubled conscience on one hand and disparaging barbs that puncture all academic posturing and self-absorption on the other. "No man at peace makes poetry," he adduces in "Confessions of an English Opium Smoker" (Enright *CP 87*, 53). And his fundamental honesty never allows him to use his wit as a means to avoid the issue at hand.

One of the most poignant poems from the period is "Misgiving at Dusk":

> In the damp unfocused dusk
> Mosquitoes are gathering.
>
> Out of a loudspeaker
> Comes loud political speaking.
> If I could catch the words
> I could not tell the party.
> If I could tell the party
> I would not know the policy.
> If I knew the policy
> I could not see the meaning.
> If I saw the meaning
> I would not guess the outcome.
>
> It is all a vituperative humming.
> Night falls abruptly hereabouts.

Shaking with lust, the mosquitoes
Stiffen themselves with bloody possets.
I have become their stews.
Mist-encrusted, flowers of jasmine glimmer
On the grass, stars dismissed from office. (Enright *CP 87*, 71)

Enright's next two volumes, *Unlawful Assembly* (1968) and *Daughters of Earth* (1972), are a continuation of his spare verses: "Plain speaking was in order, / Plain speaking was merely truth" (Enright *CP 87*, 80). According to William Walsh, "they do manifest, if not a new, an increased or developed authority and power. Weight in the line, the pressure of a nearly insupportable experience, a poetic rhythm sometimes at the farthest remove from song – these are the qualities of the poetry which speak of an effort to be bare, hard, essential. Even the wit is undecorative and austere."[12]

Throughout his career Enright has developed the themes of insignificance that Larkin so compellingly explored, and they became the core of his modern satires on the Faust and Adam myths. His work is typically aphoristic yet equivocal; and he is willing to look upon himself both as unimportant creature, as in "Misgiving at Dusk," and as deity, as in "The Faithful":

The insects love the light
And are devoured. They suppose
I punish them for something,
My instrument the spring-jawed dragon.

It isn't difficult to be a god.
You hang your lantern out,
Sink yourself in your own concerns
And leave the rest to the faithful. (Enright *CP 87*, 87)

The poems in *Unlawful Assembly* and *Daughters of Earth*, though sad, retain a tragicomic quality that heightens their informality. Enright's droll view of the academy and his modest position within it is central to a number of the poems. "What became of What-was-his-name?" "Cultural Freedom," "Board of Selection," "More Memories of Underdevelopment," "Royalties," and "Memoirs of a Book Reviewer" are poignant and humbly autobiographical; no Movement poet seems to write so achingly and honestly about him-

self. That Enright should write a verse autobiography of his childhood, then, is unsurprising.

While Larkin felt his childhood too unexceptional to be worth
recording, *The Terrible Shears: Scenes from a Twenties Childhood*
(1973) is a merciful remembrance of Enright's boyhood. The title
refers to the shears Enright's grandfather used to prune the church-
yard cemetery, and accordingly recollections about death are the
substance of many of the poems. Each death brought an additional
hardship to a family already heavily burdened. Nor was any generation immune; the experiences undergone by Enright were common
to all families. He recalls his grandparents died, then his infant sister:
"the baby quietly / Disgorged a lot of blood, and was taken away"
(Enright *CP 87*, 124). Her Christmas gift, a rolling music box, was removed from its hiding spot on top of the cupboard. When Enright's
postman father, a nonsmoker, died of lung cancer – he had been
gassed in France in World War I – his mother became a housekeeper
to support the family. Pets and friends also met with calamity.

Although the 1920s were clearly a dire decade for many families,
Enright frequently writes of those experiences with affection and a
lack of prejudice. Although the poems are clearly Enright's most confessional work, chronic misery, because it is ordinary and unexceptional, did not bring him closer to religion. "I cannot recall one elevated moment in church" (Enright *CP 87*, 134), he asserts in
"Sunday," yet Enright was sent to church nonetheless because his
mother, a non-Catholic, felt that somehow the experience "might
come in useful later on" (Enright *CP 87*, 133). The poem's theme and
childhood simplicity are reminiscent of Blake's "Holy Thursday," in
which children are marched to church for their own good.

Enright's view of religion is tellingly revealed in a disturbing
group of Christmas poems. "Jingle Bells" details the death of Enright's baby sister, Valerie. In "Another Christmas" Enright's father
writes to a man named Crawford, whom he had rescued on the
Somme, clearly hoping that the reunion with his wartime comrade
would elicit a Christmas present, a belated gift of thanks for the family. The Enrights do receive a package by return mail: an assortment
of inferior cookies.

When Enright recalls the worst experiences of his early education ("Two Bad Things in Infant School"), religion is again at the
heart of his complaint.

Learning bad grammar, then getting blamed for it:
Learning Our Father which art in Heaven.

Bowing our heads to a hurried nurse, and
Hearing the nits rattle down on the paper. (Enright *CP 87*, 123)

As these autobiographical poems relate, Enright developed an appreciation for language at an early age, but in "Two Bad Things in Infant School" sacred verses lead to little more than spiritual and linguistic corruption. It is secular experience that is consecrated when the school children bow their heads submissively in the name of personal hygiene, not the Lord.

Enright is forever striving to balance life and art; in "A Sign," his defense of language is mistakenly viewed as a defense of religion. Enright retrieves an old Bible he spots in a rubbish bin, not intending to be seen as a defender of the faith. "At that tender age I couldn't bear / To see printed matter ill treated" (Enright *CP 87*, 133). There is no religious significance to his act, but he achieves a kind of neighborhood fame nonetheless for having saved religion "from the scrap-heap" (Enright *CP 87*, 133).

Now I could watch unmoved the casting
Of hundreds of books into dustbins.
But two of them I think I should still
Dive in after – Shakespeare and the Bible. (Enright *CP 87*, 133)

Shakespeare's humanity held a particular appeal for Enright, even in childhood, but his explications of Shakespeare's plays, published in 1970 as *Shakespeare and the Students*, are couched in an antiromantic Movement perspective meant to oppose "the hygienic incinerators of symbolism, imagery-computation, a curiously trite moralising, and philosophising of a sort so primitive as undoubtedly to have contributed to the discredit which literature has fallen into among the serious minded."[13]

He would save literature if only to save himself, not to establish some cultural icon before which the unread must bow. Lacking faith, he must be content with the rubbish of the world. This perspective, central to "A Sign" and "Two Bad Things in Infant School," also informs the satirical dialectic in "Anglo-Irish." When his father proclaims to be descended from the ancient Irish hero and king Brian

Boru, Enright's mother quips that her husband is merely a Catholic. "We would have preferred to believe our father. / Experience had taught us to trust in our mother" (Enright *CP 87*, 126). The dispute is more than familial; it is, more to the point, a struggle within Enright between the forces of romanticism and logical positivism. It is akin to the line of debate that occurs in other Movement poems, such as Larkin's "Poetry of Departures," and finds its poetic origins in the work of Thomas Hardy.

Though their subject matter is distinctly English, William Walsh suggests that the verses in *The Terrible Shears* resemble Japanese senryu poetry in form but are Chinese in spirit: "Japanese, that is, in being brief, spare, and if not exactly anonymous since impressed indelibly with a unique tone, at least unfussed about individuality; and Chinese in feeling, that is, coherent, solid, pragmatic, affectionate, objective" (Walsh, 103). But the satiric vein of traditional senryu is surely present in the volume as well.

Enright left teaching abroad and returned to England to give tutorials at the University of Leeds, Yorkshire, for two years. He then became coeditor of *Encounter*, occasionally contributing reviews, and joined his publisher, Chatto & Windus, in 1972, succeeding C. Day Lewis as director. Chatto issued Enright's *Sad Ires* in 1975 as part of its Phoenix Living Poets Series.

Sad Ires is a continuation of Enright's favorite themes. There are profound poems on religious uncertainty ("The Stations of King's Cross") and quizzical ones about literary matters ("The Ageing Poet," "Origin of the Haiku," and "Literary Party"); there are poems with foreign settings (some about the war in Vietnam) and poems about commuters in the London underground. The collection opens with a semantically rich catalog of crimes and punishments from the purview of a post-Edenic Adam. Having named the animals, he may now name modern horrors. The list is long; from humankind's one original transgression are now committed innumerable infamies. In Enright's words these include simple simony, manducation of corpses, infringement of copyright, champerty and malversation, hypergamy and other unnatural practices, free verse, terrorist bombings, bed-wetting, and the transporting of bibles without a license. But there are commensurate punishments: blinding with science, death by haranguing, palpation of the obvious, retooling of the economy, boredom of the genitals, sequestration of the funny-bone, and so on. The reader is frightened and intrigued by Enright's wit.

Now, four decades removed from the origins of the Movement, Enright has become a kind of active elder statesmen among English poets. A Fellow of the Royal Society of Literature, he received the Cholmondeley Award in 1974 and in 1981 was conferred the Queen's Medal for Poetry for his *Collected Poems*. He remains a vigorous editor and anthologist, having released four useful and curious anthologies in the 1980s – *The Oxford Book of Contemporary Verse, 1945-1980* (1980), *The Oxford Book of Death* (1983), *Fair of Speech, The Uses of Euphemism* (1985), and *The Faber Book of Fevers and Frets* (1989). During the decade he also issued three collections of literary essays – *A Mania for Sentences* (1983), *The Alluring Problem, An Essay on Irony* (1986), and *Fields of Vision: Essays on Literature, Language, and Television* (1988) – and one candid collection of verse, *Instant Chronicles, A Life* (1985). Additionally, he has published nearly 200 reviews on a wide range of topics for the *New Statesman, London Magazine*, the *New York Review of Books*, and other periodicals.

While, like Conquest, Enright believes that television and other forces of crass philistinism may contribute to an unseemly narcissism, he is no bluenose. He is intrigued by the ludicrous, the vulgar. He admits that language may not prove an effective social corrective, particularly in a time that resists the poetic, but continues to find social power in the printed word. His colloquial asides are frequently provocative. "After all, if words can lead to war, why can't words avert war? (As one might ask, if great literature can elevate, why can't pornography debase?) No condition is closer to events, more profoundly related, than feeling responsible for them, however 'fictively.' . . . The writer pursues nothingness only to find, and to mark for others, a way out of it."[14] This was at the root of the Movement all along – a way out of the poetic nothingness of the 1940s.

Chapter Five

Robert Conquest

The poetry of Robert Conquest reminds us just how inherently opposed to authority Movement writers were. George Robert Acworth Conquest was born on 15 July 1917 in Great Malvern, Worcestshire, the son of Robert Folger W. Conquest, a Virginian who lived on a private income and occasionally wrote for *Punch* and other magazines. Young Robert spent much of his childhood in the south of France, but he enrolled in prep school in Great Malvern. He then attended Winchester College and the University of Grenoble before graduating in 1939 from Magdalen College, Oxford, where he read politics, economics, and philosophy. He eventually took his M.A. from Oxford in 1972 and his D.Litt. in 1974.

From 1939 to 1945 Conquest was a member of the Oxfordshire and Buckinghamshire Light Infantry and served in Italy and the Balkans during the Soviet takeover of Bulgaria. Wearied by army life but fascinated with politics, he joined the Foreign Office in 1946 as an expert in postwar Eastern European politics. Conquest spent a decade in the Foreign Service; he served as first secretary in Sofia, Bulgaria, and was a member of Britain's delegation to the United Nations before leaving diplomatic life to become a free-lance writer and research fellow at the London School of Economics and Political Science. He subsequently held scholarly appointments at the University of Buffalo, Columbia University, the Woodrow Wilson International Center for Scholars at the Smithsonian Institution, the Hoover Institution at Stanford, the Heritage Foundation in Washington, D.C., and the Ukrainian Research Institute at Harvard. In his prestigious career as a cold-war Kremlinologist, Conquest has written and edited more than two dozen books on Soviet ideology.

Although trained as a social scientist, Conquest published his first poems in *Twentieth Century Verse* in the late 1930s. His literary career received a significant boost in 1945 when he won the P.E.N.

Brasil prize for his long poem "For the Death of a Poet," an elegy for Drummond Alison. Buoyed by this success, Conquest began to publish in the *Listener*, the *Spectator*, and *London Magazine*, and in 1951 he won the Festival of Britain verse prize. But Conquest's first book of poems, simply titled *Poems*, did not appear until 1955. Employing traditional meters and rhyme schemes, the book is decidedly political and is dedicated to the memory of Maurice Langlois ("poet, died in the hands of the secret police of the occupying power"). Two of the four sections – "War and After" and "The Balkans" – draw upon Conquest's experiences as a soldier well acquainted with Russian oppression. His rhetorically controlled, reserved style keeps the poems from sentimentality, and his protestations, when they occur, are more intellectual than emotional objections to tyranny. He feels a deep attachment for the frozen Balkan scenery and the inhabitants who dwell under the weight of Soviet totalitarianism, but politics is not the sole impulse of Conquest's art. There are love poems in the collection that do not depend on a properly political point of view. In "Aegean," for example, romantic love serves as a vehicle for a discussion of art rather than dictatorial oppression: "You were the first and only one to show me / The relation between a woman and a poem."[1]

Generally speaking, *Poems* is a collection of idiomatic occasional lyrics, war being but one of life's occasions, and it exhibits the characteristic Movement reluctance to speak with authority on life. *Poems* probes modern landscapes that, though perhaps lacking lasting political direction, are awash in myth and associative meaning. Conquest's technique is particularly strong in the volume's second section, "Arts and Contexts," in which echoes of the classical past continually infuse his ideas about art. The formal control in the poems contradicts somewhat the delicate sympathies they express. "The Rokeby Venus," "A Painting by Paul Klee," and "The Classical Poets" express how art variously pours forth images to shed light on a darkened world.

This light/dark imagery, while pronounced throughout the volume, is especially important to "Epistemology of Poetry" – "poems attempt / Light reconciling done and dreamt" (RC *Poems*, 35) – "Antheor," and "Humanities," in which light's effect on the landscape becomes a metaphor for the verbal lens of poetry. This

consideration of optics and the nature of perception is at the philosophical core of many poems in the volume and suggests that for
Conquest science and poetry are inextricably bound together. The
precision of Conquest's diction in exploring hypotheses – the
vocabulary, though rendered in ordinary language, is often drawn
from technical and scientific realms – triggers conclusions that become the bases of his ironic observations on art and poetry.

> Is it, when paper roses make us sneeze,
> A mental or a physical event?
> The word can freeze us to such categories,
> Yet verse can warm the mirrors of the word
> And through their loose distortions represent
> The scene, the heart, the life, as they occurred.
>
> – In a dream's blueness or a sunset's bronze
> Poets seek the images of love and wonder,
> But absolutes of music, gold or swans
> Are only froth unless they go to swell
> That harmony of science pealing under
> The poem's waters like a sunken bell. (RC *Poems*, 37)

Particularly interesting in *Poems* are Conquest's musings on
technological subjects, where his subdued coolness and clarity seem
especially appropriate as counterbalances to his strong humanistic
concerns. Although his poems are mostly lyrical, the genre most
identified with self-expression, he enlarges their traditional margins
by voicing a rationalist view on matters of scientific inquiry and
thereby achieves both an intellectual and emotional quality simultaneously. He notes strong similarities between artists and scientists,
claiming "that with any poet or almost any creative man, I mean
artist, scientist or anybody else, the interest is on the frontier between what he knows and what he doesn't know, rather than in organizing what is known. Only the empirical view, the scientific
method, if you like, though *scientific* is a narrow word, can cope"
(*Speaks*, 46).

His sonnet "Guided Missiles Experimental Range" considers the
horrific implications of scientific study, but the key to understanding
this ballistic achievement turns on a classical reference, as its sestet
contrasts the "loveless haste" of rockets speeding to their targets
with the avenging deities of Greek drama.

Stronger than lives, by empty purpose blinded,
The only thought their circuits can endure is
The target-hunting rigour of their flight;

And by that loveless haste I am reminded
Of Aeschylus' description of the Furies:
"O barren daughters of the fruitful night." (RC *Poems*, 4)

Similarly "Another Klee" examines a shocking painting under a microscope; "The Psychokinetic Experiments of Professor Rhine" surveys experiments in extrasensory perception in light of Kantian epistemology; and "The Landing in Deucalion," one of the earliest poems to disclose Conquest's abiding interest in the poet's relationship to the phenomenal universe, associates a landing on Mars with the poet's drive to create:

And why this subject should be set to verse
Is only partly in what fuels their hearts
More powerful than those great atomic drives
(Resembling as it does the thrust of poetry –
The full momentum of the poets' whole lives)
– Its consummation is yet more like art's:

For as they reach that unknown vegetation
Their thirst is given satisfaction greater
Than ever found but when great arts result;
Not just new detail of a changed equation
But freshly flaming into all the senses
And from the full field of the whole gestalt.

And so I sing them now, as others later. (RC *Poems*, 13)

Although his interest in technology underscores the Movement's interest in establishing a practical urban poetic, the "civilized" voice of Conquest seems even more impressive than his choice of topics. As a first collection, *Poems* shows extraordinary breadth, undoubtedly due in some measure to Conquest's wide reading and extensive travels, but he creates sympathy by modulating his curiosity in the guise of traditional verse. The specificity of his language transcends his choice of topics and therefore is a major attribute of his civility, and he admitted as much to *London Magazine* in 1962 when he claimed that an imaginary collection of "The Thousand Worst Poems about the Atomic Bomb" would rival in awfulness "The Hundred Worst Poems about the Death of Dylan Thomas."[2] By denying any poetic advantage derived from his interest in science, Conquest nonetheless publicly acknowledges a major difference between his verse and the work of other poets: his topics may make him different, but only his language can make him extraordinary.

Conquest once confessed that he would rather read *Scientific American* than any literary magazine, and his science fiction novel, *A World of Difference*, also published in 1955, confirms this interest. The book touches on Conquest's favorite themes – the failure of totalitarianism, the marvels of science, and the human impetus toward art. Although the novel presages a time in which Soviets occupy space and computers generate poetry, the world is eventually liberated by a group of "Poet class" cruisers named after his Movement colleagues. In a chapter full of double meanings, Major Hartley (*Spectator* editor Anthony Hartley was a good friend of Amis's at Oxford) reports on the status of his fleet: communication has been lost with the *Amis*, the *Jennings* has been destroyed on the ground, the *Larkin* "got badly holed tackling the Icarus base,"[3] and the *Gunn*, launched with the motto of its sponsor, "the rational man is poised, to break, to build" (*Difference*, 184), has changed course and swung toward an Earth orbit. But the *Wain*, *Enright*, and *Holloway* remain in service undamaged.

The novel suggests that the failure of Soviet autocracy is tied to its mishandling of verbal symbols, and Conquest has political and literary fun at the oppressors' expense. Their PACIC computer writes pointless sonnets in imitation of the apocalyptic poets of the 1940s. One creation is "sent around with a fifty-page analysis showing the machine's brilliance in selecting the words both on a psycho-emotional basis and for their rhythmic and general sound connections with surrounding words, and with the structure of the poem as a whole" (*Difference*, 64).

Conquest's heroes are not so stodgy or somber in their approach to language. One limerick writer, begrudging the absence of certain rhymes in English, coins the neologisms "torange" and "punth," and another character concedes that the purpose of science fiction is "to help loosen up literary thinking" (*Difference*, 84). (Such literary humor extends even to *The Egyptologists*, a satire Conquest cowrote with Kingsley Amis in 1965. The pair had been jointly editing the annual science fiction anthology *Spectrum*, and in a bit of self-mockery in the novel York, a pseudoscientist and the reckless treasurer of the Metropolitan Egyptological society, reads *The Year's Best in Fantasy and Science Fiction*, a thinly veiled reference to *Spectrum*.)

Noting affinities in style, several reviewers flatteringly compared Conquest's *Poems* with the work of his Movement associates, that group with whom he so readily identified himself in *A World of Difference*. Philip Larkin's *The Less Deceived* and Donald Davie's *Brides of Reason* were published contemporaneously with *Poems*, but at the time Conquest's poetry was judged to be not so flat and dull as that of his colleagues. John Holloway even called him "the *doyen* of the 'Movement,' "[4] though he acknowledged that Conquest's verse possessed a distinctively exotic quality that set him apart from his cohorts, with their nonconformist, suburban backgrounds. He commends Conquest's rich stream of images, "which flows with brilliant sensuous amplitude" (Holloway, 596) from the volume's diverse sources of travel, pictorial art, modern science, and science fiction. Indeed, the *Times Literary Supplement* reviewer called the volume "the most impressive first book of poems by an English writer to appear for several years."[5]

The Movement's concern for order is evident even in these early poems, as they emphasize a commonsense, democratic approach to the poetic process, an approach that pervades the rest of Conquest's work. But as important as *Poems* was to the Movement, Conquest made his most significant contribution not as a poet but as the editor of *New Lines*. Excepting perhaps only Enright's *Poets of the 1950s*, *New Lines*, published a year later, in 1956, was the most consequential collection of Movement work. Although they were individuals in many respects, the nine Movement poets shared complementary attitudes about verse; they were producing work startlingly different from the romantic poets of the 1930s and 1940s, who spewed forth "diffuse and sentimental verbiage" and "hollow pirouettes" (*NL*, xii) that continued to taint modern poetry. Since none of the members of the Movement was well known before the end of World War II, Conquest could not bank on the reputation of a big-name poet to attract attention to his anthology. But claiming that "the stage needed sweeping" (*NL*, xviii), Conquest, by bringing the poets together into a single work, achieved a two-fold purpose: (1) he reestablished a literary tradition that had been interrupted by the self-consciousness of Dylan Thomas and other apocalyptic poets ("to show that, as against much of the work of the past few decades, a good deal of contemporary poetry had returned to the cardinal traditions of English verse"),[6] and (2) he presented a healthy body of modern poetry whose intellectual honesty and moderation distinguished it from poems that slavishly imitated their predecessors ("the first lesson – that a poem needs an intellectual backbone") (*NL2*, xvi).

Though not so important to his own poetry, the skepticism of the Movement is conspicuous throughout the anthology, and Conquest chose poems that clearly embraced the rational, empirical perspective so evident in *Poems*. (While the eight poems he selected for *New Lines* from his own first volume were all quite speculative and tentative in nature, they showed the broad range of Conquest's interests, for he included not only poems about science and technology but love poems and poems about his Eastern European and Mediterranean travels as well.) Although he had no intention of launching a poetry movement with *New Lines*, by restoring a kind of reason to English poetry Conquest succeeded in establishing what was to be the intellectual basis for the group. It was, as John Press observed, "a call to order, an attempt to revive certain principles that he judged to be in suspended animation: verbal control, intellectual strength, and emotional sanity."[7]

Charles Tomlinson's review in *Essays in Criticism* was typical of the negative response to the anthology. Claiming that they were inspired by an intrinsically middlebrow muse, Tomlinson contends that the Movement poets wished to be admired for an essentially negative virtue – that is, the absence of formal poetic rhetoric in their work. In general he finds the poems to be an "invitation to mediocrity,"[8] their "middlingness, lack of real poetic talent and ambition . . . [having] found yet another cosy corner . . . in our watered-down, democratic culture" (Tomlinson, 216). And he calls Conquest's poetry "slick and sentimental" and his critical powers as an editor "wholly unexceptional" (Tomlinson, 217).

In subsequent issues of the magazine Donald Davie and D. J. Enright rose to Conquest's defense. Davie rebuked Tomlinson for sneering at the democratic taste exhibited in the anthology, and Enright objected to Tomlinson's offensive tone, calling Tomlinson's remarks "a nice example of the second-generation vulgarisation which to-day passes as healthy literary criticism."[9] Although *New Lines* did meet with less than enthusiastic reports from some quarters, Enright charged that Tomlinson's critique smacked of sour grapes – Tomlinson was the only poet to submit unsolicited work to *New Lines* and *Poets of the 1950s*, but his poetry had been rejected by both editors.

The public debate over *New Lines* heightened during the next year. Tomlinson protested that his exclusion from the volumes was purely a private matter that Enright had improperly raised. Conquest, questioning Tomlinson's motives and logic, retorted that even if Tomlinson's verses had been submitted without his knowledge or approval – an avowal that Conquest openly doubted – Tomlinson was certainly aware of their rejection before he penned his attack against *New Lines*. Furthermore, Conquest reinterpreted indictments against the book's dullness as a failure on the part of his critics to believe that "there is any place in poetry for comparatively flat lines. This is rather, indeed almost exactly, as if a critic of painting should demand highlights everywhere."[10] Ridiculing his detractors' taste for "clotted poetry and contorted syntax," he adds in an insulting after-thought that "the dryer the academicism, the wetter the sentimentalism it conceals" ("Critics," 226).

The controversy generated by Conquest's first anthology focused critical attention on the Movement poets as a group for the first time, so in 1963, having become literary editor of the *Spectator* in the interim, Conquest edited *New Lines II*, a broader collection than its predecessor. Deleting one original contributor (Holloway) from the 1956 anthology, Conquest added 16 others, including Ted Hughes, whose work "falls neither into empty rant nor into bloodless chinoiserie," (*NL2*, xxviii). Conquest's introduction repeats the rational, objectivist editorial stand taken in the first anthology, and he charges that his views "are, in general, those held by most poets and most people interested in poetry, though they are not those most commonly met with in writings about poetry" (*NL2*, xiv). He argues that poets seldom hold an irrational view regarding the composition of poetry, no matter how technically and psychologically complex it may be, and that "all attempts so far made to reduce the operation to a clearly conceptualised and self-conscious process have been failures" (*NL2*, xxi). Accordingly for Conquest the vitality of poetry remains in that it is written, not for critics but for people who like

poetry. His choice of poets was intentionally narrow, following the
lead of Philip Larkin, who believed that British culture itself was inherently insular. Conquest's selection also reflects his predilection
for writers who like himself "follow the central principle of English
poetry, and use neither howl nor cypher, but the language of men"
(*NL2*, xxviii), and he endeavors to reclaim Wordsworthian romanticism for himself and his allies.

> Poetry is written in language. That language has a close relationship – to put
> it no higher – to common speech. To "heighten" speech is not in fact to de-
> part from it more than very slightly. When poetry goes bad (from the point of
> view of language) it is invariably due to the creation of "poeticism" – a vo-
> cabulary, or diction, or general phraseology, of an isolated type. This has usu-
> ally in the past taken the form of certain words becoming traditional in poetry
> at the same times as they become obsolete in common speech. But it is also
> possible – and this is the form the vice takes in the twentieth century – to
> depart from the true roots by *creating* linguistic forms equally separated from
> the natural language, and equally to be regarded as poeticisms.[11]

In this he agrees with Pasternak that the scourge of modern poetry has been its pursuit of a new language, and his study of the Russian allowed him to unite two of his favorite themes in a single study:
his interest in literary language and his distaste for Soviet oppression.
Pasternak proved a useful topic for Conquest, for both writers believed that language must be transformed from within the work itself,
and Conquest's preference for democratic poetry is evidenced as
well in *Back to Life* (1958), his gathering of poems from behind the
Iron Curtain. Issued to prove that talented writers are not servile, the
anthology is for the most part an attack against the antiintellectualism
of totalitarian regimes. An opponent of those oppressors who would
treat verse as a vehicle to excite their emotions, Conquest contends
that even when poetry reflects the chaotic timbre of the time in
which it is composed, there is still no warrant for it to fall into violent
disproportion, novelty being no substitute for intellectual balance
and symmetry.

   The Abomination of Moab (1979) furthers this strong position
and may be read as an extension of Matthew Arnold's attack on
philistinism. Conquest alleges that the Philistines (Arnold's name for
the avowed enemies of the Israelites) were no more dangerous than
the Moabites who infiltrated the temple and "set the children of light

whoring after strange doctrine" (*Moab*, viii). The dogmatic Moabites viewed literature as a form of social service and were morally bent on monitoring literary offenses through the establishment of central committees. Like their modern cold-war counterparts, particularly the Soviet tyrants Conquest had studied so intently, they demeaned and attempted to control culture by organizing it through committees that served their own "drivelling ideologies of pop" (*Moab*, ix).

Conquest distinguishes between the consumers of literature on one hand and the critical establishment on the other. Defending the Movement's preference for unpretentious verse, Conquest contends that ungarnished verse appeals to readers, ambiguous poetry to critics, although "in any reasonable sense – the more incomprehensible the poem the worse it must be" (*Moab*, 8).

The Abomination of Moab also includes Conquest's wonderfully satiric essay "Christian Symbolism in *Lucky Jim*." The essay had originally appeared in *Critical Quarterly* in 1965, the very year he collaborated with Amis on *The Egyptologists*, and it demonstrates Conquest's willingness to have fun with his art and with that of his friends. The piece interprets Jim's intoxicated lecture, for example, as a crucifixion scene, and, although astute readers likely discerned from his bogus references, particularly one to Mrs. Joyce Hackensmith's *The Phallus Theme in Early Amis*, that the essay was clearly a spoof, it was taken seriously by more than a few readers.

Donald Davie had recommended that Conquest create in *New Lines II* a section of poems by the original Movement poets to be called "Divergent Lines," implying that an evolution in Movement verse had already taken place and that what had brought the nine together in 1956 was not so strong seven years later, with the inclusion of Hughes's muscular lyrics a testimony of sorts to the Movement's dynamism. But Conquest disagreed, believing that any differences at the time were simply miscellaneous attempts to return to the basic principles of English poetry.

Conquest included only four of his own poems in the anthology, and they were all from his second collection, *Between Mars and Venus* (1962). One is "For the 1956 Opposition of Mars," which Thom Gunn claimed was written "with such calm energy, such lucidity and power, that it would be worth buying the book for it alone."[12] But *Between Mars and Venus* is less rewarding than Conquest's initial volume, although it does contain one of his boldest attempts at humor ("Vision"), a poem about a naked girl in a seaside pose seen in an issue of *Titter* magazine. Gunn admitted that some of the landscape poems left him nonplussed because he had not seen the scenery in question, but the narrator's complaint in "Vision" is precisely that – he hasn't seen naked women on his trips to the shore either. And who in 1962 could have visited a Martian or Venusian landscape save imaginatively or through Conquest's poem? (Perhaps, however, Gunn would have concurred with Conquest's assertion in "Jet over the Pacific" that "I shall not be bored by the view from space.")[13] Possibly, as one of the editors of the science fiction annual *Spectrum*, Conquest had greater opportunity to contemplate such remote vistas.

While Gunn felt that by avoiding pretentiousness Conquest also limited the potential range of his talent, he nonetheless approved of a handful of poems that vigorously combine "passion and reserve" (*Mars*, 17). Gunn claimed that Conquest was at his inventive and intellectual best when he combined both qualities, "for the reserve does not limit the passion but serves to define, concentrate, and thus strengthen it" (Gunn, 135). William Van O'Connor had noted that same quality in *Poems*, similarly calling it a search for order based on a balance between Apollonian and Dionysian impulses.[14]

As with *Poems*, *Between Mars and Venus* embraces the possibilities of scientific discovery; "Excerpt from a Report to the Galactic Council" seems a kind of poetic prototype of Conquest's science fiction novel, *A World of Difference*. But there are also poems on strictly literary matters where the voice of Auden seems to linger ("Art and Love," "The Motives of Rhythm," "The Virtues of Poetry," "Kafka's 'The City,' " "Keats in 1819," and "Birmingham," which is dedicated to D. J. Enright) and a sequence on the American Civil War. He employs classical references in a host of poems, and a lesser number of poems are love lyrics.

Conquest's later poetry, *Arias from a Love Opera* (1969) and *Forays* (1979), though they display a continuing interest in landscapes and literary subjects, do not show much poetic development. There are markedly fewer verses exploring scientific matters, and the poems at times seem inordinately mechanical and cerebral, but they are also frequently witty. Conquest fashions a curious rhyme with "Charybdis" in "The Poet's Morning," and "747 (London – Chicago)" is a satirical indictment of the horrors of modern airports.

"Seal Rocks: San Francisco" draws a clever analogy between seals and the creation of poetry, and "A Visit to the Evans Country" is a sparkling parody of his friend Amis. (Conquest frequently masked his wit under the pseudonyms Ted Pauker and Victor Gray, and Amis included a dozen of Conquest's limericks and parodies in *The New Oxford Book of Light Verse*.)

While the books' repetition of political themes, as in "Get Lost, Gulag Archipelago," smacks a bit of self-imitation, Conquest has maintained a practical approach to his craft, striving to avoid obscurity through his choice of diction and familiar poetic structures. His formidable poetic talent remains evident, particularly in "Two Housman Torsos," an attempt set forth in a 1973 issue of the *Times Literary Supplement* to turn two fragments from a Housman manuscript into finished and satisfying poems while adhering to the form and meter of Housman's drafts. Despite his achievements as poet, editor, novelist, and cold-war historian, Conquest has sought no preeminence over his Movement companions; he stakes no "claim whatever to moral or any other sort of superiority over poets who write of (let us say) an Arundel tomb. . . . Poets can only write in the way they themselves feel appropriate, on themes which form part of their properly assimilated, imaginative ballast."[15]

Chapter Six

John Wain

John Barrington Wain was born in Stoke-on-Trent, Staffordshire on 14 March 1925. His parents were low-church Christians, but he lacked the working-class background of most other Movement writers. His father, Arnold, became a prominent dentist, although he lacked formal dental training, and he was the first member of his family to rise above its working-class origins. The climb was not without its difficulties for young John, who was frequently pursued by resentful neighborhood bullies as he walked home in his school uniform. By the age of five he had already learned "(i) that the world was dangerous; (ii) that it was not possible to evade these dangers by being inoffensive, since I was surrounded on all sides by those who hated me, not for anything I had done, but for being different from themselves; (iii) that, although the natural reaction to all this was fear, I could not admit to feeling fear or I should be disgraced" (*Sprightly*, 6). These severe lessons of childhood trained him "for an adult life infinitely worse than anything I have actually experienced" (*Sprightly*, 6). They influenced his writing as well, a body of work that sees the world as "something to be feared. I cannot remember a time when everything seemed to me cosy, secure, optimistic" (*Sprightly*, 58).

As a boy Wain had no particular intellectual interests, and, though he read widely in his father's library, he was an undistinguished student; "I was backward and unteachable" (*Sprightly*, 63). But at the age of nine he began writing a series of novels in his exercise books. Most of the stories concerned a private eye, ludicrously named Smellum Owte. Wain illustrated the works with his own pen-and-ink drawings and used block capital letters in an effort "to try to achieve some of the impersonality of print" (*Sprightly*, 162). He also published a magazine called *Hot Stuff*, which carried violent, parodic serials. "My vocabulary at nine years old was as large, and apparently as much under control, as it is today" (*Sprightly*, 163).

Wain attended high school in Newcastle-under-Lyme, where his wit blossomed further. "I grew finally into a 'character,' one of the school notabilities, able to break conventions and get away with it, tolerated and even, within strict limits, admired" (*Sprightly*, 69). Although he joined the Officers' Training Corps, Wain was rejected from military service because of poor eyesight; he had suffered a detached retina as a teenager, and he never fully regained his vision in the damaged eye. Wain then enrolled without scholarship in St. John's College, Oxford, where he took a B.A. in 1946. Though he did not serve in the war, it affected him profoundly. "It made me more Pharisaical, it confirmed me in my pessimism, and it hampered my education . . . one of the least qualified seventeen-year-olds ever to go up to Oxford" (*Sprightly*, 83). Still, he became a star pupil in college and graduated with highest marks.

He continued his studies as a research fellow at Oxford, receiving his M.A. in 1950. In college he met Kingsley Amis and Philip Larkin, friends to whom he has acknowledged a lasting literary debt. Wain's tutor at Oxford was C. S. Lewis, who conveyed to him the "theory that, since the Creator had been fit to build a universe and set it in motion, it was the duty of the human artist to create as lavishly as possible in his turn" (*Sprightly*, 182). Lewis insisted that the artist who invents a world worships God more intrinsically than the realist who analyzes a world that already exists. So Wain left Oxford with the desire to create, but he also carried with him "one great disability: my settled, middle-aged pessimism, my conviction that the hordes of barbarians were already within the gates and that the only thing left was to guard the few fragments in one's possession and accept a backward-looking, stoical melancholy at one's portion in life. . . . All I wanted to do was to dig in, cultivate my knowledge of the glorious past, and stand firm as the tidal wave of modernity swept over me" (*Sprightly*, 158).

Following his graduate studies, Wain taught at Reading University where, as a lecturer earning 400 pounds per year he also learned the hard lessons of poverty. Still burning with the desire to write, he left teaching after eight years to try to support himself entirely through his writing. The adjustment was made less difficult by two factors: his salary as a lecturer had been quite small, and he intensely disliked authority and wished to escape the confines of daily employment. "The thing I have always been bad at is taking orders," he writes. "I

am not the kind of person who finds it easy to work out a happy relationship with those whom he must obey. When I see Authority, I
reach for the custard pie. . . . My life would have been far smoother
and happier if I had found it easier to accept authority" (*Sprightly*,
64).

Wain had been readying to free himself from teaching for some
time. He began reviewing books and free-lancing, primarily for the
Observer, and despite the uncertainty of his income managed to
avoid the financial snares that befell many serious writers. In 1953,
while lecturing at Reading, he was asked to become host of the BBC
poetry program *First Reading*, which had succeeded John
Lehmann's *New Soundings* project, begun the previous year.
Lehmann, through *New Soundings* and his *Penguin New Writing*
collections that preceded it, had introduced the work of Davie,
Gunn, Jennings, Holloway, and Wain to a wide audience, and on his
first program Wain similarly announced an intention to promote a
group of young, disciplined writers attentive to the traditions of English letters. He read an excerpt from Amis's *Lucky Jim* on that inaugural broadcast, and was then attacked for it by Hugh Massingham,
the *New Statesman*'s radio critic. A subsequent *First Reading* in-
stallment presented the work of Philip Larkin. Wain's radio series
lasted only six months, but the six programs broadcast work by some
important new authors. Wain proudly boasted, "If I drew up a list of
the writers who first reached a wide public through *First Reading*, it
would be a fairly comprehensive roll-call of the younger established
writers of today" (*Sprightly*, 168).

Wain enjoyed their work because it was tough, witty, distrusting,
and coolly informal. Sharing Donald Davie's appreciation for Augustan restraint, they, like Wain, were not much interested in romanticism or in emotional nature poetry or the treacly love poems
spawned in its name. "The last thirty years have been the hey-day of
the poetic charlatan," he lamented. "The situation has been with us
for many years, but it is getting worse. Thirty years ago, F. R. Leavis
said of the Sitwells that they belonged to the history of publicity
rather than of poetry. . . . But one of our new-style poets can build
up a big reputation in the absence of anyone who likes, or even
reads, his work" (*Sprightly*, 189-92).

The *First Reading* experience left Wain with an extreme disdain
for critics. Noted literary figures, including Graham Greene and V. S.

Pritchett, were brought into the fray and for the most part opposed the Movement sensibilities endorsed by Wain's program. Wain unexpectedly became spokesman for the group's most compelling authors (Amis in fiction and Larkin in verse); being both a novelist and a poet as well as a critic, he was probably the most qualified member to speak on the Movement's behalf. Wain's antipathy to criticism was in part an intellectual dislike for what was popular and journalistic, but it was also born from that distinction between artist and critic imparted to him by Lewis. "There must be the artist, there must be the professional go-between (publisher, art dealer, impresario), and there must be the public" (*Sprightly*, 190), but Wain felt that in poetry the triangle had collapsed altogether. Wain was academically trained himself and had written numerous critical pieces, but his first allegiance was to the craft of creative writing.

Wain had published his first poems in *Mandrake*, the Oxford literary magazine he founded in 1945, and his first critical piece appeared in the undergraduate magazine the *Cherwell*. But for the most part his interest in creative writing had languished until, when he was 26 Reading University brought out his first book, a paperbound volume of 19 poems called *Mixed Feelings* (1951). Only 120 copies were printed.

He then began writing a novel solely for the purpose of trying to get his work into print. "My avowed aims were to get the book published and to make a hundred pounds from it" (*Sprightly*, 165). Secker & Warburg bought the book, *Hurry On Down*, in 1953 and gave him a 250-pound advance. The book sold modestly – 5,000 copies – but its effect was considerable.

The story of Charles Lumley, a recent graduate in history, *Hurry On Down* (released in the United States as *Born in Captivity*) chronicles Lumley's "descent" into success. Like Wain, Lumley seems unfit for life. Unable to find employment appropriate to his talents, he moves through a series of menial, even criminal, occupations: window washer, smuggler, chauffeur, bouncer. Like Amis's Lucky Jim, Lumley despises the residue of 1930s intellectualism, but he eventually triumphs as a radio gag-writer, a job that transcends traditional class distinctions. A largely reactive character, Lumley exhibits Wain's distrust of destiny and class as forces that shape human life. Lumley is in fact best defined by what he opposes – his middle-class background, his schooling, and cheerless British society. He is naive and innocent, he is not very likable, and his ignorance proves a large burden to him.

Although the novel's final scene finds Charles being happily visited by Veronica, a beautiful woman with whom he is enamored and who is well above him socially, *Hurry On Down* paradoxically brought Wain the label of Angry Young Man. Beneath its wit and humor critics detected an undercurrent of outrage and anger, perhaps abetted by the childhood remembrance at the book's core. "The mood at its centre was born that afternoon in 1935, as I scrambled to my feet, dazed, nursing my knee, and saw, on one hand, the glowering faces of the elementary-school boys, and on the other the aloof backs of my schoolfellows – and wondered how, between the two of them, I was ever going to find a place to live" (*Sprightly*, 62).

Always ready to thwart society's tendency to restrict and categorize, Wain persistently rejected the label of Angry Young Man. His publishers even put out a display card bearing Wain's picture with the inscription "John Wain is *not* an Angry Young Man." Wain felt the designation had been fabricated by journalists who knew and cared nothing about literature, and, while he admitted that his early criticism, particularly the essay on William Empson he wrote for *Penguin New Writing* (1950), had been unnecessarily aggressive, he believed that being labeled an Angry Young Man, while it enhanced sales of his work, prevented people from holding serious opinions about his art. When the Soviet Union imported and translated *Hurry On Down*, presumably perceiving it as a diatribe against Western capitalism, Wain protested vigorously, even though the book sold 250,000 copies there. His anger toward the Soviets was later expressed in *The Young Visitors* (1965), a novel that ridiculed what he perceived as their failed efforts at diplomacy and their bungling bureaucratic system.

Although he acknowledged the presence of anger in his work and was an admirer of the other Angry Young Men – Amis, Alan Sillitoe, Malcolm Bradbury, John Osborne, and John Braine (who has often been confused with Wain because of the phonetic similarity of their names) – Wain complained, "I have never described myself as an Angry Young Man . . . but everyone is angry at something, and one of the things that angers me is the thought that I am living in a civilisation so completely dominated by the journalist and his cousin the ad. . . . Instead of the artist, we have the journalist. Instead of the voice, the loudspeaker. Instead of the man, the machine. Productivity instead of work. Sex instead of love. The pop-disc instead of the folk-song. Housing estates instead of villages. Plagiarism, staleness, envy, discontent, gossip, malice, instead of a genuine free play of the imagination."[1]

When Wain began to have bouts of illness, he asked the university for a year's leave to spend the winter in the Swiss Alps. With no teaching salary to sustain him, he wrote a second novel in 1955. "The less said about this book, *Living in the Present*, the better. The months during which I worked on it were some of the worst in my life. . . . I slowly forced my way through the novel, gritting my teeth and making myself write a certain number of pages each day" (*Sprightly*, 170). But he persevered and completed the work, though it was denounced by the critics. Based on the promise of *Hurry On Down*, Wain was called a flash in the pan, a one-note bird.

Both comic and dour, *Living in the Present* concerns a suicidal London teacher named Edgar Banks. His girlfriend has left him, and he detests his job. He can find no spiritual or philosophical solace. Determined to kill himself, Banks decides to take with him the most morally despicable person he can find – an effete fascist poet and critic named Rollo Philipson-Smith. Banks pursues Philipson-Smith across Europe, but in a series of melodramatic episodes his quarry avoids extermination. Edgar abandons his venture when he falls in love with Catherine, the sweetheart of his good friend Tom Straw. The book is fundamentally dissatisfying as Edgar marries Catherine and returns contentedly to his old job.

Wain's third novel, *The Contenders* (1958), also concerns a homecoming of sorts. The book again takes up the theme of competition, though it develops it more on a personal rather than an economic or class level. The "contenders" are three friends from a Midlands pottery town who vie with one another for success in business and romance. The hostilities that erupt between the artist (Robert Lamb) and the businessman (Ned Roper) are smoothed over by the book's overly romantic, moral ending in which the local journalist (Joe Shaw) settles down with Pepina, a country girl whom Robert has brought back with him from Italy.

Wain, however, was not ready to return home. Empson and others wrote encouraging him not to forsake his teaching post, but he declined to return. Though his books were not necessarily critical successes, he had proven to himself he was disciplined enough to survive as a professional writer, and because of his poor vision he did not want to resume the vast amount of reading that was required of a university teacher. He also had private reasons for not returning to the classroom. He was at the time undergoing a divorce from Marianne Urmstrom, whom he had married in 1947 and who also taught at Reading, and he "wanted to spare the university the embarrassment of witnessing a divorce between two members of its teaching staff" (*Sprightly*, 171). Although Wain married again in 1960 to Eirian James and has fathered three children from their happy union, the failure of his marriage to Marianne remains "the central crisis of my life, which broke so much in me that a dozen lifetimes would not suffice to mend it all. . . . Parting from someone you care for is the worst kind of pain, the slowest to heal and the most deeply felt" (*Sprightly*, 261, 161).

Over the years Wain served from time to time as visiting professor at various colleges and for five years in the 1970s as the esteemed Professor of Poetry at Oxford. Wain admits he doesn't think teaching is "good employment for a writer," yet when he tries to imagine "a suitable framework for a literary life, there is always a university in it somewhere. . . . The university is the only place left where young people can meet in an atmosphere of freshness and idealism" (*Sprightly*, 186, 189).

In the next seven years Wain published three novels, four books of nonfiction, and three books of poems. Perhaps most interesting among the novels is the polemical *Strike the Father Dead* (1962), which concerns the struggle of jazz pianist Jeremy Coleman to overthrow the influence of his father, a professor of classics. Wain's ironic vision distinguishes the book. In a generational rebellion Coleman takes on a surrogate father and pursues his music as a form of defiance. But he, too, must in the end make way for a new generation; ultimately Coleman is driven from the stage by up-and-coming rock-and-rollers.

Nor does Wain opt for a happy ending in *The Smaller Sky* (1967). Rather, he kills off his central character, scientist Arthur Geary. Geary, who has left his wife and children, quits his job as a researcher and moves to a hotel near Paddington Station. Suffused with a sense of loneliness over the suicide of a friend, Geary is tormented by a persistent drumbeat in his head and chest. He spends much of his time on a railway platform, where he finds his anguish abates. Geary's situation is brought to the attention of family, friends, and psychiatrists and eventually to television personality Adrian Swarthmore, a friend of Geary's wife. In a bit of shameless self-promotion Swarthmore visits the platform with a television crew to interview Geary. Attempting to escape, Geary climbs to the roof where he falls to the tracks below. The novel concludes: "As Geary died, two good things happened. The drums ceased, and the snow went on falling."[2] The ending is one of the novel's most incisive ironies.

The protagonist's dislocation also operates in *A Winter in the Hills* (1970). Philologist intellectual Roger Furnivall moves to Caefenai, Wales, to study the language but is drawn into a dispute over local bus service. Roger becomes a fare collector for a one-man bus operation, defying takeover by a capitalist ruffian named Dic Sharp. Though not readily accepted by the working-class locals, Roger wins them over when he survives a brutal attack by Sharp's henchmen. His resolve enables him to win both a moral and economic victory; the bus monopoly is broken.

As a fiction writer, Wain is an allegorist of sorts who sees himself in the realist tradition. His settings are hardly exotic, and his characters engage in commonplace activities. His poetry is more personal than his fiction, and, despite his popularity as a novelist, Wain laments that "my poems, which are the best things I have done, are naturally unknown because this is not a poetry-reading age. . . . There is some material that cries out for the poem, and there is some that cries out for the novel or the play" (*Sprightly*, 202).

His first book of poems, *Mixed Feelings*, later incorporated into *A Word Carved on a Sill* (1956), exhibits the Movement's distrust of 1940s romanticism. Wain's disapproval of unfocused imagery is the substance of his "Reasons for Not Writing Orthodox Nature Poetry." He favors clarity, restraint, and directness. Preferring the Empsonian track of order over emotion, he employs the complex verse forms (sonnets, villanelles, and terza rima) Empson used in the 1930s, but he imbues them with the concerns of the 1950s. Consequently, the poems have a distinctly academic air.

Though he had written admiringly of Dylan Thomas's *Collected Poems*, he was quick to note Thomas's deficiencies. "I think, then, that he is a fine, bold, original and strong poet whose work is marred by two great drawbacks. First, a disastrously limited subject-matter.

There are really only three subjects treated; (i) childhood, and the associated topic of what it is like to remember one's childhood; (ii) the viscera; (iii) religion. . . . The third subject, religion, seems to me Thomas's worst pitch; he never succeeds in making me feel that he is doing more than thumbing a lift from it."[3] It is not surprising that Wain's first poems avoid these three topics almost altogether.

Particularly interesting are Wain's love poems. That love is the principal topic of *A Word Carved on a Sill* is evident from the inscription taken from Robert Graves: "Yet love survives, the word carved on a sill / Under antique dread of the headsman's axe." More than any other Movement poet, Wain has taken up the romantic love lyric. In "Cameo" he compares the perfection of lovers arching like bridges to a modern city, but the poem escapes sentimentality, and "Poem in Words of One Syllable" is likewise simple and soulful. He contrasts human hearts ("Sonnet") with their "animal" counterparts, concluding "our hearts beat and ache. Theirs only beat."[4] And he merges pain and pleasure into a singular sensation in "On Reading Love Poetry in the Dentist's Waiting Room": "So, thinking of the drill, I here condone / The drill they mastered with sweet intuition" (Wain *Poems*, 176). His flair for titles, as in "Don't Let's Spoil It All, I Thought We Were Going to Be Such Good Friends," at times humorously cloaks his depth of feeling.

Though not much interested in science and technology, Wain's "Poem Feigned to Have Been Written by an Electronic Brain" is written with an electronic stammer that discloses both the machine's frustration and Wain's inventiveness. It might well be read as a statement of conscience from the poetry-writing computer in Robert Conquest's science fiction novel, *A World of Difference*.

The indeterminancy of love and Wain's homage to Empson are most cogently revealed in "Eighth Type of Ambiguity," wherein he asks, if love has ruled the world, why has the world not been subdued? Like Larkin, Wain is able to see both the enchanting and destructive aspects of love:

And so to every type love is a danger.
Some think it means no more than saying Yes,
And some turn canine when they reach the manger.

It seems a meaning we could hardly guess. (Wain *Poems*, 174)

Wain's willingness to deal frankly with matters of the heart is evident in his fiction as well. Almost all of his novels concern themselves with love affairs, especially *A Travelling Woman* (1959), which details five characters' infidelities, and *The Pardoner's Tale* (1978). In the latter, novelist Giles Hermitage is abandoned by his wife for another man. He invents a perfect, fictional woman whom he then meets in real life, but he loses her as well. The novel's plot is strikingly similar to Larkin's *Jill* in its use of an imaginary lover, and it relates the hazards of using romance as a means of escape from life's difficulties.

Weep before God (1961) is a continuation of Wain's low-key poetics, although it shows more technical versatility. His "Apology for Understatement" and "Poem without a Main Verb" epitomize the reserve of Movement verse and its reverence for a reticence that keeps "the keen equipose between *always* and *never*" (Wain *Poems*, 153). Love remains Wain's primary interest in *Weep before God*. There are poems of loneliness and heartbreak ("Anecdote of 2 A.M." and "To a Friend in Trouble") and transforming poems about miraculous love ("This Above All Is Precious and Remarkable" and "Apology for Understatement").

One of the volume's most celebrated poems is "A Song about Major Eatherly." Eatherly, who piloted the aircraft carrying the second atomic bomb to Nagasaki, suffered severe depression for his hand in the death of thousands. Although awarded a monthly pension of $237, Eatherly refused it on principle and turned to petty thievery, for which he was sent to prison. For Wain, the poem represents a technical departure from his reliance on the three-line stanza. More visionary than his previous work, "A Song about Major Eatherly" nevertheless possesses Wain's familiar social irony. It opens:

> Good news. It seems he loved them after all.
> His orders were to fry their bones to ash.
> He carried up the bomb and let it fall.
> And then his orders were to take the cash. (Wain *Poems*, 165)

Eatherly becomes an emblem. His punishment for theft is imprisonment, but there is no assuaging his moral guilt. Wain intends Eatherly's case to serve as a social corrective: "Eatherly, we have your message" (Wain *Poems*, 170).

Wildtrack (1965) is an even greater philosophical departure from the Movement's rhetorical stoicism. A difficult concert of poems in a mixture of metrical keys, *Wildtrack* contrasts man's day-self – that is, his social identity – with his night-self, that inward-looking spirit that separates him from others. "The day-self is the self which copes with exterior reality, which acquires skills and responsibilities, which learns languages and procedures, and the day-self is balanced by the night-self which is, of course, instinctual, primitive – in touch with the archetypal realities."[5] The personal and the historical blend to form a singular shape of human personality. Images of permanence and impermanence interpenetrate. Stalin, Rousseau, and astronauts affect history no more incontrovertibly than do snowflakes and beggars.

Wain's promenade through human history extends into *Letters to Five Artists* (1969). After his lengthy "Introductory Poem," Wain addresses letters to two poets (Movement colleague Elizabeth Jennings and British poet Anthony Conran), an American junk sculptor (Lee Lubbers), an English painter (Victor Neep, whom Wain further celebrates in his "Victor Neep: 1921-1979" sequence in an issue of the *Antagonish Review*), and an American jazz musician who lived in Paris in the 1930s (trumpeter Bill Coleman, perhaps the nominal inspiration for the rebellious Jeremy Coleman in *Strike the Father Dead*). But they are merely bridges to the past; his allusions to Ovid and Villon suggest historical unity, just as the poems' epistolary form is employed to achieve an artistic one.

Feng (1975) is a more successful long poem. An incomplete sequence of 17 dramatic monologues, it was issued in a limited edition of 600 copies. Six of the poems and a seventh excluded from the sequence had appeared in *The Shape of Feng* (1972). *Feng* is a compelling version of the Hamlet myth taken from Saxo Grammaticus. Horwendil, governor of Jutland, wins fame by killing the King of Norway in combat, but he is murdered by his brother, Feng, who then marries Horwendil's queen, Gerutha. Like Shakespeare's Claudius, Feng must deal with his hallucinatory sickness and his powerful ambition, while Horwendil's son, Amleth, under the guise of madness plans retribution. After sexually assaulting Amleth's beloved, Feng retires to a tower to await Amleth's revenge.

Wain's interest in Shakespeare and his familiarity with Shakespearean analogues is evident in *Feng*, *The Living World of*

Shakespeare: A Playgoer's Guide (1964), Wain's most popular critical work, and in his two casebooks on Shakespearean tragedies. But Wain's technique proves more interesting than the substance of his narratives. *Feng* demonstrates just how far from *New Lines* strategies his verse had grown. He mingles new forms and old as he connects stanzas of verse with prose passages in modernistic fashion, and *Feng* seems closer to Pound's *Cantos* than it does to Larkin's *The Less Deceived*. Although Wain claims that Larkin is one of two modern poets – John Heath-Stubbs is the other – who "make a satisfactory amalgam of form with content" (*Professing*, 154), he reserves special praise for Pound. "If there could ever be such a thing as a stylist pure and simple – a man in whose work style counted over and above matter," Wain writes, "Pound would be that man" (*Preliminary*, 160).

Over his career John Wain moved from considering the isolation of the individual in personal terms to historical ones, and his attachment to the Movement seems enigmatic. While he has since the early 1980s forsaken the long poem for those between 75 and 150 lines, he has strived to hold onto the attributes found in shorter Movement poems, particularly their linguistic precision and logical coherence. "As for the so-called 'Movement,' " Wain observes, "I only wish my writing really did have the virtues of the 'Movement' as, say, Philip Larkin's does. But I know, inwardly, that I don't fit in properly anywhere" (*Sprightly*, 205). While carping that too many writers under 40 still "write endlessly about themselves and their own feelings" (*Sprightly*, 222) and compose "a kind of loose-knit verse which presents carefully chosen images in carelessly chosen words,"[6] Wain is also willing to write about profound personal experiences, but his approach is decidedly more cerebral.

Perhaps it is his ambivalence that most differentiates him from the others. His poem "In the Beginning," for example, is typically lyrical in its exploration of the first hours of love. He does not deny the moment's perfection, only his ability to speak of it. Reserve and balance attend even in times of strongest emotion.

> This equilibrium,
> most rare and perilous balance, leaves me dumb
> to say it all, to name the gems and metals
> (flame of a butterfly before it settles)
> before the troubles and the questionings come. (Wain *Poems*, 86)

Wain's maverick nature prevents him from accepting any doctrinaire position, and he refuses identification with any movement or program.

> I must have freedom to do my work as effectively as possible, and a label narrows that freedom from the outside, as a programme narrows it from the inside. In my opinion, a writer has no business with programmes because his job is to keep himself alert and able to deal with truth in any form in which it may confront him. His object is merely to understand, and pass on to his readers, as much truth as he can comprehend. . . . Programmes are bad because they almost inevitably lead the writer to over-simplify. A programme is an abstraction from human experience, and the truth is always richer, more various, and more contradictory than an abstraction. . . . For myself, I refuse to have a programme, or even (if I can help it) to become associated with one particular type of subject-matter." (*Sprightly*, 206-8)

While as a young man he welcomed the Movement's impulse toward popular poetry, Wain believes that its promise of liberation has gone unrealized. "At this point, the modern academic steps in again, to remind me that my values are based on an obsolete regard for the individual. In an age of collectivism, here am I, quaintly, still making the unargued assumption that it is better for human beings to think and feel as individuals than as a mass" (*House*, 208-9).

Such hidebound academicism was also what prompted the Movement to give poetry a necessary injection of straightforwardness. "It was rare, at that time, to read a new poem which could have been recited to an audience with any hope that they would pick up its meaning. The key to 'success' in the little-magazine world of that time was to pile on the obscurities. If the editor couldn't make head or tail of your poem, he would probably print it, on the grounds that if it was 'difficult' it was probably a genuine poem. Or, at any rate, near enough to pass for one" (*House*, 16).

Wain feels that his best work, that created and understood outside the boundaries of any group labels, has yet to be realized. "Perhaps one day I shall begin to emerge. Perhaps the next book I write . . . will put me in a position that critics will be able to define in its own terms, without any roll-call of other names. But I doubt it" (*Sprightly*, 205-6). The struggle to write well seems task enough, and it is unlikely that John Wain shall be muzzled.

Chapter Seven

Elizabeth Jennings

Elizabeth Jennings is unique in two particular ways: she is the Movement's only woman and its only Catholic. Born Elizabeth Joan Jennings in Boston, Lincolnshire, on 18 July 1926, she was the daughter of Henry Cecil Jennings, a physician. As a teenager she studied poetry in school and was swept up by G. K. Chesterton's battle poem "Lepanto." She wrote an essay on the work and soon was eagerly studying the great romantics – Wordsworth, Coleridge, Keats, and Shelley. Her godfather-uncle was a poet, and he encouraged Elizabeth to write poems herself. She recalls that her first one came to her almost automatically at 13 while she was waiting at a bus stop. From the start Jennings was intrigued by the fascinating variety of poems that could be produced from formal metrical patterns, so she turned her interest to sonnets, ballads, and odes, though she admits that only one four-line poem of her juvenilia warrants preservation. At 15 she began sending out her verse with no success, but she was encouraged by a handwritten rejection from the now-defunct *New English Weekly*, which affirmed, "These poems show talent."[1]

Even in Jennings's earliest poems a sense of form predominates, and the primary characteristics of her mature verse – regular rhyme and meter – are evident. Moreover, they frequently display the simple vision of childhood in an emotionally honest, clear manner.

Jennings moved to Oxford as a child and was educated at Oxford High School and later St. Anne's College, taking an M.A. in English language and literature with honors in 1949, having earlier failed her B.Litt. studies, which concentrated on Matthew Arnold as both a romantic and classical poet. At Oxford she met Philip Larkin and John Wain and enrolled in a court handwriting seminar with Kingsley Amis. Despite his youth Amis already held strong opinions on literature and art, and he introduced Jennings to jazz. They spent hours together in record shops and cinemas, but he was never critical of her conventional preference for classical music. Amis also read and admired her poetry, and both had poems in the 1948 Oxford anthology. When Amis and James Michie edited it the following year, they looked for hard, modern poems to print. They selected six of Jennings's poems for publication.

After graduation her verse began to appear in various magazines, including the *Spectator*, the *New Statesman*, and the *Poetry Review*. Jennings worked for a short time as an advertising copywriter, employment which she believes made her style increasingly slick, relaxed, and more publishable. But Jennings was fired from the agency, and in 1950 she hired on as an assistant at the Oxford City Library, where she worked until 1958. Oxford undergraduates interested in her poems or in writing poetry themselves visited her there regularly and often invited her to dinner and the theater. Among those students were Geoffrey Hill, Adrian Mitchell, Anthony Thwaite, and Alan Brownjohn and Americans Donald Hall and Adrienne Rich, all of whom were to achieve their own recognition as poets and critics.

When Jennings had assembled enough poems for a book, she sought a publisher. In time she was introduced to Oscar Mellor, a private printer living in the small village of Eynsham outside Oxford. Mellor issued a pamphlet of her work, thus beginning the Fantasy Press Poets Series, which would come to include works by Gunn, Davie, Larkin, Amis, and Holloway among its distinguished contributors. The success of this inaugural volume prompted Mellor to put forth a full-length book of Jennings's verse, *Poems*, which included three of her poems from *Oxford Poetry 1949* and earned her an Arts Council prize in 1953. Fantasy Press also issued the first full-length books of poems by Gunn (*Fighting Terms*, 1954) and Davie (*The Brides of Reason*, 1955).

As a result of her Arts Council award Jennings was interviewed and photographed by local and London reporters and became one of the first Movement writers to have her fame established primarily through poetry, although Amis and Wain had both published novels by then, and Davie's *Purity of Diction in English Verse* had received considerable critical attention. She began to feel that she should have at least one poem or book review a week in the important journals. She nearly succeeded. *Time and Tide* and the *Spectator* asked her to contribute articles and reviews, and Stephen Spender asked her for poems for his new magazine, *Encounter*. John Lehmann's

New Soundings radio program had included a poem by Jennings in its first broadcast, and he included three more by her in the first issue of *London Magazine*, prominently placing her work alongside that by Thom Gunn and T. S. Eliot, who wrote a special introduction for the issue. And she was included in Enright's *Poets of the 1950s* and Conquest's *New Lines* anthologies, the two collections that fixed the roll of membership in the Movement, although Conquest humorously claimed that Jennings's relationship with the Movement was comparable to that of a schoolmistress with a bunch of drunken marines.

From the outset her lyrics were distinguished by their brevity (usually fewer than five stanzas in length) and simplicity. Her vocabulary resists strange and unusual words, and there is a noted absence of proper nouns in her work. Preoccupied with the themes of the individual's fears and essential loneliness, her poems became noted for their wit, lyrical innocence, and exploration of nuances of the spirit.

"Delay," the opening poem in the volume, exhibits the tentativeness and rationality commonly found in Movement verse. The poem is one of her best; Jennings chose it for her *Collected Poems* and *Selected Poems* and Larkin included it in *The Oxford Book of Twentieth Century English Verse*. The poem, a short formal lyric, seems well suited to Jennings's talent as she fashions an analogy that compares the speed of light to the speed of love. Despite its emotional subject, the poem's regular stanzas and exactness of language enhance its logic. Jennings emphasizes the colossal distance between lovers by springing from the first stanza to the second on the word love.

> The radiance of that star that leans on me
> Was shining years ago. The light that now
> Glitters up there my eyes may never see,
> And so the time lag teases me with how
>
> Love that loves now may not reach me until
> Its first desire is spent. The star's impulse
> Must wait for eyes to claim it beautiful
> And love arrived may find us somewhere else. (Jennings *CP*, 3)

Her diction is plain and exacting, yet the understatement in the poem's last line is both tender and poignant.

Jennings's preference for such emotional and syntactic spareness is consistent with the erudite attitudes of other Movement poets, although she was the only member of the group who never worked full-time in academia. While her poems occasionally seem detached in their attempts to demystify emotions, Jennings did not wish to be limited by an intellectual aesthetic. A cradle Catholic, she maintained a lifelong faith in Christianity, which Enright failed in doing, and poems of religious belief always occupied an important place in her work.

Jennings published her second volume, *A Way of Looking*, two years later in 1955. Its 40 poems also display the cool, natural, uncontrived style found in *Poems*. As its title suggests, the volume is interested more in probing ways of looking than in developing particular subject matter. Even when her topics are factually based and drawn from historical record, she rarely employs detailed settings and considers actuality merely a point of departure from which self-understanding may be abstracted. Physical reality serves more as a speculative premise in these poems than as a reminder of verisimilitude. "Not in the Guide Books," from the book's last section, is one such lyric, a travel poem in which public experience gives rise to private understanding. The formula is comparably employed in "For a Child Born Dead" and "The Recognition." And in "Tribute" she directly acknowledges the importance of poetry to this associative process:

> The poem is enough that joins me to
> The world that seems far to grasp at when
> Images fail and words are gabbled speech:
> At those times clarity appears in you,
> Your mind holds meanings that my mind can read. (Jennings *CP*, 35)

In their reviews of *A Way of Looking*, some critics denounced the unfulfilled potential promised by Jennings's first collection. She reflected, "A second book of verse is always a hazard. Critics are waiting to pounce and declare, 'It doesn't live up to the promise shown in her first book.' If you have enlarged your scope in the matter of theme and form you are unlikely to win even then, for journalists will say, 'She is uneasy with her new subject matter' " (*Contemporary*, 110-11). Nevertheless, the book won the Somerset Maugham prize for 1956; the award stipulated that the recipient must spend at least three months abroad in a country of her choosing. The financial remuneration of 400 pounds enabled her to spend three months in Italy, which she declared to be the happiest and most worthwhile time of her life, and to return to England with 80 pounds left over.

The poems she wrote in Rome became the basis of her third book, *A Sense of the World* (1958), and naturally many of them, such as "Fountain," "St. Paul Outside the Walls," and "Letter from Assisi," contained Roman themes. The poems record her love for Italy and her Catholic heritage, but they are more than postcards intending to conserve the itinerary and topography of her travels. The settings also provide juxtaposition for her spiritual dislocation. Jennings's poetry was becoming decidedly less confessional, and her concerns turned to children, old men and women, storms, religious motifs, and the passage of time. Unlike her Movement colleagues, Jennings never felt comfortable writing poems about popular issues and current events, believing that successful poems absorb writers wholly and completely and not just for the moment. While she admitted that good poems might be written about such matters as nuclear warfare, modern art, popular advertising, and scientific experimentation – all of which had served as topics for Conquest, Larkin, and other Movement writers – she found those subjects generally less compelling than the familiar themes of love and death with which poets had traditionally dealt. "The best poets writing today are those who are most personal, who are trying . . . to examine and understand their own emotions, behaviour or actions, or those of other people" ("Comments," 32). By writing about familiar subjects in orthodox ways Jennings felt she was participating in the proud English tradition of Chaucer, Shakespeare, Wordsworth, and Eliot.

Moreover, satisfied with no single political party, Jennings was not interested in writing political verse, though unlike her *New Lines* colleagues she was devoutly committed to exploring themes of Roman Catholicism. Her Catholicism is especially conspicuous in *A Sense of the World*. While her religiosity and absence of social correctives may at first glance appear uncharacteristic of Movement verse, she explains their relevance. "I believe firmly that every poet must be committed to something and, if his religion or political convictions mean anything to him at all, I do not see how they can fail to affect his poems" ("Context," 51).

Although the verses in *A Sense of the World* are primarily lyrical, she began to experiment with other poetic forms, including free verse, the prose poem, and a good deal of terza rima. She returned to England but visited Rome again in February 1957; she then quit her job, and in April 1958 returned to Rome for 13 weeks.

Upon coming home she became a general reader for Chatto and Windus, the publishers of William Empson and F. R. Leavis, and the position afforded her the opportunity to attend literary teas with T. S. Eliot and Edith Sitwell. Her reputation grew, earning her a membership in the Royal Society of Literature in 1961, and her work was included in the first Penguin Modern Poets series, published in 1962, which also contained the work of Lawrence Durrell and R. S. Thomas. The book went through three additional printings in the next five years and spawned subsequent volumes in a long-running sequence of titles.

In her second year at Chatto and Windus, Jennings suffered a severe mental breakdown and attempted suicide. She consequently left Chatto's and would eventually write two books devoted to her struggle with depression, which are discussed later in the chapter. But during her recovery she completed work on *Every Changing Shape*, a book about mysticism and poetry, reviewed novels for the *Listener*, and worked on four other books: a new book of poems, *Song for a Birth or a Death*; a poetry book for children, *Let's Have Some Poetry*; a translation of Michelangelo's sonnets; and a pamphlet she was editing for the British Council, *An Anthology of Modern Verse 1940-60*.

Song for a Birth or a Death (1961) was composed in Italy, and it deviates from the Movement themes of insularity and secularity. The poems are profoundly religious, at times even mystical, and they display a distinct lack of irony. In "To a Friend with a Religious Vocation," she struggles to articulate her religious vision:

> I see
> Within myself no wish to breed or build
> Or take the three vows ringed by poverty.
>   And yet I have a sense,
> Vague and inchoate, with no symmetry
> Of purpose. (Jennings *CP*, 114)

In "A World of Light" she basks in "A mood the senses cannot touch or damage,/A sense of peace beyond the breathing word"

(Jennings *CP*, 92), and in another poem she derives a calming tranquility from a Roman mass, even though she does not understand Latin. Though mystical experiences are by nature fundamentally private, Jennings suggests in "Men Fishing in the Arno" that they can become the basis for a whole community with

> Each independent, none
> Working with others and yet accepting
> Others. From this one might, I think
>
> Build a whole way of living. (Jennings *CP*, 117)

Jennings justifies religion's close connection to her art, believing that the host, wine, and offering contribute to a sacrosanct vision "of art as gesture and as sacrament, . . . art with its largesse and its own restraint" (Jennings *CP*, 104).

Jennings laments that the sense of the sacred is vanishing from modern life, "so the poetic gift, which still remains something mysterious and inexplicable has tended to be ignored along with many other intangible things."[2] Her obeisance to the idea of salvation through art prompted Wain to dedicate his "Green Fingers" to her, claiming "Your art will save your life, Elizabeth."[3]

In contrast to *Song for a Birth or Death*, her anthology seems a clear celebration of Movement virtues. Beginning with the publication of Eliot's last great poem, *An Anthology of Modern Verse 1940-60* (1961) covers "twenty years of suffering, restlessness and uncertainty,"[4] a period marked by an urge for formal order and clarity in verse in defiance of the chaos and confusion of postwar society. Most of the poets she includes were children or adolescents when World War II began. "The war was for them, therefore, little more than a rather vague, unhappy memory. They began to write their mature poems in an atmosphere of political and, indeed, cosmic uncertainty. Yet, paradoxically, it is in their work that we can see the most striking evidence of the desire for form, style and order, and also of a wish to stress the dignity of human personality" (*Anthology*, 9).

Believing that such ruthless honesty and underlying passion had been best exemplified by poets whose love of simplicity and disdain for poetic artifice were common to her own work, Jennings selected all nine Movement poets for inclusion in her anthology: two poems apiece from Amis, Conquest, Davie, Enright, Holloway, and Wain, three from herself (one each from her first three volumes, including her favorite poem, "Fountain"), and four from Larkin and Gunn.

But *An Anthology of Modern Verse 1940-60* notwithstanding, Jennings's gradual dissatisfaction with the characteristic Movement style was becoming apparent. Writing in *London*, she paid homage to the past but also declared her intention to break with its traditions:

> I don't myself always want to write the rhyming lyric of thirty-odd lines. Indeed, I do at times feel positively inhibited and exasperated by the form. At the moment, I am extremely eager to write longer poems, dramatic verse (I would, for example, like to write the libretto for an opera), and prose poems. But I am still as fascinated as I was when I was thirteen by the marvellous variety within strict English lyric verse. As for the "poetic language" of today – there are times when I feel that it is too dry, too intellectual, sometimes, even, too facile. Maybe it needs a little rough treatment, though I can see absolutely no virtue in confusion or obscurity for their own sake. ("Difficult," 51)

Jennings worried that she was becoming too slick and feared that her talent might dry up before she mastered her craft. She sought to be less an observer and commentator and more a vehicle for her personal experiences, perhaps as a curative for her mental illness. Her tortuous recovery from depression through hospitalization and analysis was detailed by Jennings in *Recoveries* (1964) and *The Mind Has Mountains* (1966). The verses in these two collections are remarkable, given their subject matter, for their lack of sentimentality; they are not the ravings of a broken spirit, nor do they display an open sense of self-pity. Rather she views all those in the mental hospital – patients, doctors, and nurses – with detached compassion, and they are hardly the type of commonsense poems on which the Movement was established.

Jennings's best poems always seem contemplative in nature, and the hospital setting was appropriate for her meditations on psychological pain. The remarkable stillness in these poems is achieved by her clear, spare language. She concentrates meaning in the poems' fluent final lines as momentary stays against disorder, allowing her to transcend for a time the hurt that prompted the utterance. In this way Jennings uses her art to exorcise the demons of her breakdown by transforming the chaos of her dark dreams into a kind of serenity. In "Works of Art" she asserts that, although art so often "appears like an escape . . . We want more order than we ever meet / And art keeps driving us most hopefully on" (Jennings *CP*, 137). Though these poems are frequently disquieting, Jennings retains control in them. She examines her illness lucidly and without resorting to self-confession or linguistic confusion.

The Mind Has Mountains, which won the Richard Hillary prize, derives its title from Gerard Manley Hopkins's explorations into the abyss of mental despair. Identifying with other creative artists who have suffered extreme mental distress, Jennings proclaims in "Van Gogh" that madness may be an important component of art's tranquility:

> There is a theory that the very heart
> Of making means a flaw, neurosis, some
> Sickness; yet others say it is release.
> I only know that your wild, surging art
> Took you to agony, but makes us come
> Strangely to gentleness, a sense of peace. (Jennings *CP*, 176)

Jennings's sympathy with her fellow sufferers and patients is strong. She insists in "Madness" that

> It is the lack of reason makes us fear,
> The feeling that ourselves might be like this.
> We are afraid to help her or draw near
> As if she were infectious and could give
> Some taint, some touch of her own fantasies,
> Destroying all the things for which we live. (Jennings *CP*, 173)

Jennings was hospitalized on several occasions, and she attempted to gain some peace through the efficacy of poetry, believing "the act of writing a poem is itself an implicit affirmation of the possibility of order" ("Difficult," 30). The composure which she sought in her own verse and valued in that of others became the goal of her personal life, and her poetry often seems a courageous effort to discover a sense of order within, although she confesses in "In a Mental Hospital Sitting Room" that "It does not seem a time for lucid rhyming" (Jennings *CP*, 171), and she laments in "On a Friend's Relapse and Return to a Mental Clinic" that "It is the good who often know joy least" (Jennings *CP*, 188). *The Mind Has Mountains* displays a heroic dedication to return to the placidity of the poems she wrote before her breakdown. She bravely tries to come to terms with her turbulent illness, but some poems offer little more than pious pronouncements. And while the poems are highly personal in nature, they retain a formality antipodal to their subject and are never particularly revealing in an autobiographical kind of way.

Jennings's *Collected Poems* was issued in 1967, drawing its material from the seven books she had written over a 14-year period. The collection reprints 207 of her 243 previously issued poems. Its publication renewed critical interest in her work, and it was reviewed widely as critics used it as a benchmark to assess her artistic development. Anthony Thwaite noted her "steady and persistent contemplative gift"[5] and appreciated her unsentimental lyrical verses. He proclaimed that the volume "shows a remarkable unity of tone and theme, repetitive and yet gaining strength from that very fact. The most notable development has been one of giving greater prominence to the immediate and circumstantial, and yet clearly the later poems of mental agony and illness come from the same person who wrote such pure and clear lyrics and meditations as the early 'Delay,' 'Reminiscence' and 'The Island.' "[6]

Julian Symons praised her ingenuity and wit and remarked favorably on her ability to construct metaphysical conceits. He found sources for her organization and technical clarity in Robert Graves and A. E. Housman. Although he charted little stylistic development in Jennings's verse, Symons observed a change in her subjects. Even the mental illness poems "are composed with the cool firmness of the early poems. Nobody can have written less hysterically about hysteria, yet the sense of personal involvement is always there."[7]

The themes of her next book, *The Animals' Arrival* (1969), are decidedly shopworn, however, and the verses themselves shrill as Jennings sought to emerge from the writings about her breakdown by creating what seemed to her more vital poetry. The book is dedicated to her friend poet Peter Levi, but her concerns here are less personal and more aesthetic. In "Of Languages" she demands a new poetic, believing that the hour is nearing when language must be made sudden and new and images sharp and still. A call for honesty also appears in "Resolve," where she vows not to write so glibly of the ill, choosing instead warmth, sanity, and health. But on the whole, the poems are not especially engaging.

Jennings's poetic decline continued in *Relationships* (1972), which Alisdair Maclean labeled "catastrophic."[8] He blames the decrement on her use of Emily Dickinson for a poetic model. Although the resemblance of Jennings's verse to Dickinson's had been approvingly noted by John Thompson in his review of *A Sense of the World*, Maclean complains that "for Emily Dickinson's apparent simplicity, however, Miss Jennings too often supplies bathos, and for phrases like 'zero at the bone' substitutes a language colourless to the point of invisibility. The trouble seems to be a lack of any real pressure in the creation of these poems" (Maclean, 389). He also faults her language as stilted, inverted, and awkward, as in "Simply because they were human, I admire"[9] ("In Memory of Anyone Unknown to Me"). Only her pain and vulnerability, best articulated in "Sympathy," keep the poems from seeming overly didactic.

A stronger Jennings emerged in *Growing-Points* in 1975, one admittedly determined to gather strength from her pain. She continued to experiment technically with a variety of verse forms, and the volume seems aptly named. The poems themselves have grown longer, thereby freeing up her diction from the restrictions of regular meter while still remaining essentially pure, and her poetic line has been lengthened as well (though sometimes leading to irksome run-ons, as in "An Abandoned Palace," where the lines sometimes exceed 20 syllables). Experiments with free verse and prose poetry alternate with traditional poems in an attempt to bring a new force to her work. The poems still frequently end in aphorisms, but the volume shows just how far Jennings had begun to stray from Movement dictum. Her trademark homilies and quiet lyricism are still visible, but her realizations are more labored, muddled, wistful, and complex than before.

Her divergence from Movement themes and techniques is quite evident in her myth poems on Orpheus, Persephone, and the Minotaur and in her muted, unfocused imagery, which all too often falls into clichés and stereotypes – sunsets, falling leaves, and the like. Her poems of tribute and direct address to famous artistic, literary, and religious figures are on the whole sanctimonious and sentimental. The volume includes poems to Mozart and Hopkins, homage to Van Gogh, Thomas Aquinas, Mondrian, Rembrandt, Wallace Stevens, and Auden. And there is a bold but ill-considered monologue projected by Christ on the cross.

Religious themes compose the dramatic substance of *Conse-quently I Rejoice* (1977), an ample collection of 88 meditations on Jennings's Christian faith. As in *Growing-Points*, she records the pain and suffering of a convalescing Catholic, and there are again dra-matic monologues from religious figures, here Christ and Mary. While still an intensely personal, lyric poet, in *Consequently I Rejoice* Jen-nings turns a bit abstract in her longing for faith, for the book at-tempts to universalize her campaign against despair. It begins simi-larly to her previous collections by documenting her nightmares, and there are the familiar lines of self-flagellation, as in "Elegy for Aldous Huxley" – "You put away / The novels, verses, stories where the 'I' / Dominates, makes us masochists"[10] – and of pleading, as in "Cradle Catholic" – "O take my unlove and despair / And what they lack let faith repair" (*Consequently*, 36). But she expands the scope of her study beyond the personal as she traces her spiritual and in-tellectual development through a year-long cycle. Seasonal and cycli-cal patterns (poems of parents and infants, images of sun and moon and night and day) accent the soul's passage until at the cycle's end the last nightmares are no longer uniquely hers but every-one's – especially the elderly, who either dwell in or remain bereft of lasting spiritual peace. Her "Old People's Nursing Home" is mind-ful of Larkin's "The Old Fools"; though her poem is more compas-sionate and intuitive than Larkin's, it surely lacks his distinctive irony.

By compressing the journey of the soul into one year's time, Jenning's book invites comparison to *In Memoriam*, though it was certainly conceived on a smaller scale. Tennyson's "swallow flights of song" are designed to chart the soul's passage. Jennings too avails herself of bird metaphors, for her poems are haunted by auguries of flight and birdsong meant as hopeful reminders that her spirit may one day again soar. "Wisdom is in our bloodstream not in brain," she affirms in "Song for the Swifts" (*Consequently*, 15).

Throughout the poems Jennings equates religious doubt with her self-doubt as a writer, and in penning poems of tribute to other artists (Huxley, Edward Thomas, D. H. Lawrence, Paul Klee, Cézanne, and Virginia Woolf her examples here) she actually seeks self-illumination and understanding; the artists' identity seems con-sequential to her own. Tennyson felt himself a lesser artist than Hal-lam, but for Jennings it was Thomas ("For Edward Thomas") who embodied the quiet, principled, amiable nature she wished to capture in her verse. Her meditations on other artists are but another form of self-reflection, and it is instrumental to both her faith and poetic achievement in that she views the relationship between the individual soul and God akin to that between artist and creation.

The title of her next offering, *Moments of Grace* (1979), refers to those brief occasions when despair and frustration are eclipsed by moments of spiritual transcendancy. Jennings's religious verse consistently subscribes to the Wordsworthian notion that daily human experience is laden with potential revelations. Suspending the soul between the natural and supernatural seems her aesthetic goal, but all too often she depicts her aloneness and sorrow without achieving that measured balance. Jennings openly acknowledges that prayer and the sacraments of her faith have not always sustained her. That her devoutness could not allay her religious dismay proved especially troubling; a life-long Catholic, she struggled perpetually for the protection and blessings of God.

Moments of Grace is not about her mental illness, and it includes Jennings's first poem to address a public issue, "Euthanasia." More than in her earlier works, she attempts to witness the unification of God and nature. As a result the strong lyricism of prior volumes is diminished by her emphasis on what is essentially more ponderous, philosophic matter. Perhaps she had previously been afraid to explore such deep, ruminative questions, but in *Moments of Grace* she is ill at ease with her speculative subject matter. She confesses her awkwardness and alienation, and is uncertain when probing the grace afforded by the natural world. Undoubtedly Jennings believed the Wordsworthian premises articulated in her verse, but she is a gentle arguer and seems envious of those able to overcome their estrangement and attain those rare "moments of grace."

Perhaps her reticence is strategic, meant to suggest that she is unworthy of spiritual consolation, that she is to remain in awe forever before God. In any case, the poems are often interrupted by mild interjections that reverse the course of her ideas but allow her to adhere to her metrical pattern (her fondness for terza rima persists). She seems as restive with her fellow humans as she does with herself, and is at times overly apologetic and colloquial, as if her vicarious experiences were more important than her personal ones.

Selected Poems appeared in the same year as *Moments of Grace*. Ninety-one poems from her *Collected Poems*, three with slight verbal changes, appear in *Selected Poems*. That few changes appear in the poems is unsurprising, for 12 years earlier she conceded in an interview with John Press that she wrote swiftly and revised little. Surprisingly, though, three-quarters of the poems written between her *Collected* and *Selected Poems*, that period of her great mental torment, were omitted presumably because Jennings felt they lacked the impact of her earlier work and thereby did not warrant inclusion.

In the 1980s Jennings was again drawn to Italy and southern travel, issuing *Italian Light and Other Poems* in 1981 and the Bibbiena poems, *Celebrations and Elegies*, the following year. Her Lincolnshire childhood is the subject of her fourteenth book of poems, *Extending the Territory* (1985). Her more recent poetry, like that in her first books, is marked by restraint and understatement. Elizabeth Jennings "is not the kind of poet who is likely to find it acceptable to 'say something a bit more interesting' than she means."[11] She has remained a quiet, readable poet preoccupied with suffering and pain, and she has a musical ear, a talent fashioned out of decades of plumbing her own ephemerality and isolation. Her growth as a poet has been modest, though she is still craftsmanlike in her approach to verse and continues to prefer rhyme and traditional meters as ways to balance form and content. A lyrical writer who shuns lengthy descriptions, Jennings is more a temporal than spatial poet; her romanticism and imagery tend toward intellectualization and allegory and away from plot.

Consequently, she continues to receive the complaints, long leveled against Movement verse, that her work is emotionally diffident and self-conscious, that it is frequently too literal, didactic, and banal, and that it lacks vivid descriptive appeal.

William Blissett assesses her contribution to the period as follows: "The student of literary history will discern in Elizabeth Jennings the marks of her generation and The Movement – the continuity of rhyme and reason, of syntax and stanza (as if Ezra Pound had never lived), the easy rhythms, the eschewing of decoration, the control of metaphor; but he will also notice how the one woman and the one Catholic stands apart from the others, in the special insights given her by the enjoyment of Italy and the suffering of illness, by her librarian's nonacademic love of literature, and by her lifelong religious concern."[12]

Chapter Eight

Donald Davie

If Philip Larkin was the most important poet of the Movement, Donald Davie was surely its preeminent scholar. A prolific and dedicated writer, he has spent a lifetime writing and explaining erudite poetry, a commitment he easily defends: "This stuff (poetry) is dangerous and double-edged; if it were not so dangerous, would we spend so much time trying to learn how to handle it?" (*Companions*, 106).

Oddly enough, Davie's erudition emerged from firmly working-class origins. Born on 17 July 1922 in the coal-mining town of Barnsley, Yorkshire, he was taught early on the possibilities of bettering his social situation through hard work. His maternal grandfather was a miner who eventually became mine foreman, and his paternal grandfather was a railway signalman; their wives were both domestic servants. Davie's father, George Clarke Davie, was a businessman and his mother, Alice Sugden Davie, a schoolmistress who "had risen to become a certificated school-teacher, without benefit of college training" (*Companions*, 13). She encouraged Donald to read and for his seventh birthday gave him a collection of Robin Hood tales, which "surely did more than any other single text to make me a compulsive reader for ever after" (*Companions*, 16).

Davie attributes his ability to handle ideas and riddling abstractions to his early exposure to books, and he began writing poems at 14. Having passed his university examinations, he went to Cambridge in 1940 where he studied architecture but also read much pulpit oratory, particularly that from the seventeenth century. After one year of college he joined the Royal Navy, leaving as a sublieutenant in 1946. While in uniform he spent 18 months at three different outposts in northern Russia, and these assignments fueled his interest in Russian and Eastern European literature. At Cambridge Davie composed a long poem on Pushkin; he chose an Anglo-Russian topic for his dissertation there and afterward wrote three books on Russian literature: *The Poems of Dr. Zhivago* (a translation of Pasternak issued in

101

1965), *Russian Literature and Modern English Fiction: A Collection of Critical Essays* (also published in 1965), and *Pasternak: Modern Judgements* (translated by Davie, edited by Davie and Angela Livingstone, and published in 1969).

Davie married and returned to Cambridge after his military service, completing his B.A. in 1947, his M.A. in 1949, and his Ph.D. in 1951. A student of F. R. Leavis, he became an admirer of T. S. Eliot. Leavis taught that "one had to cultivate propriety of culture which meant necessarily, so the doctrine went, propriety of morals; one had to be a didactic person; and one had to be prepared for others to be affronted, or bored, by one's pretensions" (*Companions*, 75). Leavis based this idea of a minority culture on rational, orthodox, moral dissent, and Davie melded the concept with his own Baptist rearing – his paternal grandfather was a Baptist lay preacher and deacon, and his father was active in the congregation of the Sheffield Road Baptist Church in Barnsley – to form the idea of a gathered church of dissenters, "gathered from the world and in tension with it" (*Companions*, 76). Over the decades Davie has adamantly maintained an interest in how dissent enriches culture and literature, most notably in *A Gathered Church: The Literature of the English Dissenting Interest, 1700-1930* (1978), a work that details how nineteenth- and twentieth-century dissent have degenerated from that in the eighteenth century. The book spawned a sequel in praise of hymns, *Dissentient Voice* (1982), and an edition of Christian poetry edited by Davie, *The New Oxford Book of Christian Verse* (1981). Davie's faith waned somewhat during his service in the Royal Navy, but in the 1960s the death of his parents and some close friends sparked a spiritual reawakening. He was baptized into the American Episcopalian Church in California in 1972, and his religious aesthetic, always reflecting strong humanistic values, is evident in much of his poetry and in his essays on religious writers.

Davie's penchant for analysis has been a characteristic feature of his career as a poet and literary critic, and in 1952 as a lecturer at Trinity College, Dublin, he issued the Movement's critical manifesto, *Purity of Diction in English Verse*. In it Davie contends that good diction is based on reasonable choices, pure diction on the conversational style of a given period. Davie augments Wordsworth's observations on poetic diction by interjecting his own concerns about taste and judgment. Hence, for Davie purity of diction is determined by its appropriateness. Arguing that poetic diction has become increasingly impure since Wordsworth, Davie cites Keats, Hopkins, and Eliot as writers who abdicated their poetic responsibilities to it.

Davie outlines two primary obligations of the poet to the human voice: to preserve the works of past masters in his own verse and to purify them by using correct language. And as a critic Davie interprets the moral effect of those choices; "the poet who uses a diction must be very sure of the audience which he addresses. He dare not be merely the spokesman of their sentiments and habits, for he must purify the one and correct the other."[1]

The poet who coins new metaphors, he reasons, enlarges the language; the poet who enlivens dead metaphors purifies it. Thus purity of diction cannot be achieved simply by acknowledging old standards. (Davie claims that the metaphorical quality of eighteenth-century verse is frequently misunderstood simply because it employs an old criterion of economy.) So in defining pure diction as "the perfection of a common language" (*Purity*, 68), Davie means that "a pure poetic diction can purify the national language by enlivening metaphors gone dead" (*Purity*, 62). Ironically, then, Wordsworth ceased to be a spokesman for pure diction precisely when, having gained recognition in later life, "he saw himself more and more as, after all, a spokesman of national sentiment" (*Purity*, 114).

By claiming that verse should be both technically excellent and morally correct and that it should follow logical syntax, Davie recapitulates Movement ideology. His critique in *Purity of Diction* is but a thinly disguised declaration of motives to which the group informally subscribed. In contrast, Dylan Thomas had displayed a kind of literary amorality in violating them. But Davie's 1966 postscript admits another motive for writing *Purity of Diction* – to understand the poems he had been composing at the time.

Articulate Energy: An Enquiry into the Syntax of English Poetry (1955), begun as a sequel to *Purity of Diction* though less of a manifesto, is a more polished inquiry. It also stresses the importance of syntax in poetry and claims that "The central act, of poetry as of music, is the creation of syntax, of meaningful arrangement."[2] Verbs are particularly meaningful as energizing elements, Davie argues, but he alleges in outright admiration of Augustan verse that abstract words are the best part of English poetics. Davie's early poems show this same preference for abstractions over concrete images.

Davie identifies five types of syntax – subjective, dramatic, objective, musical, and mathematical – through which the poet humanizes his verse. "It is my case against the symbolist theorists that in trying to remove the human smell from poetry, they are only doing harm. For poetry to be great, it must reek of the human, as Wordsworth's poetry does" (*Articulate*, 165). To spurn syntax, he insists, is to renounce literary history and to abandon "faith in the power of the mind itself."[3]

While in Ireland Davie published several volumes of poetry, and his kinship with eighteenth-century poets is as obvious in these verses as it is in his criticism. In "Homage to William Cowper" he openly calls himself "a pasticheur of late-Augustan styles."[4] F. W. Bateson agreed, declaring in his review of Davie's *Brides of Reason* (1955) that an understanding of Davie and Larkin may be obtained through reading "their Augustan prototypes."[5] The volume's 27 poems employ traditional meters, "and they are also, like Pope's, uncomplicated by intruding symbols from the unconscious mind" (Bateson, 77). The images that do occur take on consequence as a result of Davie's lyrical focus, metrical control, and precise diction. The subject of these poems is often the discovery of morality ("Three Moral Discoveries") or, as in "Among Artisans' Houses," the morality of politics. "Remembering the 'Thirties" and "Hypochondriac Logic," the oldest poem in the collection, display both a sympathy for and a distrust of literary fools, while "The Garden Party" establishes "a rationale of class-hatred: it is natural for the poor to hate the rich because the rich seem permanently young to them, whereas the poor seem to themselves to have no real youth at all" (Bateson, 79). The restraint and irony in the poems question "at what point do the signs of civility . . . become so rudimentary or so vestigial that one can no longer defend them, or applaud them, or invest any hope in them?" (*Companions*, 69)

By imitating eighteenth-century poets Davie sought in *Brides of Reason* to affirm their traditional values of reasoned stability and moderation, just as his first two scholarly books advocated a return to Augustan purity in matters of diction and syntax and confirmed the connection between language and moral decadence. Although Davie admires certain modernist poets, especially Pound, his distrust of romanticism and its assertion of the individual ego typifies his own neo-Augustan temperament and his suspicion that syntactical disorder imperils society itself.

Davie's next volume of poetry, *A Winter Talent and Other Poems* (1957), is imbued with a strong sense of place. The collection contains 37 poems. The middle three of the book's five sections are entitled "England," "Ireland," and "Italy." "Via Portello" in the Italy section seems a direct response to Kingsley Amis's protestation that people are tired of poems about foreign cities. Perhaps trying to separate himself to a degree from the parochialism of the Movement's themes, Davie acknowledges Amis's complaint, then defends his own intellectual interest in the broken civilizations he has explored in his travels.

Four of the England poems are grouped under the subheading "Dissentient Voice." These concern his early upbringing outside the Church of England. "A Baptist Childhood," the first of the poems, opens with a clear reference to another poet's recollection of childhood innocence, Dylan Thomas's "Fern Hill." But the severities of Davie's Baptist training are contrasted with Thomas's ingenuous observations, and Davie shows little appreciation for the puritanical convictions of religion: "When some were happy as the grass was green, / I was as happy as a glass was dark" (Davie *CP 1950*, 46). Davie's personal observations are far different from those of Thomas.

> In the writing of Thomas and his imitators, one saw the blurring of the personal and private life of the poet as individual with the necessarily public life of the poet as the latest instance of the poetic vocation. . . . I think if readers were pressed, they would still say that the poet has a sort of duty to let down his hair in public, to undress in public, to let the reader into affairs which older generations would have regarded as private and intimate. This is bad, I believe, not only for art but for personal morality and human relations.[6]

Davie is reluctant to take on fully the mantle of lyrical poet, particularly since the author's personal experiences carry exemptions for the reader. "A lyric poet is one who is absolved from all civic responsibilities and all moral restraints on the strict understanding that by enacting his own self-destruction under the spotlights he shall vindicate his public in its resentful acquiescence to the restraints he is absolved from" (*Explain*, 64-65). The poet's duty is "to resist such seductive simplifications of his mental and emotional life; and to insist that human consciousness, though it comprehends political con-

sciousness, transcends it" (*Explain*, 56). Amis's "After Goliath" is the
only poem Davie cites that deals effectively with this issue.

Religion and foreign travel are topics not much embraced by
Movement poets, yet *A Winter Talent*, while pursuing these eccentric
subjects, retains a distinctly Movement flavor, particularly in its final
section. In "Limited Achievement" Davie questions the possibilities
of success for an artist confined to a narrow single track, a complaint
common to the group's critics, and in "Rejoinder to a Critic" he defends the absence of strong feelings in his verse. The poem expands
so that Davie becomes more than a solitary artist answering his detractors; he rises to a kind of spokesmanship, plurally concluding,
"How dare we now be anything but numb?" The final poem in the
volume, "Heigh-ho on a Winter Afternoon," correspondingly conveys an unheroic, mellowed weariness common to Movement verse.

Davie stayed in Ireland until 1957, but IRA atrocities in the 1960s
caused him to sour on the country. His disenchantment and frustration are clearly evident in "Ireland of the Bombers," a poem published in a 1969 issue of the *Irish Times*. So in 1958 Davie, like Thom
Gunn, fled to the United States, where he became visiting professor
at the University of California in Santa Barbara. In California he met
Yvor Winters, Gunn's mentor, with whom he had corresponded for
10 years; he had read Winters's *In Defense of Reason* and had written to him praising the book. Curiously enough, though, he did not
meet fellow Movement poet Gunn until he moved to California,
where he also became friends with Polish scholar Wacla Lednicki.
Lednicki, who was teaching at the University of California at Berkeley, abetted Davie's study of Polish poetry, which bore results in
Davie's *The Forests of Lithuania* (1959), an adaptation of Adam
Mickiewicz's 1834 romantic epic *Pan Tadeusz*.

Mickiewicz's poem had purportedly been written by a fictitious
exile during the Russian occupation of Lithuania in 1811. Though the
poem's subject matter is far afield from the Movement's representative interests, Davie discards the epic quality of the original in favor
of unconnected episodes, and the poem is, for the most part, less
formal than his earlier work. The lines are unrhymed and short, although in part 6, "The Year 1812," he employs a series of rhyming
tercets. Davie's rendering also bears the certain imprint of his American experience as it attempts to reconcile the teachings of Winters
with the style of Ezra Pound, whose work Gunn deprecated.

Shortly after *The Forests of Lithuania* Davie issued *New and Se-lected Poems* (1961) and *A Sequence for Francis Parkman* (1961), a response to his first visit to North America. The latter is a collection of poetic profiles of LaSalle, Montcalm, Pontiac, Frontenac, Lewis de Bougainville, and the Jesuit explorers of North America drawn di-rectly from the multivolume work *France and England in North America* by American historiographer Francis Parkman (1823-93).

As Davie familiarized himself with America and its poetry, he be-gan to discover essential differences between British and American verse. He noted distinctions in style and theme and came to believe that there were unmistakably British responses to experience. Unlike Leavis, Davie avouches the uniqueness of modern English literature; he contends that it has not been significantly influenced by Euro-pean or American tastes, though like Eliot and Pound he realized the educative possibilities of foreign literature. He finds American poets generally superior to their British counterparts (although he thinks excessive egocentrism a major defect in the American viewpoint), but judges British critics foremost in their consideration of poetic "technique."

Davie returned to Cambridge to teach the following year, and Charles Tomlinson was one of his first students there. His return to England was highlighted by a spirited argument with A. Alvarez in the first issue of *Review* (April-May 1962). Alvarez insisted that the im-portance of poetry rested in its ability to deal with serious and timely issues. Davie's position was that the chief obligation of poetry, as with any work of art, was to be tasteful and aesthetic. The debate was rejoined some years later when in a 25 May 1967 letter to the *Times Literary Supplement* he again inveighed against Alvarez for countenancing artistic extravagance and drug taking. Davie's letter, given the title "Beyond All This Fiddle," drew support from the later poems of Pasternak, whom he claims is a far better model for young writers than the poets cited by Alvarez: Robert Lowell, John Berry-man, and Sylvia Plath. Davie emphasizes that the behavioral extremes exhibited by these writers are not adequate substitutes for the famil-iar poetic pursuits of truth and beauty.

Davie transferred his academic affiliation when as cofounder of the University of Essex he assumed the responsibilities of pro-vice-chancellor. He became a university administrator "so as to help pro-duce an academic milieu in which the critic shall not be elevated above the creator, nor the two misleadingly lumped together as 'the literary intelligence' " (*World*, 357). *Events and Wisdoms: Poems 1957-1963* (1964) soon followed. These poems show a greater concern for the sensuous world than those in Davie's earlier volumes. "Low Lands," for example, describes a river delta – "Like a snake it is, its serpentine iridescence / Of slow light spilt and wheeling over calm / Inundations, and a snake's still menace" (Davie *CP 1950*, 137) – and "The Hill Field" discloses how a landscape may be turned into art – "And the miller comes with an easel / To grind the fruits of earth" (Davie *CP 1950*, 143).

His interest in foreign literature and landscapes is again pervasive; there are poems on the American West ("Agave in the West" and "In California"), Mexico ("Homage to John L. Stephens"), Europe and its Slavic republics ("Bolyai, the Geometer," "In Chopin's Garden," "A Meeting of Cultures"), and other intellectual heartlands. There is even a travel poem ("The Hardness of Light") inspired by his own earlier work, "Via Portello." In most of these poems Davie tinges his visual metaphors with the moralizing melancholy of a first-person confession. He concedes in "A Lily at Noon" that "In the marriage of a slow man / Eighteen years is soon" (Davie *CP 1950*, 144) and similarly avows in "Humanly Speaking" that "life itself / Is this one soured life I'm leading" (Davie *CP 1950*, 142).

Also in 1964 Davie released the first of his two critical studies on Pound. In *Ezra Pound: Poet as Sculptor* Davie, through close exegeses of individual poems, concludes that Pound approaches the objectiveness of Augustan poets to a greater degree than did his contemporaries Yeats and Eliot. This conclusion echoed that of another critical study, *The Language of Science and the Language of Literature, 1700-1740* (1963), in which Davie likewise resisted the notion that Cartesian philosophy was unfriendly to poetic development.

The syntactical principles Davie expressed so fervently in *Purity of Diction* are decidedly at odds with Pound's preference for images and symbols, but Davie partially recants his earlier criticism in his exploration of the neoclassical qualities of Pound's work. Davie's interest in Pound is curious; since Pound's diction does not adhere to the principles of prose syntax, Davie could hardly consider it pure. Moreover Pound's work, particularly *The Cantos*, is prophetic. But like Pound, Davie frequently employed the techniques of translation, adaptation, and imitation, most notably so in *The Forests of Lithua-*

nia and *A Sequence for Francis Parkman*, which suggest that his principles of diction serve more as guideposts than restrictions.

Davie returned to the United States and spent one year at the University of Southern California before going to Stanford in 1969. He published *Essex Poems: 1963-1967* that same year. As in his previous volume, many of the poems concern crises of identity prompted by Davie's feelings of expatriation. One of the most compelling is "July, 1964" in which he merges three deaths, actual and impending, literary and personal, into a deeply singular expression of grief. The poem was prompted by Davie's reading of Theodore Roethke. Davie had become acquainted with Roethke in London and wrote the poem only a few months after Roethke's death. While reading Roethke's verses, Davie thinks about the wife of a neighbor who has died from cancer and about his fatally ill friend, Douglas Brown. Davie naturally ponders his own mortality, but his thoughts are quickened momentarily – but only momentarily – as he considers the purposes of his art. Individual lives seem very small indeed when measured against great passages of time; only art seems capable of enlarging them. Davie's ambivalent understatement is reminiscent of much Movement verse.

> The practise of an art
> is to convert all terms
> into the terms of art.
> By the end of the third stanza
> death is a smell no longer;
> it is a problem of style.
> A man who ought to know me
> wrote in a review
> my emotional life was meagre. (Davie *CP 1950*, 183)

In *Essex Poems* Davie draws once more upon his affinity for Pasternak. Numerous poems, such as "The God of Details" and "Orford," are derived directly from Pasternak's work, which Davie had twice translated. His next work, *Six Epistles to Eva Hesse* (1970), was prompted by the work of another writer, Pound's German translator. Hesse was the editor of *New Approaches to Ezra Pound* and had reprinted some of Davie's writing about Pound. Davie had reservations about Pound, which are conveyed to Hesse in a verse-letter.

This first lighthearted letter gives way in the volume to five others. Davie's strategy in *Six Epistles* is purely Augustan; he uses the verse-letter form "to show that, despite current assumptions on both sides of the Atlantic, as much variety of time, space and action can be encompassed in one of the traditional forms of English verse as in the much vaunted 'free form' of an American tradition originating in Pound's *Cantos*" (Davie *CP 1950*, 306-7). Though a departure from his normal technique, *Six Epistles* is reminiscent of Davie's Parkman sequence and "Trevenen," his verse biography of a tragic-heroic eighteenth-century Cornish naval officer driven to madness.

In an enlightening essay Howard Erskine-Hill sees these works as interesting experiments in Davie's body of work. He calls the Hesse poems "a humorously critical response to contemporary adulation of the long and free epic line, the tradition running from Whitman through Pound and William Carlos Williams."[7] And "Trevenen," he claims, is "among the finest and most characteristic of Davie's poems and (to hazard an affirmation) a classic of postwar modernistic poetry in English" (*Responsibilities*, 118).

Yet despite his interest in Pound and Pasternak, Davie sees himself and his Movement contemporaries, particularly Larkin, as being influenced more by Thomas Hardy. In *Thomas Hardy and British Poetry* (1972) Davie attributes the narrow range and moderate tone of Movement poets as Hardy's legacy to modern verse, "an attempt to work out problems, especially social and political problems, which Hardy's poetry has posed for the twentieth century."[8] Unlike his romantic predecessors, Hardy accepted the world on its own terms, and Davie praises Hardy's scientific humanism and the liberalism it fostered. Like Hardy, the Movement rejected the prophetic role of the poet in favor of a more sensible if diminished role as "undeceived" individual. Davie admired not only Hardy's philosophic posture but his poetic technique, particularly his more asymmetrical poems, and Davie's reading of Hardy may have led to his exploration with looser forms. He claims that Hardy – more than Pound, Eliot, Yeats, or Lawrence – should rightfully be judged the most influential figure in modern British poetry.

The decade Davie spent away from England was eventful. Besides publishing various books of criticism, he traveled widely, founded *PN Review* in 1972, and authored two more important volumes of verse: *The Shires* (1974) and *In the Stopping Train and*

Other Poems (1977). *The Shires*, though a tour de force, was a poorly received reverie of his native England written in voluntary exile. Davie penned 40 poems, one for each county in England, and arranged his entries alphabetically from Bedfordshire to Yorkshire. The poems blend historical, cultural, and topographical features with autobiographical references and 18 evocative black-and-white photographs. *The Shires* attempts to go beyond travelogue and historical narrative to produce a meditative epic along the lines of Pound's *Cantos*. The collection is nostalgic, even elegiac, and it bears clear marks of Davie's expatriation.

In his *In the Stopping Train and Other Poems*, Davie displays a wide range, but he maintains the formality and control that are the hallmarks of his verse. There are the recurrent themes of his American and European travels, and he revisits five of his English shires. But all of the lyrics are essentially personal and retain Davie's predictable moral cast. He seems willing to probe each experience in the name of art. In "Portland" he sees similarities between making love and creating poetry ("Clear sound, full rhyme, and rational order take / Account of a dream, a sighing cry, a moan"),[9] and in "Ars Poetica" he articulately explains the discipline of his vision.

> Most poems, or the best,
> Describe their own birth, and this
> Is what they are – a space
> Cleared to walk around in.
>
> Their various symmetries are
> Guarantees that the space has
> Boundaries, and beyond them
> The turbulence it was cleared from. (Davie *CP 1971*, 58)

The rigor of Davie's exploration does not ensure felicitous discoveries. In "To Thom Gunn in Los Altos, California" he considers the terrors of a life in exile at the end of the world (in this case the California coast): "This is the Garden of Eden, the serpent coiled / Inside it is sleepy, reposeful. It need not flex / A muscle to take us. What are we doing here?" (Davie *CP 1971*, 69-70).

The title poem, "In the Stopping Train," recalls Larkin's "The Whitsun Weddings," for in both poems a train trip provides the opportunity for poetic reflection. Davie's poem is derived, however, from his travels in France (he and his family lived in Tours for two years in the early 1970s), while Larkin's poem remains a distinctly English experience. Still, both display the reticence and ambivalence typical to Movement verse.

Davie's poem is divided into 10 sections. His divisions, with all their stopping and starting, are meant to resemble "the slow train" (Davie *CP 1971*, 59) that he has mistakenly boarded. The journey is clearly a metaphoric one toward self-understanding, and the poet is separated from the world he sees by his art, the vehicle that emotionally transports him:

> He never needed to see,
> not with his art to help him.
> He never needed to use his
> nose, except for language. (Davie *CP 1971*, 60)

Like the train from which he views the world, the poet is reluctant to declare himself with a full head of steam. It's not getting to the end of the line that maddens him; it's all the stopping and starting.

> It's not
> the last stop that is bad . . .

> No, they said, it's the last
> start, the little one; yes,
> the one that doesn't last. (Davie *CP 1971*, 61)

What does he make of his sad journey? He concludes with a sentiment worthy of Larkin: "He knew too few in love" (Davie *CP 1971*, 66).

Davie refashioned two poems from *In the Stopping Train*, "The Fountain of Cyanë" and "The Fountain of Arethusa," to make them two of the three title poems in *Three for Water-Music* (1981), which also included all the poems from *The Shires*. "The Fountain of Cyanë" is based on the Ovidian myth in which a young girl is raped by her uncle, but Davie's poem is a far cry from Larkin's meditation on rape, "Deceptions." The classical background of the poem and Davie's formal divisions and tone abstract it from the immediacy of sexual violence. Davie in fact turns the myth into a study of his own art and romanticism's failure to nourish the modern poet. The problem for the contemporary poet, Davie says, is not that he has no mythology to use, but that he has more than one mythology to draw from. Visiting again Cyanë's spring-fed pool, he finds no fountain, "No jet, no spume, / Spew nor spurt" (Davie *CP 1971*, 88). Rather than a fountain, that exuberant symbol of nineteenth-century romanticism erupting forth like Coleridge's sacred river, Davie finds the easy lap of blue water; "temperate, temperate" (Davie *CP 1971*, 88) is the word he keeps repeating. In its advocacy of restraint the poem is nearer Amis's "Against Romanticism" than Larkin's poem. But the poem is also self-critical and laments the epiphanies that may be lost through moderation: "And some / Who missed the flash of a fin / Were keeping their eyes on rhyme-schemes" (Davie *CP 1971*, 89). While he wilts from the lack of romanticism's strong waters, Davie's art – "my plants" (Davie *CP 1971*, 90) – does not. Likewise in "The Fountain of Arethusa" he suggests that warm honesty might at last lead to "a profusion of late blossoms" (Davie *CP 1971*, 97).

Two of the best poems in *The Battered Wife and Other Poems* (1982) also examine problems of immoderation. The title poem explores the brutality of hopeless love, but the "Devil on Ice," with its spiritual overtones, is even more chilling. Drawn from an experience in the Royal Navy 30 years earlier when Davie was called to work on Christmas Eve, the poem's frigid setting in northern Russia amplifies its spiritual iciness. Required to ferry the celebratory alcohol, "the wardroom's gin" (Davie *CP 1971*, 134), through the subzero temperature, Davie, like the gin he carts, feels literally on ice. The poem's title bespeaks other meanings: disgruntled at having to work on a holiday, Davie has uncharitable, even un-Christian feelings, and feels in league with the devil; and, though still harboring spiteful feelings, he has repressed his resentment for three decades since that frozen Christmas and been "amenable, / Equable, a friend of law and order" (Davie *CP 1971*, 134). The hatred is still present, however, and, though preserved on ice, it may yet thaw. Such emotional intensity is unusual for Davie, particularly as the poem addresses his own depravity, but the poem may have been inspired by Hardy's Christmas poem "The Oxen" in which the miracle of Christ's birth is attended by devoted, kneeling oxen. Davie's poem is more refractory: "The holy babe, and lordling Lucifer / With him alas, that blessed morn" (Davie *CP 1971*, 134). While Hardy's poem beseeches optimism, Davie's ponders whether his years of rectitude are the triumph of personal restraint or merely a stalemated battle with his innate depravity.

Because his verse is generally so controlled and circumspect and because he has spent his professional life as a teacher, Davie is frequently termed a coldly academic poet. Responding to that charge, Davie retorts:

> Because I am a poet who has spent his life in universities, and because I do and always shall attack those who would set the life of poetry against the life of intellect and the life of learning, it is supposed that I do not recognize the blight of academicism. So far am I from any such complacency that I would testify from my own experience how the surest way to reputation as a critic of poetry is to have a firm and profound distrust of what poetry is, and what it does. This is only natural. For the process of explaining a poem, as practised by these pundits (I could name names, and they would be distinguished ones), consists precisely in emasculating poetic utterance until it can seem no more than a wayward variant on discursive prose. (*Companions*, 129)

As his colleague Robert Conquest says, the greatest enemies of poetry are frequently its well-meaning friends. Moreover, in one light, being an academic may not be so bad, and, as Davie writes in *The Poet in the Imaginary Museum*, may in fact be inescapable, "as the philistinism of Anglo-American society forces all artists – not just writers – back into the campus as a last stronghold."[10] The philistine, Davie reflects, has "access to legitimate pleasures which further education and refinement would only close to him" (*Companions*, 11), and he adds that antiacademicism typically arises from within the academy itself, from those who are reluctant to praise their contemporaries. The pejorative label of academicism seems even more ironic when one recalls how reactionary Davie and his Movement colleagues were thought to have been only two decades earlier, and it is a designation Davie sometimes finds offensive. Believing that erudition is not an inherent adversary of art, he draws a distinction between the scholar and the academic. "Academicism is one of the enemies of literature but nowadays it is the critic-pedagogue, not the scholar, who is the danger. (I believe that the poet and the scholar are natural allies)" (*World*, 357).

This judgment is borne out in much detail in *The Poet in the Imaginary Museum* (1977), a collection of essays written between 1950 and 1977 reiterating how poetry has yet to be revolutionized by the attention of the critical academy. Davie claims that modern poets write as if Pound and Eliot never existed, but he also insists that the modern poem is not to be trusted entirely either. Yet while distrustful of academics, Davie's work hardly appeals to a mass audience, nor is it intended to. "There are many more people than is usually acknowledged who are tone-deaf to poetry. . . . And these people, who I suspect are numerous, have the right to be left alone" (*Companions*, 8).

Even so, as Davie has grown more outspoken over the years, his verse has become less intellectual and less obscure, as if he were trying to reach some of that audience. To that end his more recent verse employs a wider range of styles than it once did. He remains skeptical, however, of romanticism's easy faults, suspicious of the cloying emotions and the affectations of excessive feeling and preferring to maintain, according to Kenneth Allott, "a more equable disposition than most poets are lucky enough to possess" (*World*, 358).

Bernard Bergonzi has called Davie "the finest critic of poetry of his generation" (*Responsibilities*, 46), for, though his criticism is frequently didactic, it is also a reminder of two significant Movement virtues: clarity and a willingness to explore equivocal perspectives. His notions about poetry have undergone continual and fastidious revision, and these changes in theory are also evident in Davie's drift toward looser forms in his own verse. Davie has consciously striven to incorporate into his poetry "more and more of the prose virtues, so as to see how near to prose poetry can come while still remaining poetry" (*Companions*, 81-82).

While a representative practitioner of Movement theory, Davie displays considerable ambivalence about his participation in the group. He alternately confers special status on the Movement and dismisses it as "the first concerted though unplanned invasion of the literary Establishment by the scholarship-boys of the petty bourgeoisie" (*Companions*, 136). Having always identified with his blue-collar, northern rearing, Davie is a great admirer of Larkin and "his refusal to go for experience outside England" (*Companions*, 123), yet Davie himself traveled widely, and his travels have visibly influenced his work. His *Purity of Diction in English Verse* is the most trenchant example of the Movement criticism, but Davie disavows the organizing principles of the group:

It wasn't like a Parisian French movement, you know, it wasn't actually dreamed up with a manifesto all afloat around a café, and so it didn't break up in vituperations on matters of abstract principle. Simply, it happened, then it dissolved itself. It's still true that some of those poets, most of those poets within *New Lines*, I still have considerable affection for; and I am always interested in their writing, where they're going, or seem to be going. I have a natural sympathy with them, though some of them now seem to be writing very differently from me. In fact one wishes that that sort of thing happened more often. (*Explain*, 206)

The sympathy is natural; they are like him. But he also likes them because they are different. In other critics such remarks would prove more puzzling than they do coming from Davie. "These men [Amis, Enright, and Larkin] are my friends and I think I know perfectly well what makes them, being finally civilized men, pretend to be barbarians; why, though they are humane persons and responsible citizens, they pretend sometimes to be cultural teddy-boys. They are putting the house of English poetry in order: not before time, too. . . . They are getting rid of pretentiousness and cultural window-dressing and arrogant self-expression, by creating an English poetry which is severely limited in its aims, painfully modest in its pretensions, deliberately provincial in its scope" (*Museum*, 48).

Davie understands why these university-educated writers became defensive when lumped together in an unsophisticated faction; the very self-consciousness that made them acutely aware of life's ironies also nearly destroyed the group's enterprise. He confesses, "We ridiculed and deprecated 'the Movement' even as we kept it going. . . . Ours was writing which apologized insistently for its own existence" (*Museum*, 72). And he admits that his early poems were designed in large part to accommodate this aesthetic. "What we all shared to begin with was a hatred for writing considered as self-expression; but all we put in its place was writing as self-adjustment, a getting on the right terms with our reader" (*Museum*, 74). This defensive and self-deprecating posture became, certainly for Davie at least, "a way of looking at ourselves and our pretensions, not a way of looking at the world" (*Museum*, 74).

Chapter Nine

Thom Gunn

Thomson William Gunn, the youngest of the Movement poets, was born in Gravesend, Kent, on 29 August 1929. His father, Herbert Smith Gunn, the son of a merchant seaman, was a journalist who worked on various provincial newspapers before becoming editor of the *London Evening Standard*; his mother, Ann Charlotte Thomson Gunn, the daughter of a tenant farmer, also worked as a journalist until Thom was born. Because of the World War II blitz and his father's moving from job to job, young Thom attended a number of schools before moving to Hampstead, where his parents soon divorced. He attended University College School, London, and, according to his father, was better read at 11 than most people are at 35. At 12 he created *The Flirt*, a "novel" illustrated with pictures he had cut from magazines, for his mother's birthday. She lived only two more years.

Gunn served in the National Service from 1948 to 1950, which he thought "largely a matter of boredom, drudgery, and endurance."[1] He believed it was good training, however, for a would-be poet in that the tedium of performing his duties gave him ample practice in dealing with life's boredom.

After military service Gunn spent six months in Paris, where he had a low-paying office job with the metro and worked on another unfinished novel, his third. He then attended Trinity College, Cambridge, where he studied with F. R. Leavis, whose "discriminations and enthusiasms helped teach me to write, better than any creative-writing class could have. His insistence on the realized, being the life of poetry, was exactly what I needed" (*Occasions*, 160). At the end of that initial year at Cambridge, Gunn published his first poem in an antiwar issue of the student magazine, *Granta*, and while studying for his B.A., which he took in 1953, he wrote the poems that were to become *Fighting Terms*.

Gunn was 25 when Fantasy Press issued *Fighting Terms* in 1954, and he drastically reedited it for Jerome Rothenberg's 1959 Hawk's Well Press edition. But feeling that he had overrevised it for American audiences, he restored most of the changes to the original for the 1962 Faber edition, although he did omit two poems from the original volume that he thought too dull and unintentionally comic to warrant reprinting. Two or three other poems, most noticeably "Round and Round," remain significantly altered from their appearance upon initial publication. Gunn's habitual rewriting of *Fighting Terms* underscores his continuing dissatisfaction with it. "I'm a bit puzzled," he wrote, "by the way that certain critics – Alvarez is the one I'm thinking of particularly – who like *Fighting Terms* more than anything else I've written. I can see that it has a kind of youthful clumsiness, and clumsiness can look like genuineness, but there is very little in it that I would particularly want to keep. About six or seven poems out of 25 perhaps" ("Conversations," 68).

Fighting Terms abounds in allusions to combat and warfare and was heavily influenced by Gunn's reading of Donne and Shakespeare. In "A Mirror for Poets," for example, he interestingly poises the violence of Elizabethan England against the glorious literature that rose from its misery. "The Wound," the first poem in the volume, is the one Gunn feels is the book's best. "I think it's about the breakdown of control over oneself" ("Conversations," 68). It is constructed in five five-line iambic pentameter stanzas with lines alternately rhymed. Its narrator is a wounded soldier in the Trojan war who, having served on both sides, is a kind of male counterpart to Helen. But where Helen finds sorrow in every battle, he primarily feels rage. That the wound from which he suffers is in his head suggests that it is as much a spiritual injury as physical one, and, when he is called once again to armor, his reluctance causes the wound to break wide open.

Taken by the image of the soldier – "the soldier who never goes to war, whose role has no function, whose battledress is a joke . . . attractive and repellent" (*Occasions*, 173) – Gunn employs a wounded soldier again as spokesman in "Incident on a Journey," the final poem in the collection. In between these first and last poems, the military metaphors are tempered by Gunn's fundamentally reflective sensibility, though in a series of contemptuous love poems ("To His Cynical Mistress," "Helen's Rape," and "The Beach Head")

women's bodies are treated as enemy territory that must be con-
quered militarily. The poems achieve an interesting dynamic; Gunn's
metaphysical conceits bring an intellectualism to his martial topics,
and the potency of his intellect typically prevails. That clash is further
explored in "Carnal Knowledge," in which sex is seen as a conflict
between emotional energy and rational will. Like the soldier in "The
Wound," Gunn supplies both sides of the argument:

> Even in bed I pose: desire may grow
> More circumstantial and less circumspect
> Each night, but an acute girl would suspect
> My thoughts might not be, like my body, bare.[2]

Ultimately for Gunn the knowledge of sexuality surpasses carnality,
demonstrating that Gunn's "fighting terms" are essentially linguistic
and thereby show the superiority of language over action. But in the
poem's conclusion, when the woman objects to her lover's sending
her away, her perceptive protests are overruled by still another pose.

Such mythological and sexual posing is found in Gunn's other
work, and he has been attacked for it, especially for writing under
the guise of heterosexuality when he is homosexual. John Press for
the most part has lauded Gunn's ability to develop philosophical
themes, "thereby giving full scope to his enormous poetic talents,
the chief of these being lucidity of thought, the power of controlling
the ramifications of an elaborate metaphor, the tautness and poise of
his Metaphysical wit, and a poetic language that is swift-moving,
weighty, supple, and incisive,"[3] but he also finds Gunn's work at
times "contrived and faintly rebarbative" (Press, 191). Gunn's ex-
travagant posturing is unique to the Movement, yet these poses em-
anate from familiar sources. Like his Movement contemporaries
Gunn equivocates between a romantic call to action and an Augustan
call for reflection. And being the youngest member of the group,
Gunn was familiar with the Movement stance before *Fighting Terms*
was issued, although he has continually downplayed its influence on
him.

It was around the time of the original publication of this book, 1954, or perhaps a little earlier, that I first heard of something called the Movement. To my
surprise, I also learned that I was a member of it. . . . It originated as a half-
joke by Anthony Hartley writing in the *Spectator* and then was perpetrated as

a kind of journalistic convenience. What poets like Larkin, Davie, Elizabeth Jennings, and I had in common at that time was that we were deliberately eschewing Modernism, and turning back, though not very thoroughgoingly, to traditional resources in structure and method. . . . The whole business looks now like a lot of categorizing foolishness. (*Occasions*, 174)

Gunn had met Elizabeth Jennings in Oxford and John Wain when he spoke to a club at Cambridge. Wain had read some of Gunn's poems in the campus literary magazine, and he invited him to London to meet other poets who were writing in a similar fashion. But Gunn took no such trips.

I wasn't quite sure who these other chaps were. And then, I think it was about 1954, Anthony Hartley referred kiddingly to something he called The Movement in an article in *The Spectator*, and to everybody's surprise this got taken up. And taken seriously. Then in 1956, Robert Conquest brought out *New Lines* but by that time the Movement had been born, had flourished and was fading. Nobody any longer was making claims for the similarity between the different poets. There is a certain amount of similarity between those eight poets but solely a similarity of the times. . . . I never subscribed to any programme. . . . The big joke about the Movement was that none of the people had ever met each other and certainly never subscribed to anything like a programme. There were a few chance resemblances, but they were pretty chance." ("Conversations," 69-70)

In 1954 Gunn accepted a writing fellowship to Stanford enabling him to work for a year with Yvor Winters, whose poetry, like Gunn's, emphasized reason over passion. The two argued frequently in his first months there, but eventually they became fast friends, and Gunn praised his mentor in "To Yvor Winters, 1955" for keeping "both Rule and Energy in view, / Much power in each, most in the balanced two . . . Built by an exercised intelligence."[4] Winters used Renaissance masters as his models, and he required his students to emulate their techniques as well. The effect on Gunn was pronounced, for this training from Winters resulted in his producing editions of Ben Jonson (1974) and Fulke Greville (1968) and confirmed his own notions about the importance of technical balance in verse. Gunn slowly began to rephrase his elitist academic education in a more powerful, lyrical pulse. Through Winters's instruction he learned to distrust overly rhetorical poems and Whitmanian ones that expressed overstuffed or superficial feelings. Poetry became for him a means to explore truth with a verbal exactness absent from prose.

Gunn believed that both formal and informal diction could be natural modes of expression, and by mixing them he was essentially melding two traditions: one old, one current, but both vital. "Informality has been used with imagination and sensitivity by Amis and Larkin," Gunn declared, "while the potentialities of formal language are as rich as ever. . . . What is important is that two kinds of diction can at least co-exist – and they must continue to, if we are to get away from the boring up-and-down of alternating fashions in poetry" ("Context," 40).

Gunn had intended to study in California for only a year, but he stayed on and has lived near San Francisco ever since. He was awarded the Levinson Prize by *Poetry* in 1955, and he issued *The Sense of Movement* in 1957, a collection of 32 poems whose title owes more to his fascination with the leather fetishism popular among the San Francisco homosexual community than to any alliance of British poets. "On the Move," the first and most anthologized poem from the volume, sets the tone of the collection. It concerns a restless band of motorcyclists reminiscent of those in Marlon Brando's *The Wild Ones*. They are posers who have adopted leather and "uncertain violence" (*Sense*, 11) as their uniform. In "On the Move" they scare only a field of birds, but the power between their legs hurtles them forward as symbols of immanent human will. Gunn's reliance on more than two dozen present-tense verbs propels the poem like the speeding motorcyclists he describes. The continual action causes both poem and riders to seem eternally present, beyond a past that would restrain them. Similarly, Gunn observes in "The Unsettled Motorcyclist's Vision of His Death" that "My human will cannot submit / To nature, though brought out of it" (*Sense*, 28). The cyclist's death, though natural, will be self-imposed. Elvis Presley, like Gunn's leather-jacketed boys, also adopts a combative posture; he is a poser capable of transforming "revolt into a style" (*Sense*, 31).

The poetic persona in these poems seems to be that of an individual at odds with his human self. His machine is a complement to his finite flesh, to his need for strong convictions, and it offers movement if not direction. "I must / Find out the limitation / Of mind and universe," he asserts in "Human Condition," fearing that he is "condemned to be / An individual" (*Sense*, 18). He repeats the curse of individuality in "Legal Reform," concluding, "For law is in our hands, I realise: / The sentence is, condemned to be condemned" (*Sense*, 51).

Even in literary matters Gunn sides with his surly toughs. "Lines for a Book," written mockingly in praise of "those who would not play with Stephen Spender" (*Sense*, 30), closes with a parody of Spender's "I Think Continually of Those Who Were Truly Great": "I think of all the toughs through history / And thank heaven they lived, continually" (*Sense*, 30). Even love, purposeful and purposeless, is viewed cynically as a threat to the assertion of individual identity ("The Corridor"). Though Gunn's poems themselves are reflections on action, Gunn unmistakably prefers action.

Gunn thought his first books were reviewed more kindly than they deserved "because London expected good poets to emerge from Oxford and Cambridge" (*Occasions*, 167). The callousness of his poems and the compassionless thugs he focused on as central characters resulted in critics' measuring his success by his "ability to handle the extreme unpleasantness of atrocity."[5] But John Thompson objected to the misleading nature of the poems, proclaiming most of them

> dull and priggish in the worst contemporary manner. . . . If writing poems were like writing examinations, and had to be done, then Thom Gunn would get good marks. He is intelligent, ingenious, and formally capable within the limits that would be expected, say, in Advanced Verse Writing. The meters, alas, have all been smoothed out and the lines move in that approved, familiar rhythm of the 1940s in which nothing real can be said anymore. . . . How many times have you started to read a poem about a landscape, a house, a frontier, and then realized with a sick surmise that here was no landscape, no house, no frontier, but only another little allegory. . . . These simple correspondences have the effect of destroying both the visible world and the idea; the objects are not real, the thoughts, encountering no resistance from the outside, ripple along in their familiar way; a meaningless exercise of small ingenuities. Even more unfortunate, though, is Gunn's open preaching. . . . The pulpit is not really congenial to him. . . . But most of these poems are manufactured things that pass for poetry, and this is a pity; clearly Gunn has the intelligence to do better if he thought he had to.[6]

Others find Gunn "perverse yet compelling," (Press, 194) particularly in his rendering of the modern city and the toughs who inhabit it. While the city may be an unfinished enterprise in Gunn's work, his topics, as in *Fighting Terms*, are handled in compressed, fairly traditional, and metrically strict lines.

Gunn had taken an M.A. from Cambridge, but he left Stanford without a Ph.D. for the University of California in Berkeley in 1958 and served as poetry reviewer for the *Yale Review* until 1964, when he gave up reviewing because he found it distasteful to criticize his contemporaries. He won the Arts Council of Great Britain and Maugham awards in 1959 and traveled to Berlin the following year. He issued *My Sad Captains* (1961), his third book, upon his return.

My Sad Captains is a transitional work, although it expounds a familiar theme in its epigraph from Chaucer's *Troilus and Creseyde:* "The will is infinite and the execution confined, the desire is boundless and the act a slave to limit."[7] A number of the poems are unsurprising attempts to fashion identity through will, even when the endeavor leads to violence. His characters demonstrate Gunn's continued beguilement with soldiers and his nostalgia for violence, though they seem thoroughly incapable of abstracting experience. In "Innocence" a young Nazi watches without protest while a Russian partisan is burned alive, and "The Byrnies" are little more than medieval fascists in chain mail. Alan Bold claims "the soldier seems to typify for Gunn the one member of society who can act like an animal without having to suffer mental agony over violent acts because his are sanctified by society. Neither does the soldier have to conduct a . . . search for an identity: he puts one on with his uniform."[8] When contemplation does occur in these poems, it generally comes to little even when, as in "The Annihilation of Nothing," Gunn considers the frightening possibility of "purposeless matter" in the absence of will.

Curiously, Gunn penned two poems with the same title, "Modes of Pleasure." Both are perspectives on a middle-aged "Fallen Rake," a man who is constrained to a life of sensual pleasure and "cannot contemplate the past / Cannot discriminate" (*Captains*, 62). But the poem "In Santa Maria del Popolo" finds a more deliberate and thoughtful figure visiting the Roman church housing Caravaggio's "The Conversion of St. Paul." The shadows in the chapel merge with the shadows in the painting to leave Gunn's persona in shadowy doubt. There is some enlightenment in the darkened church, for he contemplates both women and art there, but his contemplation becomes but another means of resistance, just "the large gesture of solitary man" (*Captains*, 52).

The first half of *My Sad Captains*, 16 poems, is quite traditional. The lines are regularly accented, and most stanzas are rhymed. But the second half is a dramatic departure for Gunn. The poems are far gentler than those in his previous volumes. The volume concludes with the title poem, which seems a clear farewell to "the wasteful force" (*Captains*, 91) redolent in his first books, and "Waking in a Newly Built House" muses on a world that may be lacking "even potential meanings" (*Captains*, 77). Reflecting on this change in tone, Gunn observed:

> I'm trying to show how the celebration of energy can lead one to a kind of commitment where one finds that energy is not just in a vacuum; it is very often destroying the energy of other people and is therefore maybe not such a great energy. I suppose this is one of the main problems of being alive; how can one show the most of oneself, whatever you call it, without destroying the most in other people, infringing on the most in other people and possibly destroying them. Often in quite quiet ways without actually killing them. ("Conversations," 67)

Not only does *My Sad Captains* represent a softening in philosophy, but the poems are also looser in form, more syllabic than metric, and they prefigure the more informal but complex poems of his succeeding volumes. "When I began writing poems in syllabics," Gunn recalls, "I found that I suddenly had access to a certain spontaneity of language and perception that I hadn't been able to get when using traditional metres. Yet I feel uneasy about the split in my work between the two kinds of poems I write, the metrically intense and the syllabically casual. Each excludes too much of the other" (*Context*, 40). According to Gunn, Robert Lowell was the only poet able to blend the two forms successfully, but Gunn acknowledges shortcomings with each style: "It [metrical verse] is poetry making great use of the conscious intelligence, but its danger is bombast – the controlling music drowning out everything else. Free verse invites a different style of experience, improvisation. Its danger lies in being too relaxed, too lacking in controlling energy" (*Occasions*, 179).

Much of his poetry from the early 1960s dissatisfied Gunn because it lacked intensity on one hand and he had yet to discover what he could accomplish in free verse on the other. He issued *Selected Poems* (1962) with Ted Hughes and *Positives* (1966) in collaboration with his brother, Ander. The latter is little more than a collection of captions to 39 of his brother's photographs commemorating urban English life, but Gunn's emerging poetic may be glimpsed within it nonetheless. The book opens with the photo of a baby and closes with one of an old lady, and the theme of transformation is as much technical for Gunn as it is thematic. The photographs punctuate Gunn's point that social forces may serve to limit an individual's choices. Alan Bold called *Positives* "a superb minor achievement, a plain-speaking meditation on the wastage of so much human life" (Bold, 79).

Gunn left Berkeley in 1966, one year after receiving tenure, and his next volume, *Touch* (1967), was daringly innovative. Gunn felt that the title poem, a love poem on the importance of an embrace, was his first successful attempt at free verse poem, and thematically it is one of his most expansive and universally affirmative (love is a "wide realm where we / walk with everyone").[9] The volume contains two extended poem sequences, "Confessions of the Life Artist" and "Misanthropos." The first, a first-person account written in 10 sections, explores the danger of the creative writer who in seeing art in people loses respect for their humanity and thereby also dehumanizes him- or herself. The second, "Misanthropos," is one of Gunn's most ambitious and sustained works.

"Misanthropos" is a fantasy made up of 17 lyrics organized into four parts, with a varying number of sections in each part. "The Last Man," written in five sections, deals with a lone survivor of a holocaust. No longer aware of who he is, he hears only his own echo and comes to detest his consciousness. He would prefer to remake himself into an animal lacking all history and self-awareness. In the six sections of "Memoirs of the World" the last man is victim to his memory; his nightmares take him without mercy back to his unicellular beginnings. "Elegy on the Dust," written in a single section, scrutinizes man as a builder who constructs to compensate for what he lacks naturally. Fearing extinction, he nonetheless creates the tools of his own destruction. The five sections of the final poem, "The First Man," occur after a passage of years. Man has regressed to the stage where animal instinct has replaced his human consciousness. Then other survivors, several dozen in fact, appear. There is a stir of sympathy and a call for human acceptance. The achievement of humanity, Gunn implies, lies in intimacy, in man's ability to live in touch with others.

"Misanthropos" is not only a rich poem, it is technically varied. Gunn moves between rhymed and unrhymed lines and between first- and third-person accounts, and he blends traditional metrical forms – blank verse, terza rima, couplets, and quatrains – with free and syllabic verse. By reining his measures he deftly controls the poem's movement, and his achievement is not meager. And it is truly different from the work of his Movement contemporaries.

Gunn's experimentation is also evident in *Moly* (1971). Borrowing on the Homeric episode in which Odysseus's men were turned into swine, the title poem is spoken by one of Odysseus's mariners, who awakens transformed. "Moly" has generally been read as a celebration of hallucinatory drugs in the search for mind-expanding, spiritual enlightenment. Gunn sees LSD as a kind of modern moly; like the black-rooted herb that protected Odysseus against the enchantress Circe, it frees the individual from being reduced to the fundamental baseness of physical need. Writing in *Poetry Book Society Bulletin Number 68*, Gunn asserts:

> We can all take on the features of pigs – or what humans interpret as those features – we all have in us the germs of the brutal, greedy, and dull. And we can all avoid becoming pigs, though to do so we must be wily and self-aware. Moly can help us to know our own potential for change: even though we are in the power of Circe or of time, we do not have to become pigs, we do not have to be unmanned, we are as free to make and unmake ourselves as we were at the age of ten. (Bold, 90)

The opening poem, "Rites of Passage," also concerns just such a metamorphosis toward freedom.

> Something is taking place.
> Horns bud bright in my hair.
> My feet are turning hoof.
> And Father, see my face
> – Skin that was damp and fair
> Is barklike and, feel, rough. (*Captains*, 5)

Besides exploring psychedelics (there are some half-dozen poems on the LSD experience), *Moly* concerns other aspects of the hedonistic, West Coast, counterculture lifestyle of the 1960s. Gunn's "Discovery of the Pacific" follows a Kansas couple trekking nature's trail to California, where they bathe in the Pacific; "Sunlight" celebrates the sun's "original perfection" (*Captains*, 44), and Gunn's analogy (the sun, like man, was born in perfection before falling into finiteness) calls to mind Blake's sunflower.

These verses seem remote from the conservative stance of the Movement, and Donald Davie for one attacked Gunn's poetics in *Moly*. "Gunn's metre here and his rhymes, so determined to draw attention to themselves, deter the reader who wants poetry to spur him into feeling. . . . The subjects that he treated with this aggravating coolness were precisely those which the modern reader supposed he had a special right to feel tempestuously or intensely about."[10] Michael Fried concurred: "The *Moly* poems are dead" (Davie, 84). The desire that *Moly* might synthetically unite flagging romantic inspiration with the informed rationalism of the Movement was not achieved.

Gunn followed *Moly* with *Songbook* (1973), a despairing offering of eight songs by self-pitying personas, and a series of other slight collections. Though weightier, *Jack Straw's Castle* (1976) is a particularly brooding retreat from the bright unsophistication of his 1960s poems. Its grotesqueries are reflective of the dark period of the U.S. involvement in the Vietnam War. As in *Touch*, the volume is dominated by two long sequences: "The Geysers," a nightmarish account of communal bathing in Sonoma County, and the title poem, "Jack Straw's Castle," a loose narrative containing "obsessive images of the poet being assaulted, imprisoned, burned up, annihilated."[11] Jack Straw was one of the leaders of the Peasants' Revolt of 1381, and the name has come to mean scarecrow. Gunn's persona seems to be that of an unsubstantial revolutionary, but his self-disparagement lacks the wry humor and the political certitude of his Movement contemporaries, particularly Conquest and Amis, whose politics were generally more reactionary in support of the war.

Although there were oblique references to it in earlier poems, Gunn did not write candidly about his homosexuality until *The Passages of Joy* (1982). In this sense the work is Gunn's most mature and confessional. The title has dual allusions. While it is taken from Samuel Johnson ("Time hovers o'er, impatient to destroy, / And shuts up all the Passages of Joy"), it also refers to the nine bodily orifices, the nine passages through which physical joy may come. According to Davie, although Gunn was able to combine "unchaste subject-matter . . . with a remarkably lean and unadorned, style . . . *The Passages of Joy* isn't in the least a joyous book" (Davie, 179-80). He laments that Gunn, a poet who once commanded a public, has become in his later work a poet with merely a following.

John Press also called attention to flaws in Gunn's work: his lack of tenderness; his seeming indifference to the natural world; his inability to convey sharp, sensual images; and his disregard for those protean modes of being that defy categorization. Although not coupling Gunn's poetry to a Movement program, Press insists that Gunn's work "lacks any satisfactory social framework or terms of reference. The myth of toughness is a poor substitute for traditional religious beliefs and codes of conduct, nor is it possible to confer heroic stature on such shoddy figures" (Press, 199).

Still, there are virtues. Gunn remains a serious poet who has proven more venturesome than his Movement colleagues in matters of versification and subject matter. To be sure his topics have been more brutal and less philosophical, but they have also been impassioned and startlingly candid.

Chapter Ten

John Holloway

Like Donald Davie and John Wain, John Holloway is an important, original critic (in his case perhaps more interesting as a critic than poet) whose work is informed by the Movement desire for lucidity. Although John Holloway was an important contributor to *Poets of the 1950s* and *New Lines* and was acquainted with most of the Movement poets by 1954, he was the only original member of the Movement not included in Conquest's *New Lines 2*. Despite Holloway's early alliance with the Movement – he believed it was part of a social revolution, "a stand against having a political stand"[1] – his work was omitted from the anthology. From that time forward Holloway remained on the edge of the group, for the most part pursuing his own path as a critic, poet, and essayist.

Christopher John Holloway was born in London on 1 August 1920, the only child of George and Evelyn (Astbury) Holloway. His mother was the daughter of a country schoolmaster. His father, who served in the army and was later a furnace stoker at Queen's Hospital in Hackney, had little formal education, but he managed to lift his family into the lower middle class. Holloway's early years are touchingly recalled in his autobiography, *A London Childhood*, which covers his life from 1920 to 1929. In the preface to *A London Childhood* Holloway claims his early years were dull and unextraordinary; he writes of his fondness for bird watching and auto racing and of his playing the violin in the school orchestra. But the book is full of charming remembrances. At six, for example, Holloway was incorrectly diagnosed as having an enlarged heart. He details the special treatment he received at home and at school, where a bed was set up for him in the classroom. His earliest memory is of staring at a hot fire, probably in Mrs. Newby's kitchen where his mother worked; this early association with fire recurs frequently in his early poems.

Holloway was educated at the local grammar school, County School, Beckenham, in Kent, and he attended Oxford as a scholarship student. He took his degree in modern greats (politics, philosophy, and economics) with honors in 1941 and then served in the British Army as an antiaircraft gunner and an intelligence officer. Returning to school after the war, he received an M.A. from New College, Oxford, as an Open History Scholar in 1945 and his D.Phil. in 1947.

Although formally trained as a social scientist and philosopher, Holloway eventually became a fellow of the Royal Society of Literature and earned two doctorates in literature: one in 1954 from the University of Aberdeen, Scotland, where he taught for five years, and another in 1969 from Cambridge, where he has maintained an academic affiliation since 1954. A peripatetic lecturer, he has held academic appointments in the United States as a Francis E. Powell Traveling Fellow in 1952, as Alexander White Professor at the University of Chicago in 1966, and as visiting professor at Johns Hopkins in 1972, and he delivered the Virginia Lectures at the University of Virginia in 1979. He was appointed Byron Professor of English at the University of Athens from 1961 to 1963, which allowed him to travel throughout Greece, Turkey, the Balkans, the Near East, and Egypt, and he visited the Indian subcontinent (Ceylon, India, and Pakistan) in 1958 and the Middle East in 1964. In addition, he has toured France, Italy, and Spain several times.

Holloway married in 1946 and left Oxford for Aberdeen over his friends' objections, lured by the prospect of teaching literature. He enjoyed Scotland very much and achieved early academic success as he began publishing poems in established magazines, his first one in the *Listener*. His poetry was included in the *Hudson Review*'s collection of "Five British Poets," and in 1951 he read the sole paper at the first English Lecturers' Conference, now a well-established annual event. He also published an article in *Essays in Criticism*, an important platform for Movement writers that had already published essays by Amis and Davie earlier that year. He then issued his first book, *Language and Intelligence*, a revision of his doctoral dissertation on the philosophy of language.

In *Language and Intelligence* (1951) Holloway displays a tempered disposition, although he takes a fundamentally romantic position that finds its philosophical roots in John Locke, George Berkeley, and David Hume. Believing that in one form or another "meaning is a derivation from imagery,"[2] Holloway claims that symbolism is an activity of special interest to scholars. He dispels Wordsworth's notion of the poet's employing the language of common man, for "ordinary language is the language of persons unacquainted even with the idea of conforming to a dictionary" (*Language*, 123) and could for that reason hardly be considered poetic. How might contemporary poets find utility in the words of a man who never heard an internal combustion engine? Holloway concludes that the reliance of classical writers on epistemology and logic is actually much narrower than is generally claimed.

He alleges that natural language follows deductive patterns, particularly when attempting to state matters of fact, but any logical attempt to systematize language will ultimately prove unprofitable. Linguistic studies of poetry will yield results only in occasional, specific situations. But if modern poets, as the first representatives of the machine age, cannot be Wordsworthian worshipers of nature, their poetry can be a springboard for an unprogrammed romanticism nonetheless by employing intuition as a means of embodying past traditions.

According to Holloway, contemporary poetry need not be mechanical or merely a rearrangement of older styles, and his own verses shows a nostalgia for eighteenth-century Augustan attitudes and a repudiation of the popular poetry of Dylan Thomas and the other apocalyptics of the 1940s, whom Conquest claimed "were encouraged to regard their task simply as making arrangements of sex and violence tapped straight from the unconscious . . . or to evoke without comment the naivetes and nostalgias of childhood" (*NL*, xiv). Holloway's autobiography, in contrast, records daily life without such neoromantic excess and therefore qualifies as serious literature.

Even before his first book of verse was published, Holloway had received significant critical attention. In 1953 he read for *New Soundings* to an estimated audience of 100,000 and in June was among the first Movement poets to appear in the *Spectator*, Donald Davie having appeared in its pages the previous month. His work was soon accepted by *Encounter*, the *New Statesman and Nation*, the *Times Literary Supplement*, and other weighty periodicals. In August 1953 Davie and Holloway read on the penultimate broadcast of Ludovic Kennedy's *First Reading*, and his work was also broadcast on George Hartley's *New Verse* and Edwin Morgan's *New Poetry* programs. Holloway's first collection was issued the following year, his *Poems* becoming the pamphlet 26 in the Fantasy Poets series.

Though brief, *Poems* is thoroughly characteristic of the Movement. His "Journey through the Night" familiarly echoes Larkin's "The Whitsun Weddings":

> At the first hour from dawn
> The traveller in the window seat
> Rubbed his eyes, woke from a daze,
> Brushed his rough hair back with great
> Podgy fingers, gave a yawn,
> Cleared the pane's white dewy haze,
> Then stared so eagerly, it might
> Have been his home place come in sight.
>
> But at the second hour from dawn
> The traveller in the window seat
> Suddenly turned away from the world
> As though he saw some thing too sweet
> Or too bitter to be borne;
> And when he met my glance, he curled
> His body to the wall, and wept
> I thought; but it may be he slept.
>
> At the third hour from dawn
> The ticket man rolled back the door:
> The traveller blurted out that he
> Wanted another ticket for
> Some other place, somewhere further on;
> He spoke shortly, confusedly;
> But I saw he did not know,
> Now, where in the world to go.[3]

The protagonist's confusion is representative of widespread postwar incertitude. Other poems in the collection demonstrate Holloway's erudition and interest in myth, neither of which is typical to most Movement verse. The first two poems in the collection concern Hephaistos and Ulysses, and all of the poems display an intellectual heaviness.

Although Holloway considered himself a northerner by temperament, he moved to Cambridge as a university lecturer after the publication of *Poems* to experience a wider scholarly environment. Two years later his first full collection of poetry, *The Minute and Longer*

Poems (1956), which includes the six poems from his Fantasy pamphlet, was issued.

In *The Minute* Holloway shares with the other *New Lines* poets a penchant for traditional verse forms, but these early poems have a peculiarity all their own. His work is more visionary and decidedly more somber and obscure; it lacks the irony and social correctives that infuse many Movement poems, although he approximates Larkin's wit to a degree in "The Petty Testament of Peter the Clerk" and "The Life and Adventures of Heroic Mr Clubman." Holloway's poetry is as disciplined as that of his confederates, but it suffers from an obvious and calculated scholastic stiffness. His language rarely seems imaginative, spontaneous, or vibrant in contradistinction to the pointed obscurity of much modern poetry. Moreover, the anguish in "Recognition Scene" is hardly the cry of a common man:

> O now I see
> My monstrous child is born, the plant in flower
> Like fire, that fed on dark, the hawk burst free,
>
> Grief's clawed revengeful hawk, mad to devour
> The keeper, being itself both hawk and dove
> And falling on him like a glittering shower
>
> When the tired hand throws off the hawking-glove
> Despairing in a forest of despair
> That stifles hate: because its root is love.[4]

William Meredith, however, appreciated the craftsmanship of these poems and has praised the Movement qualities conspicuous in Holloway's verse. He approvingly notes that "Holloway's poems have the same emotional integrity as Larkin's: they are all about something that has happened and been experienced, none of them about feelings that have been induced. Poetry, which is our most accurate form of intelligence, responds gratefully to the justness of mind, of academic mind, which is brought to bear on these experiences."[5] Peter the Clerk possesses the same indecision, lack of sureness, and desire for roots exhibited by Larkin's poetic persona:

> For the blind groping of the root
> To find its soil, strikes everyone
> At first for lack of, then through friends.

And mine (although I'm glad to call
Them friends) aren't more than typical. (*Minute*, 50)

Holloway's affection for Movement poetry is most evident in his *Hudson Review* critique of Davie's *Brides of Reason*, Larkin's *The Less Deceived*, and Conquest's *Poems*, all of which appeared shortly after *The Minute* debuted. Holloway claimed that publication of these books should serve

> as a landmark, and the line of poetic movement along which that landmark stands is now hard to miss. "Movement" in fact is just what, over the last three years, this line has come to be called. These three poets are not the only runners: Mr. Kingsley Amis, Mr. John Wain, Mr. Enright and Miss Elizabeth Jennings have already published books of verse (slim volumes by private presses chiefly) along the line too; novels by the first three of these make easily the best-known part (though I think a very distinct part) of the trend; and Mr. Davie's *Purity of Diction in English Verse* is a notable critical contribution. Certainly, the Movement writers toe no rigid party line. Even the three poets under review here diverge a good deal. But: the distinctive group of writers, writing activity over a broad front, critical re-thinking that serves it (and in fact also personal acquaintanceships which lie, one knows, behind it) – to fail, still, to see that something is happening is simply to reveal lack of interest: which is not to pre-judge the value of the "Movement," nor to assert that nothing else is happening. ("New Lines," 592)

Holloway's appreciation for Movement virtues is readily apparent, and he identifies all the members of the group by name except for Gunn and himself. But since his own poems had been issued by the two presses most closely identified with the Movement and since his review is a clear endorsement of Movement principles, his inclusion in the group should certainly be inferred.

The poetic "landmark" of the Movement emanates, Holloway asserts, from "the great post-Eliot paradox of English poetical development" ("New Lines," 592), created, on one hand, from a kind of avant-garde political romanticism rooted in the poetry of Auden, Spender, and Day Lewis and, on the other, from what he calls "a private, Dylan-Thomas inspired, Id-Romanticism: Mr. Barker, Mr. Gascoyne and others" ("New Lines," 592). While the Movement identified more with a left-wing, public-university poetic than with any bohemian and Bloomsbury counterparts, the backgrounds of its members were as a rule lower middle class from the industrial Midlands and North and were nonconformist in matters of religion. Holloway acknowledges that the Movement altered these two strains of English romanticism in part by blending them. While Movement poetry was often learned and university spawned (Holloway especially refused to compromise on matters of exegetical difficulty), it also came to be identified with the country's provincial rather than elitist universities. Though influence by the academy, Movement poets tended to stay in the regions where they were reared rather than near the universities in which they were educated, thereby interrupting "the automatic decanting process into upper-class England" ("New Lines," 593), which Amis and Wain had pointedly ridiculed in their *Lucky Jim* and *Hurry On Down*.

Even in its earliest days Holloway was already theorizing that the Movement's aesthetic portended a dramatic change in the tradition of English letters; "we are witnessing the end of something which has been established ever since the death of Keats and Hazlitt" ("New Lines," 593). He calls attention to the two languages of modern poetry: "the language that points towards inspiration or abandon, and that which points towards a dry, even cagey intelligence."[6] He reproves exponents of the first (Hopkins and Dylan Thomas) for their limited, recurring images and their diction, which edges "away from ordinary language towards declamation or meditation or incantation" ("Two Languages," 15), which discounts the rational faculties of the common man. Although language of the second sort is more commonly associated with the Movement, Holloway traces the origin of the poetic intelligence "back long past John Wain or Kingsley Amis to Empson; more still . . . to Auden; and further again, to the beginning of the vogue for Donne, to Eliot's early quatrain verse, and to the Rise of the Critic as Analyst" ("Two Languages," 16).

Modern society could accommodate the poet in his various roles as rebel, bohemian, and prophet, but Holloway suggests that the second type (the poet as clerk) carries an age-old status. Some poets belonging to the first group more appropriately warrant inclusion in the second. The second kind of poet gravitates to the universities and related arenas (Jennings in her library, Conquest in diplomacy, Enright in the foreign service) and his or her language dominates modern verse. Holloway points out in example that Dannie Abse and Howard Sergeant's *Mavericks* anthology was practically identical to the *New Lines* verse it intended to challenge. But anticipating the

Movement's critics and his own growing distance from the group, Holloway also contends that "the virtues promoted by this second language of poetry – shrewdness, adroitness, professionalism, freedom from excess – are mainly negative ones; and consequently prove old-fashioned much more easily than seems at first likely" ("Two Languages," 17-18).

Holloway's criticism addresses the conflict between traditional and modern poetry and points out the limits of New Criticism. In *The Charted Mirror: Literary and Critical Essays* (1962), this conflict is represented by two common misunderstandings about poetry: "its being either a personal effusion of soul, or an undifferentiated loftiness" (*Charted*, 170). His study categorizes the failure of romanticism's lyrical intent and examines the Augustan legacy of grandiloquence, lamenting that the contemporary poet all too often relies on the poetic diction that his fellow poets have been accumulating in compensation for their lack of originality. It is precisely this diction that "will be most likely by its very brilliance and difficulty to bluff readers for a time, even when there is nothing in it" (*Charted*, 67).

Recapitulating the position taken in *Language and Intelligence*, Holloway reiterates that literature is always more highly organized and suggestive than ordinary speech. He sees no need for contemporary poets to continue repeating their failures when traditional forms should have already proven their aptness. He calls for "a more intent, trained attention" (*Charted*, 185) to penetrate the difficulties of modern verse.

Though his own poems are often difficult, Holloway suggests that much misreading of poetry arises "from the application to large-scale works of an approach, alert for paradox, irony, ambiguity, unexpected combinations of image and idea, of thought and feeling, which was derived perhaps first from Mr. Eliot's essays on the language of Elizabethan dramatists and the metaphysical poets."[7] Holloway calls clarity the chief virtue in good poetry, and, speaking more as writer than critic, he scolds Eliot for believing that difficulty is an unavoidable feature of good verse. Poems should be read closely, but they should not be inherently so complex as to require some sort of reductive scientific scrutiny.

The poem – the successful poem, that is – decides because, being not an object for quasi-scientific routines of dissection, mechanically applied, but a work of art, it progressively shapes and prescribes its own interpretation. It requires, and indeed can tolerate, no supplementation from outside, no external clues. As the work of comprehension proceeds, the poem creates a fully defined reality which is what it is; and it is this which progressively shows, more and more clearly, what still waits to be added to reach that full and final definition, and what is alien to it. (*Charted*, 179)

Holloway distrusts the methods of textual analysis employed by I. A. Richards and the New Critics, believing they encourage the reader to adopt the mechanical processes of moralizing and theme detection. As an admirer of Leavis and Arnold, however, Holloway approves of moral criticism on the whole, though he does not contend "that moral seriousness or the carrying of a moral message can . . . in the last analysis, be the defining quality of literature" ("Dual," 367). The verities of art are more likely to be derived from a less arbitrary critical practice that does not rely on the axioms of science and logic or the constructs of social rectitude for substantiation.

Holloway presented these contentions poetically in *The Minute*. His first of "Two Friendly Sonnets" confirms,

> Look, we desire evidence. Evidence is found
> By thought; persistence; suspicion; enquiry. Drudging
> Through rubbish for the occasional jewel. Trudging
> Backwards and forwards over the same ground
> Till people ask you satirically what you've found.
> But they blench white, when you tell them. (*Minute*, 64)

And his 1960 volume, *The Fugue and Shorter Pieces*, though not as brooding as *The Minute*, shows the same dispassionate, analytic approach to poetry. In "A Letter to a Writer" he challenges Archibald MacLeish's sensuous "Ars Poetica," claiming "Poems dare not merely be. They mean. / They yield. They yield."[8]

Holloway's Shakespearean criticism, *The Story of the Night: Studies in Shakespeare's Major Tragedies* (1961), emphasizes meaning as well by drawing a distinction between a literary work's emotional and moral significance. He perceives a unifying pattern in the fall of Shakespeare's heroes and insists that the power of Shakespeare's tragedies rests more in their structure than in their psychological insights. Their moral statements are less important than the audience's participation in the ritual of tragedy, as the alienated victim is redeemed through his sacrifice and his isolation is transformed into community. Frank Kermode called the study "the best essays on the tragedies I have ever read,"[9] and he agreed with Holloway that Shakespeare's critics are plagued by a dearth of intellectual rigor and are often misguided by their own terminology.

Holloway focuses on moral concerns in *The Landfallers* too, his 1962 poem about displaced refugees being held for trial. It is a modern terza rima epic in 12 parts modeled after Dante's *Divine Comedy*, and it dramatizes the conflict between the individual's private and social obligations. Like Dante's opus, the poem examines the nature of good and evil, and in the fifth section, "Line and Colour," Holloway questions, "What can uprooted creatures do, but fail?"[10] In their trial his two main characters, Plennick and Vine, take on allegorical significance. When a third refugee, a woman named Anna, falls in love with Johnson, the judge's subordinate, Holloway celebrates their love as a victory of natural goodness. As in *The Story of the Night*, the poem affirms the value of lives commuted by tragedy. Holloway considers *The Landfallers* his best work, but, while set in the twentieth century, the work is plagued to some extent by its allegorical framework, its frequent borrowings (one section, "A Game of Chess," flaunts Holloway's familiarity with Eliot's "The Waste Land"), and its formal and archaic diction.

Holloway published two more books of essays in 1964: *The Colours of Clarity: Essays on Contemporary Literature and Education* and *The Lion Hunt: A Pursuit of Poetry and Reality*. In the first he thoughtfully considers the traditions of British poetry and calls attention to the demand for clarity in verse. While clarity as a prerequisite necessarily limits poetic experimentation by impelling poets to write on a smaller scale, all poetry, no matter how restricted, possesses significant power. Holloway laments that some poets have denied poetry as "an original source, a primal energy. This is the insight that, for poetry, has gone out of sight. . . . A work of art is an event, before it is a meaning: as also it is power, before it is beauty."[11] A narrow focus may make poetry appear somewhat unambitious, but Holloway maintains that the best modern poets don't even ask for their works to be included in a grouping of the world's great poems.

According to Holloway, the main failing of modern verse is structural; "most discussion of poetry today, most comments on it, would read equally well, even were the stanzas (say) of the poem to have been printed in jumbled order" (*Colours*, 93). He speculates that critics are too concerned with decorum, realism, and moralism which may not be essential values of poetry at all. "Today we do not have that defiant new start in literature, and ought not to expect it in criticism" (*Colours*, 146).

Holloway uses the frieze of the Lion Hunt of Assurbanipal, which once crowned the Parthenon in Athens, as a touchstone for his discussion of art's importance to life. Amplifying upon *The Colours of Clarity*, Holloway maintains that all art, no matter how modest its intent, "is written for ever,"[12] and he complains that in modern times art, science, intellect, and love have been perverted into means for making money. He accounts for how literature's power has been deflected toward base ends:

> The university student is taught the skills of the critic (though he cannot win the critic's maturity except by a lapse of years perhaps five times the span of a university course) so as to care for what is strong and reject what is sham. Later, in his advertisement-copy office, he turns those skills to writing what he must still know is trash (at fifty he will have forgotten) but thinks will sell. Just so, the power to coin words, the right of mintage, has now passed to those backers of Gresham whose concern is not to maintain, but to exploit, the currency of our tongue. (*Lion*, 52-53)

Like Davie, Holloway calls for a pure diction that separates the functions of poet and critic. Poetry orders reality through its surcharged vision and so should be approached not as "a lawyer going over a case, but a woman dancing with a man" (*Lion*, 32). It is not an interpretation of life but is life itself. He defends his dedication to literary study, postulating that "we are not – at least not yet – as lost as how our language seems to say. . . . But it is not me that is to blame, when I wish to speak of the delight of art, and am stopped by the language" (*Lion*, 27).

The writer's consciousness of language, therefore, must be like that of Hopkins, a "consciousness of everything – a quick and caring interest for detail" (*Lion*, 50). And in recalling Wordsworth's desire to be thought of as a teacher or as nothing, Holloway points out the failure of contemporary poets as teachers. Although they vouch that poetry is language, they do not understand what shapes their language and where its powers lie; they relegate themselves to proceeding "along the minor axis of poetry; a verse of assumptions and acceptances rather than of exploring and meditating; of resting not running. Since Eliot, the poet has been seen as a defender and even reformer of language; but this has meant only a loose and unenquiring respect for the 'real language spoken by men'; and what this meant has gone unquestioned too, so that 'vernacular' English has signified how persons who have graduated in English talk when they have not lost their calm or temper" (*Lion*, 76).

Holloway thinks language should provide both enrichment and regulation, inspiration as well as order, and he enumerates what specifically must be taught, calling them the three great duties of writers, critics, and teachers:

> to learn the absolute nothingness of any difference between humans save that between good and evil (race, religion . . . no one deserves to have the disgusting list so much as recapitulated); to recognize the new duty of an all-powered *homo sapiens*, custodian of a precarious, self-made Eden, to undertake the guardianship of all planetary life (when he was no more than one among its species, he might fend for himself, no more); and to realize that it now lies in his power alone to surround his existence with order and beauty. . . . Self-evidently, these three things are not yet to be learned from literature. (*Lion*, 67-68)

If modern man fails his duties, his art will be "not bankrupt but penniless" (*Lion*, 79). His concluding remarks address the poet/reader personally: "So, when you have read this small book, poet, do not pass it on . . . to someone else you think may be interested. Throw it away. Better a live Prince than a Dead Lion. Better a dead essay and a live poet. Better Poetry than a Programme" (*Lion*, 80).

The experiences at the University of Athens that inspired *The Lion Hunt* also flavored many of the poems in *Wood and Windfall* (1965), including a sequence of eight poems written for *The Greek Anthology*. He struggles with romantic idealism in the long poem "Reflections on a Journey," in which he returns home to England from Greece only to discover "Nothing had changed."[13] But the latent romantic tendency in the Movement to search for meaning in simple daily activities persists into *New Poems* (1970). Mostly traditional in rhyme and meter, the poems, despite their rural topics, reflect Holloway's essentially formal approach to what are potentially sentimental subjects. By emphasizing the contemporaneity of experience Holloway expresses what is timeless and perennial, and the poems move away from complexity and obscurity toward simplicity as he universalizes unimportant topics such as farm life and household chores.

The first poem, "Yes and No," is reminiscent of Coleridge's "Frost at Midnight" in its regard for the poet's infant son. Holloway asks that he be "serene, secure"[14] with words, but not all of the verses achieve the informality of "Yes and No." There is a parody of "Cock Robin," and elsewhere Holloway falls to citing Latin. "Shakespeare and the Bible" is primarily a poetic experiment in line division that connects its three stanzas by repeating five words: night, burn, wall, blind, and gold. Still "London, Greater London," a Juvenalian satire, reminds of Larkin's landscapes in "Going, Going – " and "The Whitsun Weddings": "But here it's all underpasses, motor-ways, twelve-mile jams, and / Articulated lorries jack-knifing downhill in the smog, / And a hundred deaths on the Road each Day of National Rejoicing" (*New*, 61).

Holloway renders the world with some difficulty as if his mature, complex vision necessitated a spectrum of styles. The wordplay and variety in *New Poems* consequently carried into *Planet of Winds* (1977), his seventh collection of poems. Some of the poems are lyrical, some meditative; some intellectual, some colloquial. He composes in both metered and free-verse lines. His experimentation seems a hopeful if dispassionate attempt to restore the world through the vitality of language. And as in *The Lion Hunt*, he offers a direct invitation to the reader. In "Slack Water" he implores:

> Close your book, look up reader, and outside
>   see if the sea is quickening, sharp
> of the flood tide in outcome and inroad
>   moving with the moon toward the land: but
>
> let the easy pulse and heart's blood stream
>   truth meteor-bright, its message is
> what I hope I shall not say
>   in code or clear until dust pays for all
>
> or nothing.[15]

The Proud Knowledge: Poetry, Insight, and the Self 1620-1920 (1977) takes its title from Bacon's *Advancement of Learning*, and in it Holloway traces the process of poetic creation from the Renaissance through the early twentieth century. He calls Milton the first modern because, unlike medieval and Renaissance poets, he followed Bacon's desire to plumb the secrets of the natural world. Holloway surveys the great poets and praises their individualized nature, and he views their willingness to speak to humanity's deepest aspect as evidence of their self-directed pursuit of the truth. He readily admits, however, that poetic techniques change with time, and he cites the epiphany poem as one genus that may have been forever altered by advances in optical physics and the visual arts, which enable the twentieth-century poet to perceive objects in ways never imagined by Wordsworth and his fellow romantics.

Like Davie, Holloway sees Thomas Hardy as a contrast in greatness. Hardy's ability to identify with everyday subjects was obtained through an idiosyncratic style; because he chose not to stand apart from his subjects, his technique appears artless. "He was the first genuinely novelist-poet. In his verse we find the rich and multifarious picture of everyday, common, even humble life, which is so much a part of the great nineteenth-century novels but (Hardy aside) seldom a part of nineteenth-century poetry. . . . Hardy was the writer who established and naturalized this concept in our poetry. That is one great measure of our debt to him."[16]

He praises Hardy again in *The Slumber of Apollo: Reflections on Recent Art, Literature, Language, and the Individual Consciousness* (1983), calling him the comprehensive soul of which Wordsworth spoke and "the first English poet to present the author of the poem, not simply the protagonist in it, as an anti-hero."[17] In Hardy's work the poet regresses from a divine Apollonian awareness toward a smaller, sadder, more Dionysian consciousness. It is unsurprising then that he should be appreciated by the Movement.

The Slumber of Apollo also appraises the concept of partial randomness as one of the three important concepts in twentieth-century art and literature, the other two being "a recession of concern with the object, and especially with awareness of external reality as a whole integrated order of externality . . . [and] an emphasis on intensity, immediacy and spontaneity" (*Slumber*, 22). Although critics have frequently equated randomness with chaos, Holloway prefers to view it, as did Wallace Stevens, as a sophisticated kind of order. In illustration he points to the irregularities in *In Memoriam* that enhance the overall organization of the work. By transposing heroic couplets in apparent randomness Tennyson was able to create 132 separate poems. The seeming disorder in the poem ironically contributes to its order.

Holloway's career as a poet and critic has been marked by this constant and restless devotion to questions of intellectual inquiry and artistic structure. Though influenced by the bardic poets he studied (Blake, Yeats, and others), Holloway never achieved their visionary magnificence. Nor could he in his demand for clarity logically call for a return to classical letters. As a result his poetry is neither as pessimistic nor as witty as his Movement comrades, and it is surely less violent than that of his later contemporaries Ted Hughes and Geoffrey Hill. Holloway is a stern detractor of the dull, minimal vocabulary found in so much postwar verse, yet his own cerebrations are too crabbed, stodgy, and compressed to have earned much popularity. His work, often mythopoeic in intent, is overly and unfashionably respectful of tradition and structure, though in matters of literary criticism he remains a staunch individualist, an articulate and literate scholar, and an ardent defender of close readings.

Notes

Chapter One

1. Elizabeth Jennings, *Poetry To-Day, 1957-60* (London: Longman, 1961), 9.

2. Robert Conquest, *New Lines* (London: Macmillan, 1957), xiv; hereafter cited in text as *NL*.

3. Philip Larkin, *Required Writing: Miscellaneous Pieces, 1955-1982* (London: Faber, 1983), 71; hereafter cited in text as *Required*.

4. Robert Conquest, quoted in *Larkin at Sixty* (London: Faber, 1982), 33; hereafter cited in text as *Sixty*.

5. Blake Morrison, *The Movement: English Poetry and Fiction of the 1950s* (New York: Methuen, 1986), 134-35; hereafter cited in text.

6. Leslie Fiedler, *No! In Thunder* (New York: Stein and Day, 1972), 200; hereafter cited in text.

7. David Perkins, *A History of Modern Poetry: Modernism and After* (Cambridge, Mass.: Belknap, 1987), 423; hereafter cited in text.

8. Egbert Fass, "Ted Hughes and *Crow*," *London Magazine*, January 1971, 10-11.

9. Elizabeth Jennings, interview in *The Poet Speaks*, ed. Peter Orr (London: Routledge and Kegan Paul, 1966), 91; hereafter cited in text as *Speaks*.

10. Kingsley Amis, *Memoirs* (New York: Summit, 1991), 45; hereafter cited in text as *Memoirs*.

11. Kingsley Amis, *What Became of Jane Austen? And Other Questions* (London: Cape, 1970), 176.

12. Thom Gunn, "A Sense of Movements," *Spectator*, 23 May 1958, 661.

13. Douglas Dunn, "Underwriter," *New Statesman*, 28 June 1974, 927.

Chapter Two

1. Philip Larkin, *Collected Poems* (New York: Farrar Straus, 1989), 82; hereafter cited in text as Larkin *CP*.

2. John Bayley, "Too Good for This World," *Times Literary Supplement*, 21 June 1974, 654.

3. Jonathan Raban, *Coasting* (New York: Simon and Schuster, 1987), 267; hereafter cited in text.

4. Philip Larkin, "Four Conversations," *London Magazine*, November 1964, 75; hereafter cited in text as "Conversations."

5. Bruce K. Martin, *Philip Larkin* (Boston: Twayne, 1978), 64.

Chapter Three

1. Philip Gardner, *Kingsley Amis* (Boston: Twayne, 1981), 14.

2. Philip Larkin, quoted in *World Authors 1950-1970*, ed. John Wakeman (New York: H. W. Wilson, 1975), 45; hereafter cited in text as *World*.

3. Philip Larkin, "Introduction" to *Jill* (Woodstock, N.Y.: Overlook, 1984), 14; hereafter cited in text as *Jill*.

4. Neil Brennan, "Kingsley Amis," in *Dictionary of Literary Biography*, vol. 27 (Detroit: Gale, 1978), 17; hereafter cited in text.

5. Kingsley Amis, "I Spy Strangers," in *My Enemy's Enemy* (London: Gollancz, 1962), 101.

6. John Wain, *Sprightly Running* (New York: St. Martin's, 1963), 188; hereafter cited in text as *Sprightly*.

7. Kingsley Amis, *Collected Poems 1944-1979* (New York: Viking, 1979), 20; hereafter cited in text as Amis *CP*.

8. Elizabeth Jennings, *Collected Poems* (London: Macmillan, 1967), 3; hereafter cited in text as Jennings *CP*.

9. Kingsley Amis, quoted in *Contemporary Authors*, New Revision Series, vol. 28 (Detroit: Gale, 1990), 10-11; hereafter cited in text as *CA*.

10. Donald Davie, *Purity of Diction in English Verse* (New York: Schocken, 1967), 197.

11. Kingsley Amis, *Poets of the 1950s*, ed. D. J. Enright (Tokyo: Kenkyusha, 1955), 17.

12. Kingsley Amis, "Hock and Soda-Water," *Spectator*, 31 December 1954, 832.

13. Anthony Burgess, *The Novel Now, A Guide to Contemporary Fiction* (New York: Norton, 1967), 141.

14. Somerset Maugham, "Books of the Year," *London Sunday Times*, 25 December 1955, 4.

15. Kingsley Amis, "Editor's Notes," *Spectator*, 7 October 1955, 49.

16. Kingsley Amis, quoted in John McDermott, *Kingsley Amis: An English Moralist* (New York: St. Martin's, 1989), 29; hereafter cited in text as McDermott.

17. Paul Johnson, "Lucky Jim's Political Testament," *New Statesman*, 12 January 1957, 36.

18. Howard Nemerov, *Poetry and Fiction* (New Brunswick, N.J.: Rutgers University Press, 1963), 220.

19. Alan Brien, "Amis Goes Pop," *New Statesman*, 7 July 1967, 15.

20. Ian Hamilton, "Dead Ends and Soft Centres," *Observer*, 12 November 1967, 28.

21. Donald Davie, *These the Companions* (Cambridge: Cambridge University Press, 1982), 94; hereafter cited in text as *Companions*.

22. "Coming Obituaries: 5: Kingsley Amis: Ex-wit and Ghost," *Punch*, 28 August 1968, 297.

23. Clive James, "The Examined Life," *New Statesman*, 13 April 1979, 521-22.

Chapter Four

1. D. J. Enright, *Collected Poems 1987* (Oxford: Oxford University Press, 1987), 151-52; hereafter cited in text as Enright *CP 87*.

2. D. J. Enright, *Conspirators and Poets* (London: Chatto and Windus, 1966), 42; hereafter cited in text as *Conspirators*.

3. Donald Davie, "Hearing about Damnation: The Collected Poems," in *Life by Other Means: Essays on D. J. Enright*, ed. Jacqueline Simms (Oxford: Oxford University Press, 1990), 150; hereafter cited in text as *Life*.

4. D. J. Enright, *Oxford Book of Contemporary Verse, 1945-1980* (Oxford: Oxford University Press, 1980), xxvii.

5. D. J. Enright, *The Apothecary's Shop: Essays on Literature* (London: Secker and Warburg, 1957), 226-27; hereafter cited in text as *Apothecary's*.

6. D. J. Enright, *Heaven Knows Where* (London: Secker and Warburg, 1957), 65.

7. D. J. Enright, *The World of Dew: Aspects of Living Japan* (London: Secker and Warburg, 1955), 97.

8. Margaret Willy, "D. J. Enright," in *Contemporary Poets*, ed. James Vinson (London: Macmillan, 1980), 446-47.

9. For a discussion of Enright's treatment of the Faust legend, see Leonard Forster, "A Faust Book," in *Life by Other Means*.

10. D. J. Enright, *Memoirs of a Mendicant Professor* (London: Chatto and Windus, 1969), 108.

11. This lecture was initially published in D. J. Enright, *Robert Graves and the Decline of Modernism* (Singapore: Craftsman Press, 1960), and is reprinted in *Conspirators and Poets*.

12. William Walsh, *D. J. Enright: Poet of Humanism* (London: Cambridge University Press, 1974, 90; hereafter cited in text.

13. D. J. Enright, *Shakespeare and the Students* (London: Chatto and Windus, 1970), 10.

14. D. J. Enright, *Fields of Vision: Essays on Literature, Language, and Television* (New York: Oxford University Press, 1988), 146.

Chapter Five

1. Robert Conquest, *Poems* (London: Macmillan, 1955), 61; hereafter cited in text as RC *Poems*.

2. Robert Conquest, "Context," *London Magazine*, February 1962, 33-34; hereafter cited in text as "Context."

3. Robert Conquest, *A World of Difference* (New York: Ballantine, 1964), 188; hereafter cited in text as *Difference*.

4. John Holloway, "New Lines in English Poetry," *Hudson Review* 9 (1956-57), 595; hereafter cited in text as "New Lines."

5. "Poetic Personality," *Times Literary Supplement*, 30 September 1955, 574.

6. Robert Conquest, *New Lines II* (London: Macmillan, 1963), 13; hereafter cited in text as *NL2*.

7. John Press, "Robert Conquest," in *Dictionary of Literary Biography*, vol. 27 (Detroit: Gale, 1978), 57.

8. Charles Tomlinson, "The Middlebrow Muse," *Essays in Criticism*, April 1957, 216; hereafter cited in text.

9. D. J. Enright, "*New Lines* and Mr. Tomlinson," *Essays in Criticism*, July 1957, 344.

10. Robert Conquest, "New Critics and New Lines," *Essays in Criticism*, April 1958, 226; hereafter quoted in text as "Critics."

11. Robert Conquest, *The Abomination of Moab* (London: Maurice Temple Smith, 1979), 11; hereafter cited in text as *Moab*.

12. Thom Gunn, "Things, Voices, Minds," *Yale Review*, October 1962, 135; hereafter cited in text.

13. Robert Conquest, *Between Mars and Venus* (New York: St. Martin's, 1962), 29; hereafter cited in text as *Mars*.

14. William Van O'Connor, *The New University Wits and the End of Modernism* (Carbondale: Southern Illinois University Press, 1963), 106.

15. Robert Conquest, "Ten Comments on a Questionnaire," *London Magazine*, November 1964, 28-29; hereafter cited in text as "Comments."

Chapter Six

1. John Wain, *Essays on Literature and Ideas* (London: Macmillan, 1963), 178-79.

2. John Wain, *The Smaller Sky* (London: Macmillan, 1967), 142.

3. John Wain, *Preliminary Essays* (London: Macmillan, 1957), 181-82; hereafter cited in text as *Preliminary*.

4. John Wain, *Poems 1949-1979* (London: Macmillan, 1980), 179; hereafter cited in text as Wain *Poems*.

5. John Wain, *Professing Poetry* (London: Macmillan, 1977), 274-75; hereafter cited in text as *Professing*.

6. John Wain, *A House for the Truth: Critical Essays* (New York: Viking, 1973), 29; hereafter cited in text as *House*.

Chapter Seven

1. Elizabeth Jennings, "Elizabeth Jennings," in *Contemporary Authors Autobiography Series* (Detroit: Gale, 1987), 107; hereafter cited in text as *Contemporary*.

2. Elizabeth Jennings, "The Difficult Balance," *London Magazine*, November 1959, 28; hereafter cited in text as "Difficult."

3. John Wain, *Letters to Five Artists* (New York: Viking, 1969), 55.

4. Elizabeth Jennings, *An Anthology of Modern Verse 1940-60* (London: Methuen, 1961), 7; hereafter cited in text as *Anthology*.

5. Anthony Thwaite, *Twentieth-Century English Poetry: An Introduction* (New York: Barnes and Noble, 1978), 44.

6. Anthony Thwaite, "Elizabeth Jennings," *Contemporary Poets* (London: St. James, 1970), 559-60.

7. Julian Symons, "Clean and Clear," *New Statesman*, 13 October 1967, 476.

8. Alisdair Maclean, "Marble Fun," *Listener*, 22 March 1973, 389; hereafter cited in text.

9. Elizabeth Jennings, *Relationships* (London: Macmillan, 1972), 19.

10. Elizabeth Jennings, *Consequently I Rejoice* (Manchester: Carcanet, 1987), 54; hereafter cited in text as *Consequently*.

11. John Matthias, "Pointless and Poignant," *Poetry*, March 1977, 350.

12. William Blissett, "Elizabeth Jennings," in *Dictionary of Literary Biography*, vol. 27 (Detroit: Gale, 1978), 170.

Chapter Eight

1. Donald Davie, *Purity of Diction in English Verse* (London: Chatto, 1952), 16; hereafter cited in text as *Purity*.

2. Donald Davie, *Articulate Energy: An Enquiry into the Syntax of English Poetry* (London: Routledge, 1955), 19; hereafter cited in text as *Articulate*.

3. "Donald Davie," in *Literary Critics*, ed. Elmer Borklund (Detroit: Gale, 1982), 152.

4. Donald Davie, *Collected Poems 1950-1970* (New York: Oxford University Press, 1972), 1; hereafter cited in text as Davie *CP 1950*.

5. F. W. Bateson, "Auden's (and Empson's) Heirs," *Essays in Criticism*, January 1957, 76; hereafter cited in text.

6. Donald Davie, *Trying to Explain* (Ann Arbor: University of Michigan Press, 1979) 28; hereafter cited in text as *Explain*.

7. Howard Erskine-Hill, "Two Hundred Years Since: Davie, the Eighteenth Century and the Image of England," in *Donald Davie and the Responsibilities of Literature*, ed. George Dekker (Manchester: Carcanet, 1983) 117; hereafter cited in text as *Responsibilities*.

8. Donald Davie, *Thomas Hardy and British Poetry* (New York: Oxford University Press, 1972), 358.

9. Donald Davie, *Collected Poems 1971-1983* (Manchester: Carcanet, 1983) 57; hereafter cited in text as Davie *CP 1971*.

10. Donald Davie, *The Poet in the Imaginary Museum* (New York: Persea, 1977) 73; hereafter cited in text as *Museum*.

Chapter Nine

1. Thom Gunn, *The Occasions of Poetry* (London: Faber, 1982), 172; hereafter cited in text as *Occasions*.

2. Thom Gunn, *Fighting Terms* (London: Faber, 1962), 20.

3. John Press, *Rule and Energy* (London: Oxford University Press, 1963), 192; hereafter cited in text.

4. Thom Gunn, *The Sense of Movement* (London: Faber, 1967), 45; hereafter cited in text as *Sense*.

5. Martin Dodsworth, "The Climate of Pain in Recent Poetry," *London Magazine*, November 1964, 87.

6. John Thompson, "A Poetry Chronicle," *Poetry*, November 1959, 110-11.

7. Thom Gunn, *Moly and My Sad Captains* (New York: Farrar, Straus, 1973), 49; hereafter cited in text as *Captains*. Though once published separately, *Moly* and *My Sad Captains* were released in one volume in 1973; all citations are to this edition.

8. Alan Bold, *Thom Gunn and Ted Hughes* (Edinburgh: Oliver and Boyd, 1976), 38-39; hereafter cited in text.

9. Thom Gunn, *Selected Poems 1950-1975* (New York: Farrar, Straus, 1979), 79.

10. Donald Davie, *Under Briggflatts: A History of Poetry in Great Britain 1960-1988.* (Chicago: University of Chicago Press, 1989), 84-85; hereafter cited in text.

11. Blake Morrison, "Thom Gunn," *Dictionary of Literary Biography* 27 (Detroit: Gale, 1984), 126.

Chapter Ten

1. John Holloway, *The Charted Mirror: Literary and Critical Essays* (London: Routledge, 1960), 137; hereafter cited in text as *Charted*.

2. John Holloway, *Language and Intelligence* (London: Macmillan, 1951), 1; hereafter cited in text as *Language*.

3. John Holloway, *Poems* (Oxford: Fantasy Poets Number 26, 1954), 4.

4. John Holloway, *The Minute and Longer Poems* (Hessle, England: Marvell, 1956), 33; hereafter cited in text as *Minute*.

5. William Meredith, "Images and Reality," *New York Times Book Review*, 3 May 1959, 27.

6. John Holloway, "The Two Languages," contained in "English Poetry Since 1945," *London*, November 1959, 15; hereafter cited in text as "Two Languages."

7. John Holloway, "The Dual Role of Critic and Poet," *Times Literary Supplement*, 10 June 1960, 367; hereafter cited in text as "Dual."

8. John Holloway, *The Fugue and Shorter Pieces* (London: Routledge, 1960), 25.

9. Frank Kermode, "New Minted," *New Statesman*, 29 December 1961, 991.

10. John Holloway, *The Landfallers: A Poem in Twelve Parts* (London: Routledge, 1962), 20.

11. John Holloway, *The Colours of Clarity: Essays on Contemporary Literature and Education* (London: Routledge, 1964), 94, 144; hereafter cited in text as *Colours*.

12. John Holloway, *The Lion Hunt: A Pursuit of Poetry and Reality* (London: Routledge, 1964), 26; hereafter cited in text as *Lion*.

13. John Holloway, *Wood and Windfall* (London: Routledge, 1965), 72.

14. John Holloway, *New Poems* (New York: Scribners, 1970), 13; hereafter cited in text as *New*.

15. John Holloway, *Planet of Winds* (Boston: Routledge, 1977), 72.

16. John Holloway, *The Proud Knowledge: Poetry, Insight, and the Self 1620-1920* (Boston: Routledge, 1977), 236-37.

17. John Holloway, *The Slumber of Apollo: Reflections on Recent Art, Literature, Language, and the Individual Consciousness* (Cambridge: Cambridge University Press, 1983), 96; hereafter cited in text as *Slumber*.

Selected Bibliography

PRIMARY WORKS

Kingsley Amis

Poetry

Bright November. London: Fortune, 1947.
A Case of Samples: Poems 1946-1956. London: Gollancz, 1956; New York: Harcourt Brace, 1957.
Collected Poems, 1944-1979. London: Hutchinson, 1979; New York: Viking, 1980.
The Evans Country. Oxford: Fantasy, 1962.
A Frame of Mind: Eighteen Poems. Reading, England: University of Reading School of Art, 1953.
A Look round the Estate: Poems 1957-1967. London: Cape, 1967; New York: Harcourt Brace, 1968.
Penguin Modern Poets 2, with Dom Moraes and Peter Porter. London: Penguin, 1962.
[Poems]. Fantasy Poets Series no. 22. Swinford, England: Fantasy, 1954.
Wasted, Kipling at Bateman's. London: Poem-of-the-Month Club, 1973.

Autobiography

Memoirs. London: Hutchinson; New York: Summit, 1991.

Novels

The Alteration. London: Cape, 1976; New York: Viking, 1977; New York: Carroll and Graf, 1988.
The Anti-Death League. London: Gollancz; New York: Harcourt Brace, 1966; London: Gollancz, 1978; Harmondsworth, England: Penguin, 1980.
Colonel Sun: A James Bond Adventure, as Robert Markham. London: Cape; New York: Harper, 1968.
The Crime of the Century. London: J. M. Dent, 1987; New York: Mysterious, 1989.
Difficulties with Girls. London: Hutchinson, 1988; New York: Summit, 1989.

The Egyptologists, with Robert Conquest. London: Cape, 1965; New York: Random House, 1966; London: Panther, 1975.

Ending Up. London: Cape; New York: Harcourt Brace, 1974.

The Folks That Live on the Hill: A Novel. New York: Summit, 1990.

Girl, 20. London: Cape, 1971; New York: Harcourt Brace, 1972; New York: Summit, 1989.

The Green Man. London: Cape, 1969; New York: Harcourt Brace, 1970; Chicago: Academy of Chicago, 1986.

I Like It Here. London: Gollancz; New York: Harcourt Brace, 1958; London: Panther Books, 1975; London: Gollancz, 1984.

I Want It Now. London: Cape, 1968, collected edition, 1976; New York: Harcourt Brace, 1969.

Jake's Thing. London: Hutchinson, 1978; New York: Viking, 1979.

A Kingsley Amis Omnibus, includes *Jake's Thing*, *The Old Devils*, and *Stanley and the Women*. London: Hutchinson, 1987; Constable, 1990.

Lucky Jim. London: Gollancz; Garden City, N.Y.: Doubleday, 1954; London: Longmans, 1963; abridged, London: Macmillan, 1967; Dana Point, Calif.: Queen's House, 1976.

The Old Devils. London: Hutchinson, 1986; New York: Summit, 1987.

One Fat Englishman. London: Gollancz, 1963; New York: Harcourt Brace, 1964; Harmondsworth, England: Penguin, 1980; New York: Summit, 1989.

The Riverside Villas Murder. London: Cape; New York: Harcourt Brace, 1973.

Russian Hide-and-Seek: A Melodrama. London: Hutchinson, 1980; Harmondsworth, England: Penguin, 1981.

Stanley and the Women. London: Hutchinson, 1984; New York: Summit, 1985; New York: Harper, 1988.

Take a Girl Like You. London: Gollancz, 1960; New York: Harcourt Brace, 1961; Harmondsworth, England: Penguin, 1976.

That Uncertain Feeling. London: Gollancz, 1955; New York: Harcourt Brace, 1956; London: Panther Books, 1975.

Short Stories

Collected Short Stories. London: Hutchinson, 1980; with additional stories, 1987.

The Darkwater Hall Mystery. Edinburgh: Tragara, 1978.

Dear Illusion. London: Covent Garden, 1972.

My Enemy's Enemy. London: Gollancz, 1962; New York: Harcourt Brace, 1963; Harmondsworth, England: Penguin, 1980.

Penguin Modern Stories 11, with others. London: Penguin, 1972.

Essays and Criticism

An Arts Policy? London: Centre for Policy Studies, 1979.

The Book of Bond, or Every Man His Own 007, as William Tanner. London: Cape; New York: Viking, 1965.

Every Day Drinking. London: Hutchinson, 1983.

First Aid for ABA Conventioneers. New York: Harcourt, 1973; excerpt from *On Drink*.

How's Your Glass? A Quizzical Look at Drinks and Drinking. London: Weidenfeld and Nicolson, 1984; Arrow, 1986.

The James Bond Dossier. London: Cape; New York: New American Library, 1965.

Lucky Jim's Politics. Summer School Studies Series no. 410. London: Conservative Political Centre, 1968.

New Maps of Hell: A Survey of Science Fiction. New York: Harcourt Brace, 1960; London: Gollancz, 1961; London: Arno, 1975; Salem, N.H.: Ayer, 1975.

On Drink. London: Cape, 1972; New York: Harcourt Brace, 1973.

Rudyard Kipling and His World. London: Thames and Hudson, 1975; New York: Scribner, 1976.

Socialism and the Intellectuals. London: Fabian Society, 1957.

What Became of Jane Austen? and Other Questions. London: Cape, 1970; New York: Harcourt Brace, 1971; London: Panther, 1972. Published as *What Became of Jane Austen and Other Essays* in Harmondsworth, England: Penguin, 1981.

Editions

The Amis Anthology. London: Hutchinson, 1988.

The Faber Popular Reciter. London: Faber, 1978.

The Golden Age of Science Fiction. London: Hutchinson, 1981.

The Great British Songbook, with James Cochrane. London: Pavilion/Michael Joseph, 1986.

Harold's Years: Impressions of the Harold Wilson Era. London: Quartet, 1977.

The New Oxford Book of English Light Verse. London and New York: Oxford University Press, 1978; published in England as *The New Oxford Book of Light Verse*.

Oxford Poetry 1949, with James Michie. Oxford: Blackwell, 1949.

Poems and Essays of Oscar Wilde. London: Harvill-Collins, 1956.

Selected Short Stories of G. K. Chesterton. London: Faber, 1972.

Spectrum: A Science Fiction Anthology, annual with Robert Conquest. Vol. 1: London: Gollancz, 1961; New York: Harcourt Brace, 1962. Vol. 2:

London: Gollancz, 1962; New York: Harcourt Brace, 1963. Vol. 3: London: Gollancz, 1963; New York: Harcourt Brace, 1964. Vol. 4: London: Gollancz, 1965; New York: Harcourt Brace, 1966. Vol. 5: London: Gollancz, 1966; New York: Harcourt Brace, 1967.

Tennyson. London: Penguin, 1973.

Teleplays and Motion Pictures

Break In, 1975.

Dr. Watson and the Darkwater Hall Mystery, from his story, 1974.

The Green Man, from his novel, 1989.

The Importance of Being Harry, 1971.

A Question about Hell, 1964.

See What You've Done (Softly, Softly series), 1974.

We Are All Guilty (Against the Crowd series), 1975.

Radio Plays

The Riverside Villas Murder, from his novel, 1976.

Something Strange, 1962.

Touch and Go, 1957.

Recordings

Kingsley Amis Reading His Own Poems. London: Listen, 1962.

Poems, with Thomas Blackburn. London: Jupiter, 1962.

Robert Conquest

Poetry

Arias from a Love Opera, and Other Poems. London and New York: Macmillan, 1969.

Between Mars and Venus. London: Hutchinson; New York: St. Martin's, 1962.

Casualty Ward. London: Poem-of-the-Month Club, 1974.

Coming Across. Menlo Park, New York: Buckabest, 1978.

Forays. London: Chatto and Windus, 1979.

Poems. London: Macmillan; New York: St. Martin's, 1955.

Novels

The Egyptologists, with Kingsley Amis. London: Cape, 1965; New York: Random House, 1966; London: Panther, 1975.

A World of Difference. London: Ward Lock, 1955; New York: Ballantine, 1964.

Essays and Criticism

The Abomination of Moab, with poetry. London: Maurice Temple Smith, 1979.

Editions

Back to Life: Poems from Behind the Iron Curtain. London: Hutchinson; New York: St. Martin's, 1958.

New Lines. London: Macmillan; New York: St. Martin's, 1956.

New Lines II. London and New York: Macmillan, 1963.

New Poems: A P.E.N. Anthology, with others. London: Transatlantic, 1963.

Spectrum: A Science Fiction Anthology, annual with Kingsley Amis. Vol. 1: London: Gollancz, 1961; New York: Harcourt Brace, 1962. Vol. 2: London: Gollancz, 1962; New York: Harcourt Brace, 1963. Vol. 3: London: Gollancz, 1963; New York: Harcourt Brace, 1964. Vol. 4: London: Gollancz, 1965; New York: Harcourt Brace, 1966. Vol. 5: London: Gollancz, 1966; New York: Harcourt Brace, 1967.

Interviews

The Poet Speaks, edited by Peter Orr, 45-50. London: Routledge, 1966.

Translations

Prussian Nights: A Narrative Poem by Aleksandr Isaevich Solzhenitsyn. London: Harvill-Collins, 1977; New York: Farrar Straus, 1978.

Social Science and Political Writings

Common Sense about Russia. London: Gollancz; New York: Macmillan, 1960.

The Courage of Genius: The Pasternak Affair. London: Collins-Harvill; Philadelphia: Lippincott, 1961. Republished as *The Pasternak Affair*.

The Future of Communism. Today Publications, 1963.

The Great Terror: A Reassessment. New York: Oxford University Press, 1990.

The Great Terror: Stalin's Purge of the Thirties. London and New York: Macmillan, 1968; revised, Harmondsworth, England: Penguin, 1973.

The Harvest of Sorrow: Soviet Collectivization and the Terror-Famine. New York and Oxford: Oxford University Press, 1976, 1987.

"The Human Rights Issue." In *Defending America*, edited by James R. Schlesinger, 205-16. New York: Basic, 1977.

Inside Stalin's Secret Police: NKVD Politics, 1936-1939. Stanford: Hoover Institution; London: Macmillan, 1985.

"Introduction." In *The Ukrainian Herald, Issue 7-8: Ethnocide of Ukrainians in the U.S.S.R.*, edited by Maksym Sahaydak. Ellicott City, Md.: Smoloskyp, 1981.

Kolyma: The Arctic Death Camps. London: Macmillan; New York: Viking, 1978.

Lenin. London: Fontana, 1972; republished as *V. I. Lenin*.

The Man-made Famine in Ukraine, with others. Washington, D.C.: American Enterprise Institute for Public Policy, 1984.

Marxism Today. London: Ampersand, 1964.

The Nation Killers: The Soviet Deportation of Nationalities. London: Macmillan; New York: St. Martin's, 1970.

The Pasternak Affair: Courage of Genius. Philadelphia: Lippincott, 1962; Octagon, 1979.

Power and Policy in the U.S.S.R.: The Study of Soviet Dynastics. London: Macmillan; New York: St. Martin's, 1961.

Present Danger -- Towards a Foreign Policy: Guide to the Era of Soviet Aggression. Oxford: Blackwell; Stanford, Calif.: Hoover Institution, 1979.

Russia after Kruschev. London: Pall Mall; New York: Praeger, 1965.

The Soviet Deportation of Nationalities. London: Macmillan; New York: St. Martin's, 1960. Rev. and enl. as *The Nation Killers*.

Stalin and the Kirov Murder. New York and Oxford: Oxford University Press, 1989.

Tyrants and Typewriters: Communiques from the Struggle for Truth. Lexington, Mass.: Lexington, 1989.

V. I. Lenin. New York: Viking, 1972.

We and They: Civic and Despotic Cultures. London: Maurice Temple Smith, 1980.

What to Do When the Russians Come: A Survivor's Guide, with Jon Manchip White. New York: Stein and Day; Chelsea, Mich.: Scarborough, 1984.

Where Do Marxists Go from Here? under pseudonym J. E. M. Arden. London: Phoenix House, 1958.

Where Marx Went Wrong. London: T. Stacey, 1970.

Editions of Social Science and Political Writings

Agricultural Workers in the U.S.S.R. London: Bodley Head; New York: Praeger, 1968.

A Childhood in Prison by Petr. I. Yakir. London: Macmillan, 1972; New York: Coward, McCann, and Geoghegan, 1973.

Industrial Workers in the U.S.S.R. London: Bodley Head; New York: Praeger, 1967.

Justice and the Legal System in the U.S.S.R. London: Bodley Head; New York: Praeger, 1968.

The Last Empire: Nationality and the Soviet Future. London: Ampersand; Stanford, Calif.: Hoover Institution, 1962.

The Politics of Ideas in the U.S.S.R. London: Bodley Head; New York: Praeger, 1967.

Religion in the U.S.S.R. London: Bodley Head; New York: Praeger, 1968.

The Robert Sheckley Omnibus. London: Gollancz, 1973.

The Russian Tradition by Tibor Szamuely. London: Secker and Warburg, 1974; New York: McGraw Hill, 1975.

Soviet Nationalities Policy in Practice. London: Bodley Head; New York: Praeger, 1967.

The Soviet Police System. London: Bodley Head; New York: Praeger, 1968.

The Soviet Political System. London: Bodley Head; New York: Praeger, 1968.

Donald Davie

Poetry

Brides of Reason. Swinford, England: Fantasy, 1955.

Collected Poems 1950-1970. London: Routledge; New York: Oxford University Press, 1972.

Collected Poems, 1970-1983. Manchester: Carcanet; Notre Dame: University of Notre Dame Press, 1983.

Essex Poems: 1963-1967. London: Routledge, 1969.

Events and Wisdoms: Poems 1957-1963. London: Routledge, 1964; Middletown, Conn.: Wesleyan University Press, 1965.

The Forests of Lithuania, adapted from Adam Mickiewicz. Hessle, England: Marvell, 1959.

In the Stopping Train and Other Poems. Manchester: Carcanet, 1977; New York: Oxford University Press, 1980.

New and Selected Poems. Middletown, Conn.: Wesleyan University Press, 1961.

Orpheus. London: Poem-of-the-Month Club, 1974.

[Poems]. Fantasy Poets Series no. 19. Swinford, England: Fantasy, 1954.

Poems. London: Turret, 1969.

A Sequence for Francis Parkman. Hessle, England: Marvell, 1961.

The Shires: Poems. London: Routledge, 1974; New York: Oxford University Press, 1975.

Six Epistles to Eva Hesse. London: London Magazine Editions, 1970.

Three for Water-Music and the Shires. Manchester: Carcanet, 1981.

To Scorch of Freeze: Poems about the Sacred. London: Phoenix House, 1988.

A Winter Talent and Other Poems. London: Routledge, 1957.

Autobiography

These the Companions: Recollections. Cambridge: Cambridge University Press, 1982.

Essays and Criticism

Articulate Energy: An Enquiry into the Syntax of English Poetry. London: Routledge, 1955, 1966; New York: Harcourt, Brace, 1958; Irvine, Calif.: Reprint Services, 1988.

Czeslaw Milosz and the Insufficiency of Lyric. Knoxville, Tenn.: University of Tennessee Press, 1986.

Dissentient Voice: Enlightenment and Christian Dissent. Notre Dame: University Press of Notre Dame, 1982.

English Hymnology in the Eighteenth Century: Papers Read at a Clark Library Seminar, 5 March 1977, with Robert Stevenson. Los Angeles: William Andrews Clark Memorial Library, 1980.

Ezra Pound: Poet as Sculptor. London: Routledge; New York: Oxford University Press, 1964; London: Routledge, 1965.

A Gathered Church: The Literature of the English Dissenting Interest, 1700-1930. London: Routledge; New York: Oxford University Press, 1978.

The Heyday of Sir Walter Scott. London: Routledge; New York: Barnes and Noble, 1961.

Kenneth Allott and the Thirties. Liverpool: University of Liverpool Press, 1980.

The Language of Science and the Language of Literature, 1700-1740. London and New York: Sheed and Ward, 1963.

The Poet in the Imaginary Museum: Essays of Two Decades. Edited by Barry Alpert. Manchester: Carcanet; New York: Persea, 1977.

Poetry in Translation. Buckinghamshire, England: Open University, 1975.

The Poetry of Sir Walter Scott. London: Oxford University Press, 1961.

Pound. London: Fontana, 1975; New York: Viking, 1976.

Purity of Diction in English Verse. London: Chatto and Windus, 1952; New York: Oxford University Press, 1953; 2d ed. with postscript, London: Routledge; New York: Schocken, 1967.

Slavic Excursions: Essays on Russian and Polish Literature. Chicago: University of Chicago Press, 1990.

Thomas Hardy and British Poetry. New York: Oxford University Press, 1972; London: Routledge, 1973.

Trying to Explain. Ann Arbor: University of Michigan Press, 1979; Manchester: Carcanet, 1980.

Under Briggflatts: A History of Poetry in Great Britain 1960-1988. Chicago: University of Chicago Press, 1989.

Recordings

Donald Davie. Bournemouth, England: Canto, 1985.

Donald Davie Reading at Stanford. Stanford, Calif.: Stanford Program for Recording in Sound, 1974.

Translations

The Poems of Dr. Zhivago, by Boris Pasternak, with commentary. Manchester: Manchester University Press; New York: Barnes and Noble, 1965.

Editions

Augustan Lyric. London: Heinemann, 1974.

Collected Poems by Yvor Winters. Manchester: Carcanet, 1978; Athens, Ohio: Swallow, 1980.

Collected Poems of Elizabeth Daryush. Manchester: Carcanet, 1976.

English Hymnology in the Eighteenth Century, with Robert Stevenson. Los Angeles: Clark Memorial Library (University of California), 1977.

The Late Augustans: Longer Poems of the Eighteenth Century. London: Heinemann, 1958, 1963; New York: Macmillan, 1958.

The New Oxford Book of Christian Verse. Oxford: Oxford University Press, 1981; New York: Oxford University Press, 1982.

Pasternak: Modern Judgements, with Angela Livingstone, with verse translations. London: Macmillan, 1969; Nashville: Aurora, 1970.

Poems: Poetry Supplement. London: Poetry Book Society, 1960.

Poetics, Part 1. The Hague: Mouton, 1961.

Poetics Poetyka. Warsaw: Panstwowe Wydawnictwo, 1961.

Russian Literature and Modern English Fiction: A Collection of Critical Essays. Chicago: University of Chicago Press; Toronto: University of Toronto Press, 1965.

Selected Poems of William Wordsworth. London: Harrap, 1962.

The Victims of Whiggery by George Loveless. Hobart, Tasmania: privately printed, 1946.

D. J. Enright

Poetry

Addictions. London: Chatto and Windus, 1962.

Bread Rather than Blossoms. London: Secker and Warburg, 1956.
Collected Poems, with new poems. Oxford: Oxford University Press, 1981.
Collected Poems 1987. Enl. ed. Oxford: Oxford University Press, 1987.
Daughters of Earth. London: Chatto and Windus, 1972.
A Faust Book. London and New York: Oxford University Press, 1979.
Foreign Devils. London: Covent Garden, 1972.
In the Basilica of the Annunciation. London: Poem-of-the-Month Club, 1971.
Instant Chronicles: A Life. Oxford: Oxford University Press, 1985.
The Laughing Hyena and Other Poems. London: Routledge, 1953.
The Old Adam. London: Chatto and Windus, 1965.
Paradise Illustrated. London: Chatto and Windus, 1978.
Penguin Modern Poets 26, with Dannie Abse and Michael Longley. London: Penguin, 1975.
Rhyme Times Rhyme, juvenile. London: Chatto and Windus, 1974.
Sad Ires and Others. London: Chatto and Windus, 1975.
Season Ticket. Alexandria: Aux Editions du Scarabee, 1948.
Selected Poems. London: Chatto and Windus, 1968.
Selected Poems 1990. Oxford: Oxford University Press, 1990.
Some Men Are Brothers. London: Chatto and Windus, 1960.
The Terrible Shears: Scenes from a Twenties Childhood. London: Chatto and Windus, 1973; Middletown, Conn.: Wesleyan University Press, 1974.
The Typewriter Revolution and Other Poems. New York: Library Press, 1971.
Unlawful Assembly. London: Chatto and Windus; Middletown, Conn.: Wesleyan University Press, 1968.
The Year of the Monkey. Privately printed, 1956.

Autobiography

Instant Chronicles: A Life. London: Oxford University Press, 1985.
Memoirs of a Mendicant Professor. London: Chatto and Windus, 1969; Carcanet, 1990.

Novels

Academic Year. London: Secker and Warburg, 1955; Buchan and Enright, 1984; Oxford University Press, 1985.
Beyond Land's End. London: Chatto and Windus, 1979. Juvenile.
Figures of Speech. London: Heinemann, 1965.
Heaven Knows Where. London: Secker and Warburg, 1957.

Insufficient Poppy. London: Chatto and Windus, 1960.

The Joke Shop. London: Chatto and Windus; New York: David McKay, 1976. Juvenile.

Wild Ghost Chase. London: Chatto and Windus, 1978. Juvenile.

Essays and Criticism

The Alluring Problem: An Essay on Irony. Oxford: Oxford University Press, 1986.

The Apothecary's Shop: Essays on Literature. London: Secker and Warburg, 1957; Chester Springs, Penn.: Dufour, 1959; Westport, Conn.: Greenwood Press, 1975.

A Commentary on Goethe's "Faust." New York: New Directions, 1949.

Conspirators and Poets. London: Chatto and Windus; Chester Springs, Penn.: Dufour, 1966.

Fields of Vision: Essays on Literature, Language, and Television. Oxford and New York: Oxford University Press, 1988.

A Kidnapped Child of Heaven: The Poetry of Arthur Hugh Clough. Nottingham: Nottingham University Press, 1972.

Literature for Man's Sake: Critical Essays. Tokyo: Kenkyusha, 1955; Folcroft, Penn.: Folcroft Library Editions, 1972; Philadelphia: Richard West, 1976.

Man Is an Onion: Reviews and Essays. London: Chatto and Windus, 1972; LaSalle, Illinois: Library Press, 1973.

A Mania for Sentences. London: Chatto and Windus, 1983; Boston: Godine, 1985.

Robert Graves and the Decline of Modernism. Singapore: Craftsman, 1960; Folcroft, Penn.: Folcroft, 1974. Reprinted in *Conspirators and Poets*.

Shakespeare and the Students. London: Chatto and Windus, 1970; New York: Schocken, 1971.

The World of Dew: Aspects of Living Japan. London: Secker and Warburg, 1955; Rutland, Vt.: Tuttle, 1956; Chester Springs, Penn.: Dufour, 1959.

Editions

A Choice of Milton's Verse. London: Faber, 1975.

English Critical Texts, Sixteenth Century to Twentieth Century, with Ernst de Chickera. Oxford: Oxford University Press, 1962.

Faber Book of Fevers and Frets. London: Faber, 1989.

Fair of Speech: The Uses of Euphemism. Oxford: Oxford University Press, 1985.

The History of Rasselas, Prince of Abissinia by Samuel Johnson, with introduction. London: Penguin, 1976.

Ill at Ease: Writers on Ailments Real and Imagined. London: Faber, 1989.

Oxford Book of Contemporary Verse, 1945-1980, with introduction. Oxford: Oxford University Press, 1980.

Oxford Book of Death, with introduction. Oxford: Oxford University Press, 1983.

The Poetry of Living Japan, with Takamichi Ninomiya. London: John Murray, Grove, 1957; Westport, Conn.: Greenwood, 1979.

Poetry of the 1950s: An Anthology of New English Verse. Tokyo: Kenkyusha, 1955.

Thom Gunn

Poetry

Bally Power Play. Toronto: Massey, 1979.

Corgi Modern Poets in Focus 5, with others. Edited by Dannie Abse. London: Corgi, 1971.

A Crab. Toronto: Body Politic, 1978.

The Explorers. Crediton, England: Gilbertson, 1969.

The Fair in the Woods. Oxford: Sycamore, 1969.

Fighting Terms. Swinford, England: Fantasy, 1954; rev. New York: Hawk's Well, 1958; new rev., London: Faber, 1962.

Games of Chance. Omaha: Abattoir, 1979.

The Garden of the Gods. Cambridge, Mass.: Pym Randall, 1968.

A Geography. Iowa City: Stone Wall, 1966.

Jack Straw's Castle (poem). New York: F. Hallman, 1975.

Jack Straw's Castle (collection). London: Faber; New York: Farrar Straus, 1976.

Last Days at Teddington. London: Poem-of-the-Month Club, 1971.

Mandrakes. London: Rainbow, 1973.

The Menace. San Francisco: ManRoot, 1982.

The Missed Beat. Sidcot, England: Gruffyground; West Burke, Vt.: Janus, 1976.

Moly. London: Faber, 1971.

Moly and My Sad Captains. New York: Farrar Straus, 1973.

My Sad Captains and Other Poems. London: Faber; Chicago: University of Chicago Press, 1961.

Night Sweats. Florence, Ky.: Barth, 1987.

The Passages of Joy. London: Faber, 1982; New York: Farrar, Straus, 1983.

Poem after Chaucer. New York: Albondocani Press, 1971.

[Poems]. England Poets Series no. 16. Swinford, England: Swinford, 1953.

Poems 1950-1966: A Selection. London: Faber, 1969.

Positives, photographs by Ander Gunn. London: Faber, 1966; Chicago: University of Chicago Press, 1967.

Selected Poems, with Ted Hughes. London: Faber, 1962.

Selected Poems 1950-1975. London: Faber; New York: Farrar, Straus, 1979.

The Sense of Movement. London: Faber, 1957; Chicago: University of Chicago Press, 1959.

Songbook. New York: Albondocani, 1973.

Sunlight. New York: Albondocani, 1969.

Talbot Road. New York: Helikon, 1981.

To the Air. Boston: Godine, 1974.

Touch. London: Faber, 1967; Chicago: University of Chicago Press, 1968.

Undesirables. Youngstown, Ohio: Pig Iron Press, 1988.

Essays and Criticism

The Occasions of Poetry: Essays in Criticism and Autobiography. Edited with an introduction by Clive Wilmer. London: Faber; New York: Farrar Straus, 1982; Berkeley, Calif.: North Point, 1985.

Editions

Ben Jonson: Poems. Harmondsworth, England: Penguin, 1974.

Five American Poets, with Ted Hughes. London: Faber, 1963.

Poetry from Cambridge 1951-1952: A Selection of Verse by Members of the University. London: Fortune, 1952.

Selected Poems of Fulke Greville. London: Faber; Chicago: University of Chicago Press, 1968.

Recordings

British Poets of Our Time: Thom Gunn. Edited by Peter Orr. London: Argo, 1975.

The Jupiter Anthology of Twentieth-Century English Poetry, Part III. Edited by Anthony Thwaite. London: Jupiter, 1963; New York: Folkways, 1967; London: Audio-Visual Productions, 1975.

Listen Presents Thom Gunn Reading "On the Move." Hessle, England: Marvell Press, 1962.

The Poet Speaks, Record Five: Ted Hughes, Peter Porter, Thom Gunn, Sylvia Plath. Edited by Peter Orr. London: Argo, 1965.

Thom Gunn Reading His Own Poetry. London: Audio-Visual Productions, 1971.

John Holloway

Poetry

The Fugue and Shorter Pieces. London: Routledge, 1960.
The Landfallers: A Poem in Twelve Parts. London: Routledge, 1962.
The Minute and Longer Poems. Hessle, England: Marvell, 1956.
New Poems. New York: Scribners, 1970.
Planet of Winds. London: Henley; Boston: Routledge, 1977.
[*Poems*]. Fantasy Poets Series no. 26. Swinford, England: Fantasy, 1954.
Wood and Windfall. London: Routledge, 1965.

Autobiography

A London Childhood. London: Routledge, 1966; New York: Scribners, 1968.

Essays and Criticism

Blake: The Lyric Poetry. London: Arnold, 1968.
The Charted Mirror: Literary and Critical Essays. London: Routledge, 1960;
    New York: Horizon, 1962.
The Colours of Clarity: Essays on Contemporary Literature and Education.
    London: Routledge; Hamden, Conn.: Archon, 1964.
The Establishment of English: An Inaugural Lecture. Cambridge: Cambridge
    University Press, 1972.
Language and Intelligence. London: Macmillan, 1951; Hamden, Conn.: Ar-
    chon, 1971.
The Lion Hunt: A Pursuit of Poetry and Reality. London: Routledge; Ham-
    den, Conn.: Shoe String, 1964.
Narrative and Structure: Exploratory Essays. Cambridge and New York:
    Cambridge University Press, 1979.
The Proud Knowledge: Poetry, Insight, and the Self 1620-1920. London:
    Henley; Boston: Routledge, 1977.
*The Slumber of Apollo: Reflections on Recent Art, Literature, Language, and
    the Individual Consciousness*. Cambridge: Cambridge University Press,
    1983.
The Story of the Night: Studies in Shakespeare's Major Tragedies. London:
    Routledge; Lincoln: University of Nebraska, 1961.
The Victorian Sage: Studies in Argument. London: Macmillan; New York: St.
    Martin's, 1953; New York: Norton, 1965.
Widening Horizons in English Verse. London: Routledge, 1966; Evanston,
    Ill.: Northwestern University Press, 1967.

Editions

Later English Broadside Ballads, with Joan Black. 2 vols. London: Routledge, 1974, 1979; Lincoln: University of Nebraska, 1975.

Little Dorrit by Charles Dickens. Harmondsworth, England: Penguin, 1967.

Oxford Book of Local Verses. New York: Oxford University Press, 1987.

Poems of the Mid-Century. London: Harrap, 1957.

Selected Poems of Percy Bysshe Shelley. London: Heinemann, 1959; New York: Macmillan, 1960.

Elizabeth Jennings

Poetry

After the Ark. Oxford and New York: Oxford University Press, 1978. Juvenile.

The Animals' Arrival. London: Macmillan; Chester Springs, Penn.: Dufour, 1969.

Celebrations and Elegies. Manchester: Carcanet, 1982.

The Child and the Seashell. San Francisco: Feathered Serpent, 1957.

Collected Poems. London: Macmillan; Chester Springs, Penn.: Dufour, 1967.

Collected Poems 1953-1985. Manchester: Carcanet, 1986.

Consequently I Rejoice. Manchester: Carcanet, 1987.

A Dream of Spring. Illustrated by Anthony Rossiter. Stratford-upon-Avon: Celandine, 1980.

Extending the Territory. Manchester: Carcanet, 1985.

Folio, with others. Frensham, England: Sceptre, 1971.

Growing-Points: New Poems. Cheadle, England: Carcanet, 1975.

Hurt. London: Poem-of-the-Month Club, 1970.

In Shakespeare's Company. Warwickshire, England: Celandine, 1985.

Italian Light and Other Poems. Illustrated by Gerald Woods. Eastbourne, England: Snake River, 1981.

Lucidities. London: Macmillan, 1970.

The Mind Has Mountains. London: Macmillan; New York: St. Martin's, 1966.

Moments of Grace: New Poems. Manchester: Carcanet, 1979.

Penguin Modern Poets I, with Lawrence Durrell and R. S. Thomas. Harmondsworth, England: Penguin, 1962.

[*Poems*]. Fantasy Poets Series no. 1. Swinford, England: Fantasy, n.d.

Poets in Hand: A Puffin Quintet, with others. Harmondsworth, England: Penguin, 1985.

Recoveries. London: Deutsch; Philadelphia: Dufour, 1964.

Relationships. London: Macmillan, 1972.

The Secret Brother and Other Poems for Children. London: Macmillan; New York: St. Martin's, 1966.

Selected Poems. Manchester: Carcanet, 1979.

A Sense of the World. London: Deutsch, 1958; New York: Rinehart, 1959.

Song for a Birth or a Death and Other Poems. London: Deutsch, 1961; Philadelphia: Dufour, 1962.

A Way of Looking. London: Deutsch, 1955; New York: Rinehart, 1956.

Winter Wind. Newark, Vermont: Janus; Sidcott, England: Gruffyground, 1979.

Autobiography

"Elizabeth Jennings." In *Contemporary Authors Autobiography Series*. Detroit: Gale, 1987, 103-15.

Essays and Criticism

Christianity and Poetry. London: Burns Oates, 1965; also published as *Christian Poetry*. New York: Hawthorn, 1965.

Every Changing Shape. Philadelphia: Dufour, 1962

Frost. Edinburgh: Oliver and Boyd, 1964; New York: Barnes and Noble, 1966.

Let's Have Some Poetry! London: Museum, 1960.

Poetry Today, 1957-60. London and New York: Longman, 1961.

Seven Men of Vision: An Appreciation. London: Vision; New York: Barnes and Noble, 1976.

Editions

An Anthology of Modern Verse, 1940-60. London: Methuen, 1961.

The Batsford Book of Children's Verse. London: Batsford, 1958.

The Batsford Book of Religious Verse. London: Batsford, 1981.

A Choice of Christina Rossetti's Verse. London: Faber, 1970.

In Praise of Our Lady. London: Batsford, 1982.

New Poems, 1956: A P.E.N. Anthology, with Dannie Abse and Stephen Spender. London: Michael Joseph, 1956.

Recordings

Selected Poems. Bournemouth, England: Canto, 1987.

Translations

The Sonnets of Michelangelo. London: Folio Society, 1961; rev. ed., London: Allison and Busby, 1969; Garden City, N.Y.: Doubleday, 1970.

Philip Larkin

Poetry

Collected Poems. Edited with an introduction by Anthony Thwaite. London: Marvell, 1988; New York: Farrar, 1989.
Femmes Damnées. Broadsheet no. 27. Oxford: Sycamore, 1978.
High Windows. London: Faber; New York: Farrar Straus and Giroux, 1974.
The Less Deceived. London: Marvell, 1955.
The North Ship. London: Fortune, 1945; reprinted with introduction, London and Boston: Faber, 1966.
[Poems.] Fantasy Poets Series no. 21. Swinford, England: Fantasy, 1954.
XX Poems. Belfast: privately printed, 1951.
The Whitsun Weddings. London and Boston: Faber, 1964.

Novels

A Girl in Winter. London: Faber, 1947, 1975; New York: Overlook, 1976.
Jill. London: Fortune, 1946; Faber, 1964, 1975; New York: Overlook, 1976.

Essays and Criticism

All What Jazz: A Record Diary 1961-68. London: Faber; New York: St. Martin's, 1970, 1985.
"A Lifted Study-Storehouse": The Brynmor Jones Library, 1929-1979. Updated to 1985 with an appreciation of Larkin as librarian by Maeve Brennan. Hull, England: Hull University Press, 1987.
Required Writing: Miscellaneous Pieces 1955-1982. London: Faber, 1983; New York: Farrar Straus, 1984.

Editions

New Poems 1958, with Bonamy Dobrée and Louis MacNeice. London: Michael Joseph, 1958.
The Oxford Book of Twentieth-Century English Verse. Oxford: Oxford University Press, 1973.

Interviews

"The Art of Poetry, XXX: Philip Larkin." Interview by Robert Phillips. *Paris Review* 84 (1982): 42-72. Reprinted as "An Interview with *Paris Review*" in *Required Writing*, 57-76.

"Arts and the Staff: Philip Larkin." *Torchlight* (University of Hull) 8 (17 March 1959): 5.

"*The Beverlonian* interview." Interview by Steuart Hamilton. *Beverlonian* (Beverley Grammar School) 19 (February 1976): 10-14.

"A Conversation with Philip Larkin." *Tracks* 1 (Summer 1967): 5-10.

"Dr. Larkin's Approach to Life and Poetry." Interview by Raymond Gardner. *Manchester Guardian* 31 March 1973, 12.

"Four Conversations: Philip Larkin." Interview by Ian Hamilton. *London Magazine* 4 (November 1964): 71-77. Reprinted as "Interviews with Philip Larkin and Christopher Middleton" in *Twentieth-Century Poetry*. Edited by Graham Martin and P. N. Furbank. London: Open University Press, 1975.

"Four Young Poets, I. Philip Larkin." *Times Educational Supplement*, 13 July 1956, 933.

"A Great Parade of Single Poems: Philip Larkin Discusses His *Oxford Book of Twentieth Century Verse* with Anthony Thwaite." *Listener* 139 (12 April 1973): 472-74.

"*Green Ginger* Interviews Major Poet Philip Larkin." *Green Ginger* (University of Hull), Spring 1974, 3-4.

"Library Clamps Down. Mr Larkin Speaks of 'Stricter Era.'" *Torchlight* (University of Hull) 98 (9 March 1965): 1.

"Not Like Larkin." *Listener*, 17 August 1972, 88: 209.

"Philip Larkin Talks to *Eboracum*." *Eboracum* (University of York) 10 (Christmas 1971): 9, 16.

"The Poet-Librarian: Gownsman Meets Philip Larkin." *Torchlight* (University of Hull) 43 (21 February 1961): 4.

"A Poet on the 8.15." Interview by John Horder. *Manchester Guardian*, 20 May 1965, 9.

"Poets Talking to Mary Holland." *Queen* 426 (25 May 1966): 46-47.

"Profile: Poet Who Captures the Music of Daily Life." Interview by Douglas Oliver. *Coventry Evening Telegraph*, 6 October 1972, 30.

"Profile 3: Philip Larkin." Interview by Dan Jacobson. *New Review* 1 (June 1974): 25-29.

"Public Access an 'Unfair Burden' Says Librarian." Interview by Michael Binyon. *Times Higher Education Supplement*, 27 October 1972, 7.

"A Sharp-Edged View." Interview by Francis Hill. *Times Educational Supplement*, 19 May 1972, 19.

"Speaking of Writing: XIII." *London Times*, 20 February 1964, 16.

"Swinging, Swingeing Larkin." Interviewed by Robert Edmands. *Torchlight* (University of Hull), 6 March 1970, 12.

"The True and the Beautiful: A Conversation with Philip Larkin." Interviewed by John Haffenden. *London Magazine* 20 (April 1980): 81-95.

Reprinted in John Haffenden, *Viewpoints: Poets in Conversation.* London: Faber, 1981.

"The True Voice of Feeling: An Auto Interview." Sleeve notes on the Listen LP recording of *The Less Deceived.* Reprinted in *Philip Larkin 1922-1985: A Tribute,* 49-51. Edited by George Hartley. London: Marvell, 1988.

"The Unsung Gold Medallist: Portrait of a Poet." Interviewed by Philip Oakes. *London Sunday Times Magazine* 63 (27 March 1966): 65.

"A Voice for Our Time." Interviewed by Miriam Gross. *Observer,* 16 December 1979, 5. Reprinted as "An Interview with the *Observer*" in *Required Writing,* 47-56.

Recordings

The Jupiter Anthology of Twentieth Century English Poetry, Part III. Edited by Edgar A. Vetter with sleeve notes by Anthony Thwaite. London: Jupiter, 1963; New York: Folkways, 1967.

Martin Bell, Muriel Berry, Tony Curtis, Douglas Dunn, Philip Larkin on Record. Bradford: Yorkshire Arts Association, 1974.

Philip Larkin, "High Windows": Poems Read by the Author. Edited by Peter Orr with sleeve notes by Charles Osborne. London: Argo Records, 1974; Decca Records, 1975.

Philip Larkin Reads and Comments on "The Whitsun Weddings." Edited by George Hartley with sleeve notes by Christopher Ricks. London: Listen Records, 1965; Hessle: Marvell Press, 1965.

Philip Larkin Reads "The Less Deceived." Edited by George Hartley with an interview of Larkin by Hartley on sleeve. London: Listen Records, 1958; Hessle: Marvell Press, 1968.

The Poet Speaks. Record 8. Edited by Peter Orr. London: Argo Record Company, 1967.

John Wain

Poetry

Feng. New York: Viking; London: Macmillan, 1975.

Letters to Five Artists. London: Macmillan, 1969; New York: Viking, 1970.

Mid-week Period Return: Home Thoughts of a Native. Illustrated by Arthur Keene. Stratford-upon-Avon: Celandine, 1982.

Mixed Feelings: Nineteen Poems. Reading, England: Reading University School of Art, 1951.

Open Country. London: Hutchinson, 1987.

Poems for the Zodiac. Illustrated by Brenda Stones. London: Pisces, 1980. 12 booklets.

Poems 1949-1979. London: Macmillan, 1980.

The Shape of Feng. Illustrated by John Kerr. London: Covent Garden, 1972.

A Song about Major Eatherly. Iowa City: Quara, 1961.

Thinking about Mr. Person, etchings by Bartolomeu Dos Santos. Beckenham, England: Chimaera, 1980.

Twofold. Frome, England: Hunting Raven, 1981.

Weep Before God: Poems. London: Macmillan; New York: St. Martin's, 1961.

Wildtrack: A Poem. London: Macmillan; New York: Viking, 1965.

A Word Carved on a Sill. London: Routledge; New York: St. Martin's, 1956.

Autobiography

Dear Shadows: Portraits from Memory. Avon: Bath; London: J. Murray, 1986.

Sprightly Running: Part of an Autobiography. London: Macmillan, 1962; New York: St. Martin's, 1963.

Novels

The Contenders. London: Macmillan; New York: St. Martin's, 1957.

Hurry on Down. London: Secker & Warburg, 1953. Republished as *Born in Captivity*. New York: Knopf, 1954.

Living in the Present. London: Secker & Warburg, 1955; New York: Putnam's, 1960.

Lizzie's Floating Shop. London: Bodley Head, 1981. Juvenile.

The Pardoner's Tale. London: Macmillan, 1978; New York: Viking, 1979.

The Smaller Sky. London: Macmillan, 1967.

Strike the Father Dead. London: Macmillan; New York: St. Martin's, 1962.

A Traveling Woman. London: Macmillan; New York: St. Martin's, 1959.

The Valentine Generation. Tokyo: Hokuseido, 1968.

Where the Rivers Meet. London: Hutchinson, 1988.

A Winter in the Hills. London: Macmillan; New York: Viking, 1970.

Young Shoulders. London: Macmillan, 1982. Published as *The Free Zone Starts Here*. New York: Delacorte, 1984. Juvenile.

The Young Visitors. London: Macmillan; New York: Viking, 1965.

Short Stories

A Collection of Short Stories. Antwerp: De Nederlandsche Boekhandel, 1976.

Death of the Hind Legs and Other Stories. London: Macmillan; New York: Viking, 1966.

A John Wain Selection. Edited by Geoffrey Halson. London: Longman, 1977.

King Caliban and Other Stories. London: Macmillan, 1978.

The Life Guard. London: Macmillan, 1971; New York: Viking, 1972.
Master Richard and Other Stories. Tokyo: Hokuseido, 1960.
Nuncle and Other Stories. London: Macmillan, 1960; New York: St. Martin's, 1961.
The Two Worlds of Ernst and Other Stories. Copenhagen: Grafisk Forlag, 1982.

Essays and Criticism

Arnold Bennett. New York: Columbia University Press, 1967.
Essays on Literature and Ideas. London: Macmillan; New York: St. Martin's, 1963.
Gerard Manley Hopkins: An Idiom of Desperation. London: Oxford University Press, 1959; Folcroft, Penn.: Folcroft, 1974.
A House for the Truth: Critical Essays. London: Macmillan, 1972; New York: Viking, 1973.
The Living World of Shakespeare: A Playgoer's Guide. London: Macmillan; New York: St. Martin's, 1964.
Preliminary Essays. London: Macmillan; New York: St. Martin's, 1957.
Professing Poetry. London: Macmillan, 1977; abridged ed., New York: Viking, 1978.
Samuel Johnson. London: Macmillan, 1974; New York: Viking, 1975.
Samuel Johnson 1709-84, with Kai Kin Yung. London: Herbert, 1984.

Plays

Harry in the Night: An Optimistic Comedy. Unpublished. 1975.

Editions

Anthology of Modern Poetry. London: Hutchinson, 1963; revised as *Anthology of Contemporary Poetry: Post-War to the Present*, 1979.
Contemporary Reviews of Romantic Poetry. London: Harrap; New York: Barnes and Noble, 1953.
The Dynasts, by Thomas Hardy. London: Macmillan; New York: St. Martin's, 1966.
An Edmund Wilson Celebration. Oxford: Phaidon; also published as *Edmund Wilson: The Man and His Work.* New York: New York University Press, 1978.
Everyman's Book of English Verse. London: Dent, 1981.
Fanny Burney's Diary. London: Folio Society, 1960.
International Literary Annual. 2 vols. London: John Calder; New York: Criterion, 1958-59.

Interpretations: Essays on Twelve English Poems. London: Routledge, 1955; New York: Hillary House, 1957.

Johnson as Critic. London: Routledge, 1973.

Johnson on Johnson: A Selection of the Personal and Autobiographical Writings of Samuel Johnson. London: Dent, 1976, 1983; New York: Dutton, 1976.

Lives of the English Poets: A Selection. London: Dent; New York: Dutton, 1975.

The New Wessex Selection of Thomas Hardy's Poetry, with Eirian Wain. London: Macmillan, 1980.

The Old Wives' Tale, by Arnold Bennett. Harmondsworth, England and New York: Penguin, 1983.

The Oxford Anthology of English Poetry. 2 vols. Oxford: Oxford University Press, 1990.

Personal Choice: A Poetry Anthology. Newton Abbot, England: David and Charles, 1978.

The Poetry of Thomas Hardy: A New Selection. London: Macmillan, 1977.

Pope. New York: Dell, 1963.

The Private Memoirs and Confessions of a Justified Sinner, by James Hogg. Harmondsworth, England, and New York: Penguin, 1983.

Selected Shorter Poems of Thomas Hardy. London: Macmillan; New York: St. Martin's, 1966.

Selected Shorter Stories of Thomas Hardy. London: Macmillan; New York: St. Martin's, 1966.

Shakespeare: Macbeth: A Casebook. London: Macmillan, 1968; Nashville: Aurora, 1970.

Shakespeare: Othello: A Casebook. London: Macmillan, 1971.

Teleplays

Young Shoulders, with Robert Smith, 1984.

Radio Plays

Frank. The Monday Play series. 1982.

Good Morning Blues. The Monday Play series. 1986.

You Wouldn't Remember. Afternoon Theatre series. 1978.

Recordings

Everyman's Book of English Verse. London: National Poetry Centre, 1981.

Fifteen Poets Read Their Own Poems. London: Jupiter, 1963; released on cassette as *Jupiter Anthology of Twentieth Century English Poetry.* Part 3. London: Audio-Visual Productions, 1975.

Here Today. London: Jupiter, 1963; released on cassette as *Here Today*. Part 2. London: Audio-Visual Productions, 1975.

John Wain. London: British Council Catalogue of Sound Recordings, 1956.

John Wain. British Council. Catalogue of Sound Recordings, 342. 1960.

John Wain. London: British Council Catalogue of Sound Recordings, 1968.

John Wain and Andrew Harvey. Audio Learning English Literature Series no. 15. London: Audio Learning, 1974.

John Wain Talks to Peter Orr. London: British Council Catalogue of Sound Recordings, 1968.

Modern Poetry, with Ted Walker. Sussex, England: Sussex Tapes, 1971; Santa Monica, Calif.: BFA Educational Media, 1972.

My Work as a Novelist. Cardiff, Wales: Drake Educational Associates, 1978.

Poem for Kids. London: National Poetry Centre, 1981.

The Poet Speaks. London: British Council and the Poetry Room of the Lamont Library, Harvard University, 1968.

The Poetry of Dylan Thomas. Sussex, England: Sussex Tapes, 1979.

The Poetry of John Wain. New York: YM/YWHA Poetry Center, 1965; Guilford, Conn.: Norton, Jeffrey, 1976.

The Poetry of John Wain. Guilford, Conn.: Norton, Jeffrey, 1976.

Poets Reading. No. 5: John Wain and Ted Hughes. London: Jupiter, 1975; released on cassette as *Twentieth Century Poets Reading Their Own Poetry*. Part 3. London: Audio-Visual Productions, 1975.

Reading Difficult Poets. Sussex, England: Sussex Tapes, 1973.

Translations

The Seafarer. Warwick, England: Greville, 1980.

SECONDARY WORKS

Books and Parts of Books

Bloomfield, B. C. *Philip Larkin: A Bibliography, 1933-1976*. London: Faber, 1980. A comprehensive bibliography of the Movement's most influential poet.

Bold, Alan. *Thom Gunn and Ted Hughes*. Edinburgh: Oliver and Boyd, 1976. A biographical and critical approach to two poets whose careers have been unduly linked merely because they were initially published together.

Burgess, Anthony. *The Novel Now: A Guide to Contemporary Fiction*. New York: Norton, 1967. A brief survey of modern novels.

Byers, Margaret. "Cautious Vision: Recent British Poetry by Women." In *British Poetry since 1960: A Critical Survey*, edited by Michael Schmidt and Grevel Lindop, 74-84. Oxford: Carcanet, 1972. Discussion centers primarily on Jennings's *Collected Poems*.

Dekker, George, editor. *Donald Davie and the Responsibilities of Literature*. Manchester: Carcanet, 1983. A collection of literary essays by a group of Davie's admirers.

Dictionary of Literary Biography, Vol. 27. Detroit: Gale, 1978. Reference volume devoted to the careers of the nine Movement poets.

Fiedler, Leslie. *No! In Thunder*. New York: Stein and Day, 1972, 191-209. Chapter on "Class War in British Literature" is instructive on Amis and Wain.

Gardner, Philip. *Kingsley Amis*. Boston: Twayne, 1981. Book-length survey of Amis's fiction; includes useful bibliography.

Gindin, James. *Postwar British Fiction: New Accents and Attitudes*. Berkeley: University of California Press, 1962. Gindin's discussion of working-class novels of the 1950s offers insights into the Movement's lowbrow origins.

Hartley, George, ed. *Philip Larkin, 1922-1985: A Tribute*. London: Marvell Press, 1988. A commemoration of Larkin compiled by the editor of *The Less Deceived*; includes comments from Jennings, Enright, and Davie.

Hassan, Salem K. *Philip Larkin and His Contemporaries*. London: Macmillan, 1988. Particularly insightful in detailing Larkin's influence on Gunn, Enright, Amis, and Wain.

McDermott, John. *Kingsley Amis: An English Moralist*. New York: St. Martin's, 1989. Book-length study of Amis's work through *The Old Devils*; includes useful bibliography.

Martin, Bruce K. *Philip Larkin*. Boston: Twayne, 1978. One of the first book-length studies to argue on behalf of Larkin as a major poet.

Morrison, Blake. *The Movement*. London: Methuen, 1986. The definitive history of the Movement and its contributors.

Motion, Andrew. *Philip Larkin*. New York: Methuen, 1982. Part of the Contemporary Writers Series, this study concerns the ways Larkin revitalized English poetry by integrating the influences of French symbolism, Yeats, and Hardy into his poetry.

Nemerov, Howard. *Poetry and Fiction*. Rutgers. Book-length study offering brief sketches of Movement writers.

O'Connor, William Van. *The New University Wits and the End of Modernism*. Carbondale: Southern Illinois University Press, 1963. Considers academic influences on Movement authors.

Perkins, David. "In and Out of the Movement: The Generation of the 1950s in England." In *A History of Modern Poetry: Modernism and After*, 418-44. Cambridge, Massachusetts: Belknap, 1987. This one chapter is devoted to the Movement's development.

Petch, Simon. *The Art of Philip Larkin*. Sydney: Sydney University Press, 1981. Emphasizes the comprehensibility of Larkin's verse through detailed discussion of individual poems.

Press, John. *Rule and Energy*. London: Oxford University Press, 1963. A study of trends in British poetry since World War II; Press's discussion of Thom Gunn is especially pertinent.

Rossen, Janice. *Philip Larkin: His Life's Work*. Iowa City: University of Iowa Press, 1989. The first critical work to assess Larkin's achievement in light of the poetry made available in his *Collected Poems*.

Salwak, Dale, editor. *Philip Larkin: The Man and His Work*. Iowa City: University of Iowa Press, 1989. Eighteen reminiscences in tribute to Larkin and his work.

Simms, Jacqueline, ed. *Life by Other Means: Essays on D. J. Enright*. Oxford: Oxford University Press, 1990. Twenty-one essays on the most humanistic Movement poet.

Thwaite, Anthony, editor. *Larkin at Sixty*. London: Faber, 1982. An anecdotal birthday tribute to the best-loved poet of his generation.

_____. *Twentieth-Century English Poetry: An Introduction*. New York: Barnes and Noble, 1978. A general survey of modern English poets.

Timms, David. *Philip Larkin*. New York: Barnes and Noble, 1973. The first book on Larkin, it recognizes his talent for balancing the demands of his readers, his art, and himself.

Walsh, William. *D. J. Enright: Poet of Humanism*. London: Cambridge: Cambridge University Press, 1974. The only extensive critical study of Enright's life and work.

Whalen, Terry. *Philip Larkin and English Poetry*. Vancouver: University of British Columbia Press, 1986. Whalen explores Larkin's affinities with other authors, notably Samuel Johnson, D. H. Lawrence, Ted Hughes and the imagists, Thom Gunn, and R. S. Thomas.

Journal Articles

Bateson, F. W. "Auden's (and Empson's) Heirs." *Essays in Criticism* 7 (January 1957): 76-80. Bateson calls Davie's *Brides of Reason* and Larkin's *The Less Deceived* a refreshing return to Augustan poetics.

Brien, Alan. "Amis Goes Pop." *New Statesman*, 7 July 1967, 15-16. Views Amis as a moralist who refuses to be deceived.

Dodsworth, Martin. "The Climate of Pain in Recent Poetry." *London Magazine* 4, no. 8 (November 1964): 86-95. Sees Gunn and Larkin as important spokesmen for the poetics of pain.

Fraser, G. S. "The Poetry of Thom Gunn." *Critical Quarterly* 3, no. 4 (Winter 1961): 359-67. Fraser contrasts Gunn's first three books with

Larkin's *The Less Deceived*, calling Gunn and Larkin the best poets of the Movement.

Giles, Paul. "Landscapes of Repetition: The Self-Parodic Nature of Thom Gunn's Later Poetry." *Critical Quarterly* 29, no. 2 (Summer 1987): 85-99. Giles sees Gunn as a playfully narcissistic parodist who fuses irony with romanticism in an attempt to hammer out meanings from the world.

Hamilton, Ian. "Dead Ends and Soft Centres." *Observer*, 12 November 1967, 609-10. Review praising Amis's *A Look round the Estate* and panning Gunn's *Touch*.

Johnson, Paul. "Lucky Jim's Political Testament." *New Statesman*, 12 January 1957, 36. Considers Amis's conservatism in light of *Lucky Jim*.

Maugham, Somerset. "Books of the Year." *London Sunday Times*, 25 December 1955, 4. Contains Maugham's scathing attack on *Lucky Jim*.

Powell, Neil. "The Abstract Joy: Thom Gunn's Early Poetry." *Critical Quarterly* 13, no. (Autumn 1971): 219-27. A discussion which focuses primarily upon *Fighting Terms*.

Tomlinson, Charles. "The Middlebrow Muse." *Essays in Criticism*, April 1957, 208-17. Tomlinson's hostile review of *New Lines* set off a public debate.

Index

The Author

Jerry Bradley is professor of English and dean of humanities at Indiana University Southeast in New Albany. Reared in Texas, he holds a B.A. in English from Midwestern University and an M.A. and a Ph.D. in English from Texas Christian University. He is the cofounder of the *New Mexico Humanities Review.*

He has published several essays on Movement poets as well as criticism on the works of Samuel Beckett, William Golding, Alan Sillitoe, Edgar Allan Poe, and Wallace Stevens. A popular poet, he is also the author of the collection *Simple Versions of Disaster* (1991). He is currently preparing a comprehensive critical bibliography on the Movement.